The Evil That Men Do

Faith, Injustice and the Church

— MARCUS K. PAUL —

Sacristy
Press

Sacristy Press
PO Box 612, Durham, DH1 9HT

www.sacristy.co.uk

First published in 2016 by Sacristy Press, Durham

Sacristy Limited, registered in England & Wales, number 7565667

British Library Cataloguing-in-Publication Data
A catalogue record for the book is available from the British Library

ISBN 978-1-908381-95-8

We must face all the facts. . . . the beauty that makes us gasp with wonder and the ugliness that makes us shrink in horror, the good that makes us want to worship and the evil that makes us bow our heads in shame.[0]

G. A. Studdert Kennedy

Preface

In his classic essay of 1948, "Bias in History", G. M. Trevelyan wrote that bias in history is unavoidable. He goes on to define it as "any personal interpretation of historical events which is not acceptable to the whole human race".[1] In an earlier essay he also made clear that immense harm had been done in the modern world by one-sided history being misused. There is a case, however, to be made for a book which attempts to reverse a predominating bias while not being uncritical of its subject. This is one such book. Opposition to an idea is productive when the outcome is an improved level of argument by both parties. Passion is part of that argument and without it we would not understand or seek to convey the important truths of the past. In a sentence about the novelist Sir Walter Scott, so crafted that it could only have come from an earlier generation than our own, Trevelyan reminds us: "The impartial historian who has no feelings to control, rides a sorry nag safely to market."[2]

Foreword

In an age where it is fashionable to "bash" the church at every opportunity, it is rare to read such a clear defence of its history and ideas. Recalling the classic *apologias* of the nineteenth century, while engaging in modern disputes and arguments, Marcus Paul provides us with a compelling and fresh look at the impact of the Christian Church down the ages and educates us as to how best to navigate our way through the current fog of cultural hostility.

We live at an interesting point in history in which the student radicals of the 1960s have been dominating the political and cultural landscape for a generation and are not merely indifferent to the Judeo-Christian heritage of the West, but are actively critical and hostile. "What has the Church ever done for us?" they ask with contempt, expecting to evoke a litany of vices ranging from the cruelty of The Crusades to the more recent accusations of misogyny, homophobia and racism.

The Evil That Men Do is a lively and convincing read not least because Paul dialogues with his reader so well. The three essential, dialogical components of this book that hook, hold and land the reader are identification, prosecution and invitation.

Identification: Paul does not caricature society's queasiness about the less savoury aspects of the Church's past. Instead, he takes the time to identify the mindset that finds aspects of Christianity so odious and regressive. He engages directly with the hostile accusations that division, cruelty, ignorance and selfishness are the legacy of the Church. This identification is achieved not just in the introduction, as a mere prelude to launch a full-on defence, but throughout each historical section in which Paul understands and articulates the complaints levelled at the Church and admits culpability on a number of charges.

Prosecution: Having identified views from a wide range of sources and owned up to the wrongs and blind-spots of the historic Church, Paul then draws on his considerable research to prosecute the overreaching intolerance that lies behind so many of the revisionist takes on Church history. He fearlessly takes on the lazy, atheistic presuppositions that masquerade as new evidence and emboldens the reader to think broadly and incisively. His instinct to prosecute is perhaps the most finely tuned of the three elements and provides us with some of the boldest, provocative and empowering insights into the secular rejection of our Christian heritage.

Invitation: We are invited to look a little more sympathetically at the contributions of the Church from its unpromising beginnings, through its so-called "Dark Ages" and especially over the past four hundred years, to witness that the triumph of the West is inextricably linked to the social cohesion, compassion, education, health and altruism bequeathed to it by Christianity.

The book is something of a *tour de force*. Paul has clearly read widely, but more importantly he has reflected deeply on what he has read, making his analysis fresh, reliable and engaging. This will be a book to be returned to again and again—not simply to fill gaps in the reader's knowledge, but to help the twenty-first-century Church identify with our societal objections, prosecute innate bias and poor reasoning, and invite our dying culture once more to embrace the greatest gift it ever received. This is a vital resource for students, educators, Christian leaders and all thinking Christians—I commend it warmly.

The Revd Richard Cunningham
Director of UCCF (Universities and Colleges Christian Fellowship)

Contents

Introduction

Writing about the decisive battles of the world, one historian considered that too little attention has been given to the passing on, over the years, of *feelings* about events and people in the past, and how ordinary people experience these today.[3] The current feeling about the history of Christendom is that it is a series of shameful mistakes and iniquities for which Christians have to apologise. The most obvious of these include the wealth and corruption of the medieval Church, the Crusades, the excesses of the Inquisition, the massacres of the conquistadors, witch hunts and slavery. That is certainly quite a list. Nevertheless it is the contention of this book that the history of the Church is more full of glory than of shame but that the *zeitgeist* of our society, our feelings about it, prevent us from either seeing or reading this. One small example of this is that a generation ago it would be commonplace to hear it said, "she acted like a real Christian", because good, kind, unselfish behaviour was synonymous with Christian actions. It was still one of the definitions of the word in the *Heinemann English Dictionary* of 1979. One will seldom hear this now, however, because people's feelings about what being a Christian means have changed—but the facts of history have not. Most people have always known about the Crusades and the Inquisition, but these periods in European history, and the history of Christendom, have not, until recently, clouded their appreciation of what Christianity has achieved. Today it is hard to raise the subject of the West's history without this "dark side" being brought to the fore. As the Pulitzer prize-winning novelist and essayist Marilynne Robinson noted, we have now a cultural predisposition to protect critics from criticism whenever we sense they earnestly feel the need to challenge some sanctity.[4] This book will look at some dark episodes and periods, as well as the bright ones, but tell a rather different story; one that will take into account the context of the events rather than judging them anachronistically, perhaps hypocritically, by solely twenty-first-century standards. There are many defences or apologias for belief in God, from the early Apologists, to Aquinas, to C. S. Lewis and of course today, but too few draw attention to the magnificent achievements of Christendom through its long history. *The Evil That Men Do* will look at some of them, and consider why they are neglected today.

In 1936, in *The Allegory of Love*, his study of medieval tradition, C. S. Lewis could write: "That Christianity . . . by its insistence on compassion. . . had a tendency to soften or abash the more extreme brutalities and flippancies of the ancient world in all departments of human life . . . may be taken as obvious."[5] In the same year, H. A. L. Fisher, in his then much acclaimed *A History of Europe,* wrote in the Preface that it was a pleasure to recall "the cleansing tide of Christian ethics".[6] In 1938, John Middleton Murry, one of the most eminent literary critics of the day, wrote in *Heaven – and Earth* of the unmatchable power to edify that is found in St Paul, and said that, just as Christianity civilised the barbarians, so it was the only hope for the situation in Europe at that time.[7] John Cowper Powys, the agnostic novelist and poet, in the same year also wrote that if St Paul had not existed the "*humanizing of individuals,* would have been indefinitely postponed".[8] After six years of global war, G. M. Trevelyan wrote in *Religion and Poetry* (1945) that "religion prohibits sin and it constrains to righteous action".[9] But late in the twentieth century a sudden *volte-face* took place: it became deeply unfashionable to hold to Christian beliefs and a sort of intellectual suicide to defend the record of the Church in sophisticated literary or scientific circles. When someone as respected as A. N. Wilson returns to the fold and is critical of the overwhelming secularity of the media, some journalists, among others, get very angry.

This *volte-face* is a matter more to do with fashion, with taste, with conformity and with what Thomas Hardy called "Indifferentism", rather than to do with history. What the Church has done has not changed, nor has new evidence been unearthed; rather, a resentment that Christianity has been accorded the moral high ground in the past has taken root, and now that most people don't believe its tenets, they feel galled that Christian arrogance would still exclude them from this high ground; so their task is publicly to pull Christianity off the pedestal where Christians (mostly alone) think it sits fair and square.

Rather than joining the fashionable bandwagon that lambastes the Church for its failings, let's take a "partial" (in both senses) look at what actually happened in a not dispassionate, but less popularly filtered way.

But first, there is some clearing of the air to be done, by considering some of the worst aspects of often otherwise good journalism and other writing.

CHAPTER 1

Clearing the Air

Some falsehoods are laughable; others make us angry and these are often to do with injustice, especially injustice towards those we love or care about. One such injustice was perpetrated in a letter to *The Times* by a Professor of biblical studies at the University of Sheffield to the effect that there is no evidence that religion improves people's moral behaviour.[10] I took issue with the professor and still do with all those who think that about Christianity. Richard Dawkins also said in a Times+ event (September 2013) that he did not believe that religion was of any moral value. The humanist, A. C. Grayling, pointed at the "bloody past" of the Church in an article designed to keep historical Christianity and kindness deeply distinct.[11] Those in the Church who find themselves tempted to agree that Christians down through the ages have mostly got things wrong will find this book either a challenge or a help. Staunch believers feel the relentless pressure from our secular age to diminish society's view of Christianity's contribution to humanity's well-being, and to remove the faith's historic challenge.

Prior to the Industrial Revolution, poor roads, limited transport, the absence of newspapers and, of course, widespread illiteracy meant that small communities could sometimes form their own opinions about the world in many areas of thought. The result was often called heresy. Today, society's opinions are formed *en masse* by an astonishingly small number of TV, press and internet journalists and editors. They control what we see and read, the order and context in which we find out about it and the priority that each issue is given. Which crisis or disaster we talk about is in the hands of those with this sort of power. Sometimes it makes the reach of the politicians seem small and weak.

In this sense the media fulfil the role of the clergy in previous ages. They have access to knowledge beyond the ordinary; they interpret and select that knowledge for us; their opinion, while not above contradiction, carries enormous weight. Their critical analysis of those they aim at is repeated widely. They can make us feel both complacent and morally outraged at the same time as they point the finger at those they choose to target. The exposure of scandal in private life and corruption in public affairs gives some of them tremendous power but very seldom is the spotlight turned upon them. The Leveson Inquiry was, however, one such occasion.

Begun in 2011, "Leveson" was a response to the News International phone hacking scandal which has gone some way towards restricting illegal methods of information-gathering by journalists, but it is unlikely to alter the moral ethos of a free press. Lord Justice Leveson opened proceedings as Chairman by stating that at the heart of the Inquiry was the old and simple sounding question, "Who guards the guardians?" He concluded the nine-month Inquiry by saying that it was the politicians who would have to decide the answer to that, but was emphatic that parts of the press have "wreaked havoc with the lives of innocent people". Because there is no simple answer in balancing freedom of speech with personal privacy, the culture and practices of the press will not change despite lengthy considerations of press ethics and public shame. One thing, however, that did emerge immediately from the Inquiry was that changes in the market are putting unprecedented pressures on the industry to out-perform rivals. The largest single change of recent years is the phenomenal growth of social media (also part of the Inquiry's terms of reference). These have the threatening ability to bypass all normal editorial constraints, legal responsibilities and modes of expression in the helter-skelter race to share at viral speeds "whatever is begotten, born, and dies", in Yeats' memorable line. Lord Leveson dismissed the idea that the internet was rapidly making the Inquiry irrelevant by calling it an "ethical vacuum" which was widely known to be of doubtful integrity.

But as so often in life, we get what we deserve: we buy the papers, pull up the websites and watch the programmes which are produced. Where the copy cannot find readers it will soon change its tune. These are, of course, huge but not vapid generalisations: there are good and bad journalists and bloggers just as there have always been good and bad clergy. Nevertheless, it is worth examining the relationship between the two since society's view of the Church is founded so much on those parts of the Church's history which modernity, especially the mass media, sees fit to focus on—and as with most other stories it focuses on the negative. It is not just journalists but a variety of academics and some politicians and historians too who would write the Church's uniquely humane contribution to society out of the history books. As Samuel Butler presciently said over a hundred years ago: "It has been said that though God cannot alter the past, historians can." So can politicians. In the drafting of the European Constitution, despite repeated attempts by the Pope and others, the decision was taken not to include any reference to the Christian heritage of Europe. In the Treaty of Lisbon, the wording agreed simply speaks of a "religious and humanist inheritance". Carlyle was too optimistic in writing that "nothing worthy in the Past departs", and in believing that recognised or not, truth and goodness long buried, live on—to mould society for the better. By being deeply buried they fail to have the influence they should.

Christopher Hitchens, whose books, essays and journalism span four decades, was a prolific contributor to *The Atlantic, Vanity Fair, The Nation,* and many other publications. In his powerful book *God is not Great* (2007), he movingly tells us about his father's funeral, when he took as his text St Paul's "Finally brethren, whatsoever things are true, whatsoever things are honest, whatsoever things are just . . . think on these things" from the letter to the Philippians. Hitchens was a great fighter for truth and justice as he saw them, and undeniably very clever. But his book exemplifies modern intellectual trends. He writes this:

> Here is the point about myself and my co-thinkers. Our belief is not a belief. . . . Our principles are not a faith . . . we distrust anything that contradicts science or outrages reason.[12]

Well, so of course do many Christians, but how is it then that Hitchens could tell us that, as a boy hearing his teacher tell him that God had "made all the trees and grass to be green, which is exactly the colour that is most restful to our eyes", at the age of nine, he "simply *knew*, almost as if I had privileged access to a higher authority, that . . . the eyes were adjusted to nature, and not the other way about"?[13]

It would be hard to find a more perfect example of someone exercising faith—especially since in this case, by his own admission, he had no concept of any of the rational arguments to defend either viewpoint. Hitchens goes on to say that the "four irreducible objections to religion" are "insuperable"[14] and that they are:

1. it wholly misrepresents the origins of man and the cosmos;
2. it combines maximum servility with maximum solipsism;
3. it is both the result and cause of dangerous sexual repression;
4. it is grounded on wish-thinking.

I am tempted to say that there is hardly any need to show these are not "insuperable", but very briefly, here's why they are not:

1. No one knows the *ultimate* origins of man and the cosmos except by faith. Most of the Church has today (unlike previous ages) no quarrel with what anthropology and cosmology can tell us. To compare scientific narrative with the biblical narrative in Genesis is a category error. Just as some Christians have unwisely tried to make Genesis fit the science of the day, so some highly speculative metaphysics regarding origins is masqueraded as science.
2. This view is highly tendentious and subjective. Precisely the same observations might have elicited the wording "humility and self-awareness" from another commentator—qualities the world could do with more of.
3. This is a Freudian view which is at least widely debated (if not suspected) by many modern psychiatrists.
4. Wish-thinking is as much a weakness to be levelled at the atheist as the religious. Many people find it extremely convenient to suppose that God is not there.

When Hitchens considers the history of religions, which includes the history of the Church, he claims that no statistic will ever find that, even without the "blandishments and threats" of heaven and hell, atheists are responsible for more evil actions than religious people.[15] Of course he is right in this, insofar as, first, such statistics would be impossible to gather, and second, most of the world has been religious for most of its history. There have been few atheists by comparison to do the evil acts. He is wrong however to be so sure the evidence points the way he thinks it does when it comes to Christian history. Without attempting to be statistical, the chapters that follow will indicate that the Church has been a formative influence for social cohesion, compassion, education, health and altruism, rather than for division, cruelty, ignorance and selfishness. The fact that Christians have to concede that religion has been the cause of war, conflict of many kinds, and an excuse for persecuting others who stand in the way should not be allowed to obscure that other inconvenient fact that if religion had not been the ostensible cause or rationale behind such behaviour, the perpetrators would have found another excuse to behave that way. What is "irreducible" and inescapable is the universal fact of human greed and violence and selfishness and fear.

It is interesting that Hitchens regretfully concluded that religion is ineradicable precisely because of fear—surely part of the permanent human condition. H. G. Wells, no friend to Christian belief, had reached a similar viewpoint by 1932. Charles Taylor, in his monumental study *A Secular Age* (2007), one of the most definitive books ever written on the development of secularisation, comes to the same conclusion but without the negative stance towards religion.

My point in referring to Hitchens' book at some length is not to "rubbish" it at all (it contains some brilliant writing) but to illustrate that the rationalists with strong personalities and ready pens are not always as rational about matters of religion as they think they are.[16] Professor John Carey, in his brilliant introduction to *The Faber Book of Reportage*, extends the comparison between journalism and religion still further.[17] For previous ages he suggests religion was the permanent backdrop to existence, as reportage is to modern man. Both supply a release from triviality, a sense of communion with a reality greater than oneself, and reassurance—since the terrible events in the news convey for the reader, by contrast, an illusion of his supposed safety. Carey however is profoundly mistaken in other assertions, one of which is that both reportage and religion are taken up with death. It is certainly true of the former in terms of the content of our newspapers but surely it is not so simple with the latter.

Whether we take the Old Testament prophets, the teachings of Jesus, or the writings of St Paul, the emphasis is far more on what has to be done *now* rather than speculation about the end of life or life after death. The Kingdom of God is *among* you.

It is true that the medieval and Renaissance Church focused very much on death in its art in church buildings but the reasons for this are not hard to find. There was, of course, a political motive: it is easy to get people to behave as you want if you threaten them with an eternity of suffering. But today we are disinclined to think about alternative reasons for the Christian focus on death and the afterlife, namely the stakes involved in the issue. If you are an atheist, death is a blank, a nothingness; there is nothing there to focus *on*. This life is all there is, and death is merely the cessation of it. An atheist focusing attention on death in order to depict it makes as much sense as an artist painting total darkness. If, alternatively, you are or were a pagan, as the early Christians had been, death was literally a grey area, shadowy: not something one could think about hopefully, far less depict with confidence. By contrast, the Christian picture was both glorious, and, yes, potentially terrifying. It was part of the story that had to be told—but that story cut both ways, as a close look at some of the paintings can tell us. Richard Taylor, in his BBC Four series *Churches: How to Read Them*, demonstrated that scenes of the Last Judgement were by no means always to terrorise the faithful or manipulate them into subservience, but to give them hope.[18] In an oppressive age, the people in the pews could look up and see that those having to give account of their misdeeds before God included crowned kings, robed clergy, and the rich and poor alike. In an age where physical pain was more prevalent than now, they could see that Christ's hands were lifted not only in blessing but in revelation—of the wounds that joined him with them in their oppression by the powerful. The whole scene is depicted above the cross, a scene of terrible oppression, and yet no less than God's rescue plan in action: their salvation from misery. No wonder then that in the eighteenth century Charles Wesley could write in one of his hymns: "With what rapture / gaze we on those glorious *scars*." John Carey is a superb critic and an expert on the writings of John Donne who *was* acutely aware of his own impending death (as were so many writers in the seventeenth century), but it is not true of much of the Church's history which, whatever its paintings and literature, spent at least as much time alleviating suffering in this life as it did trying to avoid it in the next. Interestingly, Carey, having acknowledged the difficulty of preventing his book from becoming no more than a compendium of killings focusing on death, hardly fails to offset this even though there are so many other things he could have chosen to include instead. Of his last seventy-five or so pieces only five are on topics other than war and murder. Furthermore, it is difficult to follow his logic when he suggests that religion is most likely a substitute in any pre-modern age for reportage. How that which comes first and lasts longer can be considered a substitute for that which comes after and as yet has lasted only a brief time is hard to fathom. Surely the reverse is true on the very grounds that Carey earlier suggested—that it is religion that is the permanent backdrop to existence.

Professor Davies, who thinks that "history has yet to demonstrate that religious belief makes our behaviour less evil", is at best making a generalisation so broad as to be of little value, and at worst failing to acknowledge a great deal of historical evidence. Setting aside the crucial issue of what those religious beliefs are (we could hardly equate the Quakers with Hezbollah, for instance), history has yet to provide us with an era when the absence of religious belief has been a viable option for most people. The globe has been a religious place since the dawn of history. The norm has been to believe in at least one God. Unthinking assent to a set of traditional propositions which has been the position of most of the global population over the millennia is hardly a database from which to fail to "demonstrate that religious belief makes our behaviour less evil".[19] A necessary prerequisite would be to start to separate the invisible church from the visible—those who make a heartfelt attempt to live out the teachings of Jesus and those who don't. That would be a difficult task for a sociologist even today but the concept needs to be taken into account, for "by their fruits ye shall know them" when looking for the genuine article.[20] The heart of Christianity is not ritual observance or social cohesion as in some religions, but inner conviction and personal obedience to Christ. Without understanding this distinction it would be hard to say anything meaningful about Christianity.

Perhaps in, say, fifty years time we may have had a measurable period in which significant numbers have lived in Western Europe effectively as atheists, but even then how would you measure the correlation of evil behaviour and decline in religious belief? The evil that men *don't* commit because of their beliefs is hardly susceptible to recording and measurement! Famously, "The evil that men do lives after them, / The good is oft interred with their bones."[21] This is surely why, apart from normal human predilections, the appalling abuses of religion, whether Christian, Islamic or other, are in the spotlight: they are abnormal and therefore particularly terrible because of it. We didn't expect to see Stalin or Pol Pot in the seats of their local church or temple, so their appalling and violent crimes tend to shock us less. The simple acts of goodness, however, carried out every day by tens of millions, as a direct result of their faith, go unnoticed. As the Romantic poet William Blake wrote: "He who would do good to another must do it in Minute Particulars."[22] Even the sensational acts of altruism by countless agencies working from Christian compassion do not get coverage in the papers, though they are recorded in small circulation periodicals and biographies.

I cannot speak for other religions but year in and year out sees the restoration of individual lives as they "renounce evil" to find reconciliation with God and neighbour in personal Christian faith. The social impact of such faith in our prisons, to take one example, is startling among those who become Christians. And if we need a hard statistic the recidivism rate from the only Christian prison in Brazil, run entirely by Christians, is impressively low compared with the rest of Brazil and the United States.[23] We must, from the outset, take off the dark lenses through which we are so often asked to see Christian history, and Carey's anthology is a good example of how we are being asked to wear them without realising it. The Romantic poet Shelley called poets the unacknowledged legislators of the world, but surely nowadays this role has been handed to journalists and critics. Long ago, Chesterton, himself a journalist, noticed this secular bias among editors and their assumption that anything that agrees with them is universal and anything that disagrees insane: "They have a vague idea that all this stale and stagnant scepticism is now the normal air of the world."[24]

Attitudes of this sort have become the unconscious inheritance of readers today and that is always the most profound form of influence. I often found the word "cynical" used by students in essays as a term of approval. Scholars have some immunity from "the great cataract" of newspaper nonsense as C. S. Lewis put it, but even then often only in the areas of their own scholarship.[25] This is again evidenced by Carey (not an historian) when he says that there is plenty of evidence to suggest that in a pre-communication age (that is, up until the mid to late nineteenth century), most people were not religious. However, a fine professional historian, Richard Fletcher, in his authoritative book *The Conversion of Europe, 371–1386* AD, could be categorical that in early medieval Europe people of every class and ability accepted unquestioningly that the miraculous wove itself in and out of everyday experience as easily as a shuttle.[26] In an earlier generation, G. G. Coulton considered that "the marvellous and the intangible . . . filled men's minds in every department of medieval life".[27]

Most of the rest of us have so little awareness of our own history, especially that of the Church, that we are not armed to recognise unwarranted criticism or distinguish myth from history. We are also not very good at reading or distinguishing between what can be inferred from a passage because the author wants us to infer that, and what can be really established from the facts. It is unfair to compare a book like John Henry Newman's *Apologia Pro Vita Sua,* with its passion for exactitude in truth, with the picture of our intellectually sloppy society given us in (good) books like John Humphrys' *Beyond Words* and Lynne Truss's *Talk to the Hand,* but they all indicate that we are easily confused, easily cowed, and often ignorant about things that our forebears took for granted.

Unfortunately people like to hear bad news—because, ironically, it makes them feel better. This must be true because newspapers and other news media devote themselves almost entirely to it. And just as a supermarket will not stock food that does not sell, so the papers won't run stories that people won't read. They tell us what we want to know about: fraud, deceit, violence, war, betrayal, murder, and failure. The instances of humanity's inability to live contentedly, peaceably, happily, create an interminable list. Yet all over the world anonymous acts of goodness are being carried out wherever people meet—even in war zones, failed states and lawless communities. Oddly enough these acts can be most prominent where suffering is greatest—following the earthquake and after the flood. But these actions are seldom investigated and reported because those stories won't sell papers. But making people "feel better" does not in this instance allow us to occupy the moral high ground. "Bad" news—that is, news of moral depravity, criminal or arrogant behaviour, of unkindness or inhumanity—only makes us feel "better" because it makes us feel less morally inadequate. Think for a moment of reading an account of the self-sacrificing work of the Leprosy Mission, or of Mother Theresa's sisterhood in India, or all the hardship undergone by any of the "bottom billion" and those who live like them in order to help them. Such a read can be an inspiration, but it is also a challenge which raises the question: "Why am *I* not living like that, giving like that, caring like that?" Accounts like this make us uncomfortable. But to read about the way humans endlessly bring disaster upon themselves and others either evokes compassion (and compassion fatigue is never far away), or more complacently allows us to think, well, my life may be a bit of a mess, but at least I don't do that.

Now if we apply this to the Church it is easy to see why people prefer to see its failings rather than its virtues. Not only do they feel better about themselves as with every other failing they read about, but they have the added pleasure of being able to laugh at the hypocrisy, and get a real buzz from a sense of moral superiority which justifies their own irreligiosity. This sedates any remaining nagging doubts (mostly long since rendered comatose) about the foundations of their agnosticism or atheism. This also goes some way to explain why nearly every clergyman we see represented on non-documentary TV is either fraudulent, weak or inadequate.

It is hard therefore for Christianity to get good press in a world which is sensationally interesting to newspaper readers mostly because of its evil. Bad acts are often explosive, immediately visible or tangible in their impact; good ones take longer to work out, are less visible, but are no less revolutionary. Shakespeare was right when he made Mark Antony in *Julius Caesar* say, "the evil that men do lives after them". How right he was too that "the good is oft interred with their bones".[28]

For this very reason there will be surprising gaps in this partial history. Great achievements may go unremarked. As Oscar Wilde said with characteristic insouciance, a man who pays his bills on time is soon forgotten. Nevertheless, my aim will be to highlight something of the unique and unrivalled contribution Christianity has made to Europe and the world, and we need to begin by seeing whether its source documents, its foundational truths, have been the cause of this—or has it been despite them?

CHAPTER 2

Foundations

Everyone knows that if the foundations of a building are inadequate in some respect, the whole building will suffer and not function as it should. In recent years the foundations of Christian belief have come under scrutiny with an unprecedented vigour and aggressiveness. Are the foundations of the Church somehow wrong? Do the Old and New Testaments give us a picture of God more reminiscent of the work of Hieronymous Bosch than that of Holman Hunt? Have Christians down the ages been more influenced by the Old Testament than the New? And which parts of the Testaments have been most influential on human behaviour? Is Richard Dawkins right when, in *The God Delusion*, he ascribes to the God of the Bible all the nastiest qualities imaginable? The list in his emotive diatribe includes this cluster of terms: *jealousy, injustice, unforgiveness, vengefulness, misogyny, homophobia, racism,* as well as *filicide and infanticide.* As a summary God is described as capricious, bullying and malevolent.[29]

"If way to the Better there be, it exacts a full look at the Worst", wrote Thomas Hardy in defence of his pessimism, and we will take his advice shortly, since these allegations must be among the worst that can be levelled at the Bible's picture of God.[30] We shall see if they bear scrutiny. As Curdie said in George MacDonald's *The Princess and Curdie*: "We must not try to get rid of horrible things by . . . saying they are not there."[31]

The Old Testament books are classically divided into three categories: the Law, the Prophets and the Writings, and from the earliest days some of those books have been more studied, remembered and recounted than others. Most of us like and remember stories and narrative better than other sorts of information. It is novels that become blockbuster

movies; social history and philosophy do not. One well-known way of
remembering bits of otherwise dry information such as lists is to link them
into a story—funny, tragic or silly. Teachers tell stories to keep the interest
of their classes. It is no surprise therefore that in the Old Testament it is
the *stories* that have been taught and remembered more than the other
writings: the Creation and Fall, the journeys of Abraham, the turbulent
family histories of Isaac, Jacob and Joseph, the birth of Moses, the Exodus,
Joshua's campaigns. They make good reading. And of course, if they were
fiction, or more to the point here, treated as fiction, there would be no
problem. The mixture of tragedy and comedy, of violence, depravity,
lust and greed alongside heroism and bravery against the odds, some of
it told with great pathos or irony, matches the tone and content of some
of the world's greatest literature. The problem both for the sceptic and
the Christian is precisely that people have believed these stories *not* to
be fiction and therefore may have used them indiscriminately as models
for their own behaviour. Has this happened such that a foundation has
been built for the Church which has made the building disfiguring to the
landscape? We will need to consider other parts of the Old Testament
besides "the five books of Moses" (that is, books *about* Moses), and the
impact of the New Testament, to find our way towards an answer.

The first case to make is that the Bible fundamentally impacted upon
the worldview of Christians, and their experience of daily life, from the
earliest times. About this there can be little doubt. In his second letter,
Peter urges his mid-first-century readers to be "without spot or blemish"
as "brother Paul" had likewise urged, though, says Peter, the ignorant
twist the meaning of these exhortations "as they do *the other scriptures*".[32]
The clear implication is that the early Church, even in Paul's lifetime, is
already according the highest authority to the writings of Paul and trying
to live in accordance with their teaching. Clement of Rome, writing at the
end of the first century, tells the Corinthians that "the Apostles received
the Gospel *for us* from the Lord Jesus Christ".[33] The anonymous author
of the *Letter to Diognetus*, writing probably between AD 130 and 150, is
full of echoes of Paul's letters and this is a pamphlet designed to be read
by as many people as possible because it is the work of one of the early
Apologists for the Christian faith. *The Didache* or *Teaching of the Apostles*,

by an unknown writer from the first or second century, includes the Lord's Prayer, which, the writer says, "the Lord commanded in his Gospel".[34]

The Gospels, then, and the New Testament letters, seem to be central to Christian life and faith in the early post-Apostolic world. In the work of Augustine, Bishop of Hippo in North Africa (writing in the early fifth century), huge theological constructions were built—partly on his own personal experience of conversion from a worldly and indulgent life to one of rigour and self-denial, but mainly on the teaching of both Old and New Testaments. A glance at the extracts in Bettenson's *Documents of the Christian Church* shows the Bishop to be using, as the basis of his statements there, the Book of Psalms, the prophet Isaiah, the Gospel of John, Paul's letter to the Romans, and the letters of John.[35]

When St Patrick (*c.* AD 390–*c.* 460) describes his vocation in bringing souls to Christ from the ends of the earth, he quotes both the Old Testament and the Gospels as being the basis on which he acted, especially citing the end of Matthew's Gospel where Christ commissions the Apostles to "teach all nations . . . all the things I have commanded you".[36] He therefore confidently makes Scripture the authority for his actions and mission.

Significantly, when Islam was expanding rapidly through the seventh century, the *jihad* or "struggle" against the infidel was not to be extended to Jews or Christians because they were "peoples of the Book". Christians were known to be those who based their lives on the Bible.

In England, first Caedmon (seventh century), then Bede (eighth century), then Alfred (ninth century) all translated parts of the Bible with the intention that it should be either read, or sung, or recited. Medieval miracle plays brought moving or comic (and poignantly both) versions of the stories to those who could not read but who loved a story. Throughout Europe, the earliest church buildings depicted the stories on their plaster walls, and later did so in stained glass and wood carvings, and on stonework, tiles and any other available surfaces. J. R. H. Moorman, in *A History of the Church in England,* says: "by the latter part of the medieval period, every church in England was covered from floor to roof in pictures."[37]

Such was the impact of these stories depicted in medieval churches that by the fourteenth century, when John Wycliffe produced the Lollard Bible, people were able to consider the Bible to be the ultimate authority not only in matters of religious belief and practice but in all matters. Every other text, every other tradition, every other influence was secondary to all-encompassing Scripture. The Bible was the foundation of belief in every century.

It is therefore important that we understand what sort of narratives people were being told by these different and colourful media. They heard why their crops were far from perfect; that there was a link between mankind's behaviour and his suffering, and that the pattern had begun long ago in a distant garden. They heard that God had called his people to trust him despite the difficulties, to journey through desert places where evil was punished and virtue and trust rewarded. They heard that the Law had been given to restrain people's folly and protect them against social breakdown and about the winds which would follow that breakdown. For those who listened often or carefully, or were able to read, there was a detailed law code, at its heart the Decalogue, designed to check our tendency to lie or steal or kill by word or deed. They found a code designed to put what was highest and best first, and to prevent the worship of inferior gods of their own making. Only the creator God should be worshipped. All else is idolatry and vanity.

They found a law based on the assumption that the land, on which all depended, did not belong to them but to God. "In the beginning *God* created the heaven and the earth."[38] We are strangers and sojourners here, and the land should be stewarded fairly since all have equal rights to it. If borrowings have to take place they must do so without usury which, as we know far better than they, is so crippling. Liberty, the cancellation of debt, and the chance of a new start, were all written into these laws because they were based on the concept of justice. S. G. Evans shows in *The Social Hope of the Christian Church*, as many have done, that the social legislation of the Old Testament was far-reaching, covering patterns of work and rest, hygiene, housing, medicine, weights and measures, and inheritance, as well as ritual and festivity.[39] Yes, it was for a primitive society and many of the details are strange or repellent (though nothing like as much as being there would be to modern man), but it was an ethical society which put community first as part of its worship of God. Surely few, if any, societies were as advanced as this in terms of their ideals and the blueprint from which they worked. The "Torah" was not merely "the law" as we would think of it, but rather (as it may be translated) "teaching" about the way the whole of life should be lived. Marilynne Robinson has pointed out how, in distinction from other lawgivers such as Hammurabi, Lycurgus or Solon, Moses was the founder of an integrated system of religion and law which made an impact far more humane than what we know was the case in our evidence about the earliest codified Roman laws.[40] Indeed, the treatment of both theft and debt in the Mosaic code was more merciful than England's up until the nineteenth century and in some respects today. Moreover, the Old Testament did not make distinctions between classes which favoured those already privileged in the way British and American legislation did.

But of course the story of the Old Testament is the story of how this law was broken; whether a society is a good one or bad one depends not only on its laws but on how well they are kept. The history of the period of the Judges and the Kings shows how imperfectly this was done. But just as people today prefer to read sensational news about others' follies and criminality rather than the moral corrective to this, so it is with the writings of the great prophets concerned with the moral health of the nation, with justice, with the alleviation of poverty (there are over two thousand verses in the Bible which deal with the alleviation of poverty and the need for justice). Public morality and national life are more themes for Isaiah, Jeremiah, Ezekiel, Amos and Micah than is the action of people in the privacy of their homes. They bring condemnation to the ears of the Kings, the false prophets and the people, sometimes a sense of doom, and frequently a sense of righteous indignation, not because God is vindictive but because God is just, and every healthy society has needed its prophetic figures who will stand out against the prevailing corruption of the time and be prepared to pay the consequences. To be angry with, and threatening towards, those who grind the faces of the poor is simply to be doing that which the severest secular critics of the Old Testament do; in doing so, they lay claim the moral high ground. "The twin evils against which the prophets launched the condemnation of Jehovah were injustice and oppression."[41] The message of the Prophets is one of hope—that God will act, that kings and presidents do not have the final say, that God will lift up the downtrodden, and that Ahab will be made to pay for his theft of Naboth's vineyard. This hope of rescue strikes a chord with us still. The theme of the small man being taken over by the greedy corporation and then rescued by the hero has been appealing to modern filmgoers since the heyday of the Western. It's a great message to tell—that we won't have to be despised forever. Someone cares enough to do something about it, and will.

Right at the start of the prophecy of Isaiah in Chapter One, God is telling him to proclaim: "Stop doing wrong, learn to do right! Seek justice, encourage the oppressed. Defend the cause of the fatherless, plead the case of the widow."[42] The passage comes immediately after a scathing attack on any religion that is merely empty formality without any impact on justice and right living.

One passage from the prophet Ezekiel is especially interesting. God is confiding in the prophet and telling him what to say:

> There is a conspiracy of her princes within her like a roaring lion tearing its prey; they devour people, take treasures and precious things and make many widows within her. Her priests do violence to my law and profane my holy things; they do not distinguish between the holy and the common; they teach that there is no difference between the unclean and the clean; and they shut their eyes to the keeping of my Sabbaths, so that I am profaned among them. Her officials within her are like wolves tearing their prey; they shed blood and kill people to make unjust gain ... The people of the land practise extortion and commit robbery; they oppress the poor and needy and ill treat the alien denying them justice ... So I will pour out my wrath on them and consume them with my fiery anger ... declares the Sovereign Lord.[43]

There are two points of particular interest here over and above the obvious fact of the prophet's stance against every sort of injustice. The first is that his criticism of those in public office includes both priests and prophets as well as princes, that is, the *religious* establishment. The callous disregard of the lives and rights of ordinary people by those exploiting their power and influence to their own advantage has sadly impacted upon those ordinary people not only to deprive them of their well-being but also of their moral integrity as they follow the example of their leaders. The second point—which it is difficult to avoid making—is that Ezekiel's critique sounds in places unnervingly like some of the things that that the most strident secular critics are saying about the Church. What emerges from the passage is that their criticisms are misdirected when aimed at the Bible if we take a balanced view of the entirety of its message. It is worth noticing too, that Ezekiel is as concerned for the immigrant as he is for the Jew.

So far, I have tried to indicate that there is nothing shaky about the foundation of the Law and the Prophets. Both are concerned with justice, human rights and some degree of equality—though their notion of the last cannot be expected to be quite our own.

The Writings, including the Psalms (surprisingly), have come under less frequent attack despite some ghastly and bloodthirsty passages. Any close reading of the Psalms immediately reveals how passionate they are: cries for help, pleas for justice, explosions of rage and self-pity, paeans of praise, and abject confessions of failure and sin. Despite the formal care with which some are written, others seem unabashed, unedited and utterly frank: the sort of things we might confide in a private diary but nowhere else. As soon as this is realised it becomes clear that the negative and violent emotions are hardly there for us to emulate but to fear. They are cautionary tales for us to learn from, not models to copy. They also seem to give us permission to air our grievances with God in a way no other part of the Bible does. We can express our anger, confusion, and even disbelief through the words of the psalmist.

The writer of Psalm 82 envisages a heavenly court scene in which the abuse of power is confronted sharply by God. He asks those in power: "How long will you defend the unjust and show partiality to the wicked?" He commands that they must "defend the cause of the weak and fatherless; maintain the rights of the poor and oppressed. Rescue the weak and needy; deliver them from the hand of the wicked."[44] This sort of injunction is repeated hundreds of times through the Old Testament and then re-quoted regularly in the pages of the New Testament. Jesus defines his mission at its inception in these sorts of terms , when he publicly says in the synagogue that he has been sent to preach "good news to the poor" and "to release the oppressed".[45]

The positive influence of the Psalms in terms of hope, of solace, self reflection and spiritual understanding is best captured by the universality of the use of Psalm 23, and by the fact that at key moments of Christian history, from Athanasius in the fourth century to St Francis at the Crusades; from the defeat of the Spanish Armada, to Abraham Lincoln, and in state funerals today, they have been sung, quoted, and declaimed.

Having given an outline of the way the Old Testament has been read and used, perhaps we should turn more directly to Richard Dawkins' invective and see what basis it has; whether there is any justification for such ferocious hatred of the Bible.

Let's take the first four terms as a separate group since they are generalised ones used to depict the deep-seated selfishness of a personality capable of some sense of morality but demanding of others attributes you don't have yourself. The terms used to describe God are: *jealous, unjust, unforgiving, vindictive*. The first of these is the easiest to deal with.

To be jealous is to be resentful towards a rival of some kind or to want to preserve your rights with regard to something or someone. Another translation of the Hebrew is "impassioned". Dawkins is right. This is precisely the picture of the Old Testament God, but why should this suddenly be an issue when this particular attribute is one humans may be shocked by but cannot reasonably deplore? To discover this is to glimpse for the first time the God not of the gaps, nor merely of creation, but one who wants to share his heart with his people. This is uniquely the God of the Bible, a radical idea not shared by the other religions of the day, and one that some moderns find inherently uncomfortable. But in an ancient world where mortality and dependency on outside forces were so obviously part of the human condition, and where life was so much less certain than today, surely an involved, passionate God who guides, supports, and sustains, was welcome. Jealousy of course is often confused with envy; indeed the *Shorter Oxford English Dictionary* gives "envy" as one of its meanings, and when speaking of God defines it as "intolerance of the worship of other gods". Since, however, the Church, while proclaiming the goodness of God, chose to make envy one of the seven deadly sins, it could hardly be that which they understood the word "jealous" to mean! "I, the Lord your God, am a jealous God."[46]

Is God, however, *unjust*? Well, only it seems to me, if we consider that we should not be responsible for our actions to any sort of authority. We have seen that the Law was there to restrain our tendency to make standards slip in our favour and to the disadvantage of others, while the Prophets, at great personal cost, constantly brought fierce reminders to an easily corruptible society that there would be consequences of such behaviour. This is surely to uphold justice, not to negate it. A world without a God of this sort is a world condemned forever to the injustice that the poor and less privileged currently experience and always have. If God can inspire an Ezekiel or modern prophet to fight for the downtrodden, that can only be better than the alternative.

But surely God is *unforgiving*? After all, the most terrible fate happened to those who unrepentantly opposed Yahweh, first in the wilderness, then later in the towns and cities: death of every kind and mass deportation to distant countries. It is difficult not to acknowledge this, and also to square it with the picture of God that Jesus presents in the New Testament— and of course Christians are varied in their responses to the problem of reconciling these differences. We will return to this when we look at the Crusades, but initially need to remember two things: (1) society everywhere three millennia ago was brutal, and if the writers of the Old Testament are, on numerous occasions, unfeeling in their description of the deaths of both their own people and their enemies at the hand of Yahweh, they are certainly not worse than other tribal societies of their time; (2) this picture of God as implacable in his anger is balanced by frequent reminders of how he longs for his people to thrive and prosper, to love their neighbours and obey his just laws, shows a compassion not often present in a primitive and tribal society. Even in the nineteenth century, in *Eothen*, his classic account of travelling through the Middle East, A. W. Kinglake noted that "tenderness and pity" seemed to evaporate in an open air and nomadic existence.[47] But God's anger is not indifference, but a response to the wrongdoing which is hurtful to individuals and society; it is not arbitrary or capricious.

As for being *vindictive*, this is silly, as if the critic is looking for the next demeaning and derogatory thing to say, rather than weighing the evidence. It is also, of course, a very time-worn view. In 1779, David Hume quoted a writer who expresses precisely this idea about God, using the word "vindictive".[48] To be vindictive is to be given to revenge, and human revenge operates irrespective of justice and works outside any legal system. In his *Dictionary of the English Language,* the great lexicographer Samuel Johnson defined "revenge" as an act of passion, in contrast to vengeance, an act of justice. "Injuries are revenged," he wrote, but "crimes are avenged". Yahweh may be implacable on occasion, but only when the Law is broken and justice is not upheld. The well-known quotation of which Paul reminds the Romans, "'Vengeance is mine,' saith the Lord", is intended precisely to *preclude* any human behaviour of this kind; but requital fittingly belongs to a just God in a world where evil seemingly often goes unpunished. To disagree with the principle of justice and retribution altogether, a person would have to want a society without police, law courts, and penal systems. Difficult to imagine.

So the opening salvos seem to be misdirected. What about the rest of the barrage?

Misogynistic, homophobic, racist. This pretty much seems to be saying that God hates everybody—people who are men, people who are women, and people from any race that he decides he doesn't like. If that is the picture that the Bible presents, it is extremely curious that the Church has consistently proclaimed the opposite ("O God who hatest nothing that thou hast made" has been ingrained in Anglican worshippers for 400 years) though frequently failed to act in accordance with it.[49] How much the Church has succeeded is the subject of subsequent chapters, but the issue here is whether the God of the Bible is like that.

For the first charge, I assume Dawkins is thinking of certain taboos that applied to women with regard to menstruation in Old Testament law, but there are so many provisos designed to protect women that any seemingly odd or restrictive practices are easily outweighed. One whole book of the Old Testament, Ruth, dating from the time of the Judges, is given over to the celebration and affirmation of the importance of women and the need to protect the vulnerable. The Book of Esther shows just how influential and far-reaching the role of wife could be. Esther was so important that she has a feast in her honour still observed throughout Judaism today (Purim).

It is a favourite ploy of some to level the misogyny claim right from the start in the story of the Fall. After all, it was the woman who first ate the forbidden fruit. But even this is a misreading of the text, since we are told that "the serpent was more subtle than any other wild creature that God had made",[50] and Eve had far more excuse in being deceived by the serpent than Adam had in accepting the fruit from his wife who is given no such subtlety in the story. Adam was therefore more greatly to blame than Eve. This level of argument to prove God's misogyny is about as convincing as saying that the Bible is "serpentiphobic" (actually, "ophidiophobic") because of the role allocated to the serpent!

Edith Hamilton, perhaps the greatest female classicist of the twentieth century, described by the *New York Times* as clear and brilliant, and the author of major books on the ancient world, called the Bible the only book in the world up to the twentieth century which looked at women as human beings rather than as property.[51] In the ancient world the roles of women were severely restricted, but the Old Testament gives examples of them being queens, prophetesses, judges and military leaders. They show faith, determination, and courage in overcoming prejudice, as well as the to-be-expected virtues of wifely obedience and loyalty. It is interesting that the fifth commandment tells us to honour both father and mother figures equally, and the command to love our neighbours similarly makes no distinction between men and women.

In the New Testament there are many more women with important roles than most of its critics imagine. The Gospel of Luke is particularly focused on the role of women. Jesus talks about, meets, or mentions women twenty-four times in this Gospel and in every instance it is in a positive way. The woman at the well in John's Gospel becomes an ambassador for Christ, though the disciples must have been shocked by Jesus' lack of respect for the conventions of the day. When Jesus healed the haemorrhaging woman who touched his garment he did so in full view and hearing of Jairus, a synagogue ruler and pillar of the establishment, whom we can expect to have been at the least deeply disconcerted by such unconventional, indeed lawbreaking, behaviour. The treatment of the woman taken in adultery, whom Jesus forgave and sent away with a mere admonition rather than the sentence of death by stoning, is an indication of how he treated each as an individual—without reproach,

belittlement, or stereotyping. Jesus stands alone among world founders
of religions in his attitude to women. He brings prostitutes back from
the brink, supports monogamous marriage, limits the man's right to
divorce and redefines adultery to the advantage of women. No wonder
that some of his most devoted adherents were women—Mary Magdalene,
Joanna, Susanna. Dacre Balsdon in his scholarly book on Roman women
considers that in being Christianised the Roman world brought great
change to the status of women.[52] John Cowper Powys calls Luke "A really
great biographer" and with a poet's ear he continues: "In sentence after
sentence, full of a magic like that of the pictures of the Old Masters . . . he
sketches the figures of the women whose sons are to change the world."[53]

Paul has been maligned more often than Jesus for his attitude to women,
but any comprehensive reading of his letters dispels this misapprehension
quite quickly. The number of greetings he has in his letters to women who
were prominent in the church is surprising. Prisca, Junia, and Julia were
working as missionaries with their husbands and brothers. Priscilla was
a partner with Paul. Her name appears before her husband Aquila on five
occasions. Junia is named as an Apostle; Phoebe is a deaconess.[54] Of course
it is true that in writing to Timothy, Paul says "I do not permit a woman
to teach",[55] and this clearly is his own practice, born of his experience in
Corinth, but it is not enjoined on others or issued as any sort of precept.
If, in Paul's view, wives should submit to husbands as he says in Ephesians,
equally, in his view, husbands should love their wives as Christ loved the
church—in total self-sacrifice.[56] Ultimately, for Paul, there is "neither . . .
male nor female", for all are one in Christ Jesus.[57] This was reflected in
the practice of the early Church. In the Jewish synagogue women had
no part to play in the worship and sat veiled and separated. In the new
"ecclesia"—the Christian congregation—women were clearly full members.

The second charge of *homophobia* is equally off target. Presumably
Dawkins is thinking of the episode where Lot has a narrow escape from
Sodom through being rescued in a Special Forces-type raid by Abraham.
The culture of Sodom as depicted in Genesis is utterly depraved by any
standard. The men who tried to rape Lot's guests—and presumably were
subsequently destroyed in the "fire and brimstone" that rained down—
were utterly devoid of any decency, and when placed against the norms
of Middle Eastern hospitality to strangers their behaviour is shown to be

totally degenerate. To punish such absolute lawlessness severely seems neither unjust nor homophobic. Moreover, as so often is true of those on a bandwagon, distinctions are lost in a red mist and not made where they should be. We can disapprove of behaviour without being phobic about it or hating the person who does it. Paul states that homosexuals will not enter the Kingdom,[58] but given the list in which the word appears, where "the greedy" are condemned in the same way as are adulterers and "revilers", this seems to be a statement suggesting that anyone in flagrant rebellion against God, irrespective of their sexual orientation, will miss the Kingdom, rather than it being a list of unforgivable sins and sinners. He certainly makes no mention of hating them or fearing them, and does not single them out in any way above other offenders. Homophobia is wide of the mark.

What about the charge of *racism*? Racial hatred and religious intolerance are the two great cardinal sins of the twenty-first century, but it is hard to level the former at Christians on the grounds that their Scriptures incite it. From Genesis to Revelation the Bible depicts a God who intends to reach out to every nation. Abraham is told he will be the father of "many nations." The prophet Isaiah tells the people that he will establish justice "on Earth" and even "the islands" will have his law. "My servant" will be "a light for the Gentiles", so "all you ends of the earth" should turn and be saved; "for I am the Lord and there is no other". Joel sees a time when God will pour out his spirit on all people and "everyone who calls on the name of the Lord will be saved".[59]

The theme of God not showing partiality is as strong throughout the Bible as is the idea that God chose the Jews. A glance through a concordance under the heading "nations" (earlier translated as "Gentiles") gives us a picture, yes, of the greatness of the Jewish people's destiny, but it is a greatness to be shared. The nations will be invited in, gathered in, flock in. God will declare his glory to them, share his blessings with them, far more than he will pour out his wrath upon them. Indeed, God's displeasure seems more to be reserved for his "chosen people" than for others. The old rhyme ran that it was "odd of God to choose the Jews", but was it immoral or racist? Not if God has to work through individuals, which would be logical if he is the supreme personality himself. We work through *people* to change the world, to effect a plan, so why then should we expect God to work differently? God seems to start with an individual—Abraham, Moses, Joseph—and work outwards from that singularity into the whole world.

In the New Testament the idea of God not being partial is even stronger. Jesus shocked people with his failure to observe social and religious distinctions—even his enemies conceded that he was fair.[60] Some of the best-known encounters in the Gospels concern Jesus' relationship with lepers, those considered to be possessed, disadvantaged women, tax collectors, the hated Samaritans and other socially undesirable people. Paul of course is supremely the apostle to the Gentiles and the book of Acts carefully records how Peter had to painfully revise his views to come into line with Paul on this, thereby showing how unacceptable the idea originally was. Paul writes to the Romans that "there is no difference between Jew and Gentile" and to the Galatians "there is neither Jew nor Greek", while Peter told his audience in Caesarea: "I now realise how true it is that God does not show favouritism but accepts men from every nation who fear him and do what is right."[61]

The inclusion of *infanticide* refers perhaps to two episodes in the Bible. The first is when Yahweh strikes dead the firstborn of the Egyptians prior to the Exodus. This is certainly a terrible and terrifying deed and one from which anyone might recoil. How can this be consistent with the God of love? By way of answer we need to begin with a reminder of the context. The Hebrews were slaves in Egypt. The oppression of one race by another was total and constant. Not only was the population enslaved, but the conditions of that slavery were deteriorating. The Jews increased in number such that Pharaoh was finding them a threat so that further hardship in their work was imposed. Moses was called to end this oppression and did not feel equal to the task—unsurprisingly. Nevertheless, after much soul-searching he undertook it. He begins with diplomacy and tries to negotiate a release, even trying to deceive Pharaoh as to his intentions. He seeks a peaceful settlement of the problem. He then graduates to what we might call posturing, a display of power to show he means business. When all this fails to move Pharaoh he initiates other sanctions which will reach at least the borders of Pharaoh's consciousness. A variety of unpleasant measures are deployed, each in turn probably more damaging to the economy and Egypt's social stability: "the plagues". It is only when measures of this kind fail that Moses tells Pharaoh that as a final resort, if he does not release the slaves, the firstborn will die.

This is a terrible and threatening sanction, yet one that Pharaoh still does not heed. Given that all the other threats without exception had come about as prophesied, it is a measure of Pharaoh's callousness and intransigence that he does not give way. There has been a graduated approach to punishment and nothing has worked. Is this not precisely how the United Nations works today? The recognition of injustice is brought to world attention, pressure is applied and increased until finally the threat of military action either produces the required result or war ensues. People die in war. There is much "collateral" damage. Those who did not agree with the offending regime will also sometimes suffer and die. So it has been through the ages, because to be human we have to be free. To lose our free will is to lose what we have always considered our humanity. Could God not have changed Pharaoh's mind? Not if Pharaoh was determined otherwise, any more than he could have that of Hitler, Pol Pot or Saddam Hussein. Looked at in this light, the Exodus was preceded by a very modern piece of international politics and finally achieved the establishment of a people that handed down to all of us the greatest early law code.

The second episode in which God might be called infanticidal is another passage from Genesis in which Abraham appears willing to sacrifice his son Isaac at the behest of Yahweh. This is the strangest of incidents and seems morally repellent. Christians often gloss it as being a "type" or foreshadowing of Jesus' self-giving in the New Testament. Perhaps it is, but it also seems extremely worrying that God could apparently command Abraham in this way. However, no filicide actually took place and the ram caught in the thicket was provided in place of the boy. Nevertheless, there is a problem. If we allow ourselves to say that Abraham and/or the author of the account misunderstood what God was telling him, then we have to allow that other elements of the Old Testament may be recorded in such a way as will mislead us about the character of God—a disturbing thought. If the author however is not mistaken, then God takes Abraham to the very brink of an evil outrage utterly forbidden to the Jews and we naturally feel that Abraham should have been prepared to disobey such a command in the belief that the God he knew would not have issued it.

We need to remember however that at no point in the text is there the suggestion that God ever intended any sacrifice other than an animal one and that whatever Abraham believed at the time, the knife would never have been allowed to fall upon Isaac. What also does not seem to be in doubt is that no Christian group at any recorded time took this episode as a precedent for their own behaviour. Filicide did not catch on as a Christian precept or practice! Indeed, just the reverse. Unlike other societies where infanticide was practised on economic or religious grounds, the Church has always regarded it with horror and the conservative stance in the continuing debate about abortion has its roots in Christian belief and practice. Every soul is of value to God.

Of course, Christianity has its detractors who see the central event as *filicidal*: God sending his own son to the cross to be tortured and die. Christians have perhaps been too ready to see this or express it in the baldest and most simplistic terms. Indeed, one of the best-known and best loved verses of all (John 3:16) expresses the idea plainly. But as so often other parts of Scripture need to be referred to for a fuller understanding of this; the self-giving, "self-emptying" of Jesus, and the mutuality of the love between the persons of the Trinity, as well as the perfectly free willingness of Christ to lay down his life "for his friends", banishes any sense of filicidal tendencies from the New Testament picture of God.

Past generations have not found these concepts hard to accept and have always depicted the cross as a symbol of God's love, not his filicidal hatred. Throughout Christian history the cross has been seen as a place of sanctuary, forgiveness and hope, not one of divine hatred for sons or people in general. Current antagonism to the theology of the cross is reminiscent of the earliest ignorant reactions of the first and second centuries about Christians eating flesh in their rituals. Misunderstandings of this kind about the cross are based on a failure to recognise that Christians, though believing in three persons, believe in only one God. The 1662 *Book of Common Prayer* was careful to teach this of the God who, at the cross, "made there (by his one oblation *of himself* once offered) a full, perfect, and sufficient sacrifice, oblation, and satisfaction, for the sins of the whole world". Here is the God who "made himself nothing, taking the very nature of a servant".[62]

Dawkins' malevolent, capricious and bullying God therefore is actually nothing of the sort. God is seen in the pages of the Bible and in Christian theology as the opposite: consistent, loving, and self-sacrificing. It is the Church's shame that it has not always kept to that example.

As far as these particular allegations about the God of the Bible are concerned, there is not much of a case to answer. When, however, we come to the term *genocide* we must pause for further thought. To most Christians the idea that God could perpetrate such a thing is either a terrible outrage or a tragically funny mistake. God as *genocidal* is so much the opposite of the image Christians have in mind that it appears ridiculous. The reason why is not far to seek: few sermons, books or commentaries on the Bible deal adequately with the Old Testament passages that invoke the term which now we associate only with the darkest moments of human history—in the twentieth century most infamously with the Holocaust, but also with the events in central Africa and the Balkans.

Why are church leaders so reluctant to address this issue? It can surely only be because they find it so difficult to provide an answer which satisfies our belief that God is good while at the same time preserving our view that Scripture is a reliable and authoritative record of historical events—at least where it purports to be so. "A full look at the worst" here presents us with horrors we wish did not exist. But they do, and if we are to answer the charge we must examine them. Verses in Deuteronomy and the book of Joshua give us an unequivocal picture of God demanding, through the leaders he has chosen, the absolute annihilation of a race. Nothing is to be left; all are to be slaughtered: men, women and children. Neither the old, the infirm nor the infants are to be spared, as the Chosen People take over Canaanite homelands. Deuteronomy chapters 7, 20, and 32, and Joshua chapters 6, 8, 10 and 11 contain especially explicit instructions about the destruction (though there is the proviso in Deuteronomy 20 that the Israelites must offer peace terms, which if accepted are to preclude bloodshed). They are not pleasant to read. Naturally, among the Christians who do read them they produce a variety of responses.

One response is to say that God is completely "other" than us; his ways are not our ways, and anyway who are we to judge him? Job was told that since he could not answer God's questions it would be better to accept the reality that he was merely clay in the potter's hands and stop asking awkward questions. If God is good, the argument goes, then these acts of genocide are good too. We, poor mere humans, cannot fathom the mind of God. To my mind this is a very dangerous argument which could justify all sorts of evil human behaviour if accepted without some carefully thought through qualifications about the complementarity of love and severity. Moreover if we are in his image, albeit flawed, there must be some continuity of morality between God and man, or else he could not use an appeal to conscience or our sense of right and wrong as a way of showing us our failings. Yet St Paul does just this in his letter to the Romans. So does the Old Testament: "He has showed you, O man, what is good . . . to act justly and to love mercy."[63] How can we do that if his view of these things is entirely different from our own?

A second response is to consider that these things are written for our learning and learn to turn every physical action in these stories into a spiritual lesson. Thus the destruction of "evil" people becomes an object lesson in how to destroy evil in our own lives: all impurities must be laid on the altar of repentance and handed over to God for him to deal with. The passages dealing with wholesale destruction are supposed to allegorise our own spiritual battles against our own demons. The weapons of our warfare may not be "carnal" but they still destroy the strongholds of the enemy—in spiritual, not material terms. This is the way that evil is overcome now.

This response would be fine if we *were* dealing with allegory. But allegorising these events renders the Bible inoffensive and irrelevant to the same degree, as J. W. Wenham noted in *The Enigma of Evil*.[64] If, as in *The Pilgrim's Progress*, where the Castle of Giant Despair is merely a pictorial embodiment of the reality of despair, the cities of Canaan were mere pictures, this would be harmless enough; unfortunately they were not. They were filled with people not unlike us insofar as they lived, struggled, suffered and died. And they died because of God's instructions and at the hand of Joshua, according to the text.

A third response is to say that the biblical accounts of what happened vary, and so perhaps the Hebrews did in fact live and let live with the original occupants after the initial invasion of Canaan; indeed, that is what archaeological evidence suggests. The text then becomes a statement about what the writer feels should have been done if the Hebrews are to be seen as invincible. This accords with the view that, since the authorship of these books is in doubt, as well as their date, the likelihood is that they were written some time after the events they describe. Consequent upon that is the idea (attested by both the biblical record and archaeology which shows a good deal of integration between the cultures) that the books were written in a period of accommodation and compromise with the surrounding non-Hebrew peoples, and the authors therefore asserted as strongly as possible the absolute claims of Yahweh on people's allegiance. This of course does not alter the fact that the writers are claiming that God demands these things. It simply suggests that in reality they did not happen.

This response reduces the account to something less than entirely reliable, a narrative designed to exaggerate the separate identity of the invading tribes and to give their God an overridingly powerful status designed to overawe his enemies, boost the Hebrews' morale and augment such military victories as they had. This view gets rid of the actuality of genocide, but creates the equal and opposite problem of a God who has now been reduced to little more than a projection of imagination, and used for the Hebrews' own benefit.[65]

A fourth response is to believe that the land the Hebrews entered was so degenerate morally that its inhabitants deserved their punishment. Moreover, there was no way back for them, and extermination and a new start were the only way forward for humanity and salvation. Wenham and others have explored the depravity of Canaanite religion, in which child sacrifice, long discontinued by Egypt and Babylonia, seems to have been commonplace. He quotes a figure of 75 per cent of the bones found in probable ritual sacrifice areas of the late Bronze Age temple at Amman being those of children (rather than animals) aged between three and fourteen.[66] The occasional references to Molech and child sacrifice in the Old Testament are then perhaps just the tip of the iceberg: a society as corrupt as that of the Canaanites *needed* clinical extermination. Tribal societies (and more advanced civilisations) do, as we know, implode from time to time, and life was nasty and brutish and short for most, perhaps—but soldiers killing babies, women and the infirm still presents a picture hard to reconcile with a God of love.

One further way that many come to terms with these problems is to say that God gradually revealed his nature to the biblical writers, and that in the earliest days when their understanding was least developed they wrote of him in ways that were not only inadequate but actually misleading; his character was misunderstood. His presumed purposes were conceived in terms of the cultural context. It was Edmund Burke in the eighteenth century who remarked that man's first conception of God was in terms of raw power.[67] What in reality was God's desire for hearts and minds was thought to necessitate the conquest of territory and the elimination of opposition by force. War in the Near East during the Old Testament period was almost always merciless, so the perceived need for the eradication of evil in such a context would hardly have been dealt with in any way but violence. This leaves us with no more than a sketchy historical framework for the books purporting to be history, but exonerates God from the direct responsibility for the invasion, massacres and great destruction of life and property.

In her essay "The Fate of Ideas: Moses", when talking about the accounts of the invasion, Marilynne Robinson usefully reminds us that, as such things go, it was a rather modest affair in comparison with the imperial wars between Carthage or the Gallic tribes and Rome, which attract no modern opprobrium, and that we did not learn to be aggressive as the result of a largely unread Latin Bible.[68] In earlier times, Norsemen and Gauls did not learn their aggression from the Septuagint. Moreover, unlike the pagan gods' auspices of battle, the Jewish God sternly told the Jews they would likewise suffer if they acted no better than their enemies. Cato and Caesar are not eternally vilified; why then Moses and Joshua, when the society they created was answerable to a law which protected the poor and vulnerable to a degree which Rome (and Greece) never did?

What if actually, the truth were a mixture of parts of all these responses? What if none of them were entirely right or wrong but each combined with the other presented a true picture of both what happened and what Yahweh is like? How much would be lost from the traditional Christian picture of God? How much would be gained in terms of making Yahweh's actions ones that the modern world could more readily accept as being for its good? Would Christians have lost the right to claim that the whole Bible is "God-breathed" and profitable for "teaching, rebuking, correcting, and training in righteousness"?[69]

Let's take the last point first. It is surely possible to believe that the Bible is "God-breathed" and profitable for teaching, because this is not a specific theory of inspiration which demands an unthinking acquiescence in every statement of Scripture, taken at face value or in a literalistic way. The all-too-human authors of many of the books are present in their own works and are clear about their own sinfulness. Isaiah calls himself a man of "unclean lips", and St Paul calls himself "chief of sinners". Yes, the Holy Spirit directed them to write, but are we to accord precisely the same kind of inspiration to every book when the Bible itself, inspired over several millennia (if we include the original telling of the stories), makes no particular assertion about the precise nature of the authority of individual books? Can we not allow that Revelation can be progressive? Indeed it is difficult to see how it can be otherwise when Jesus alone, more than a millennium later than the events under discussion, is the full revelation of God, the very "image of the invisible God".[70] "For in Christ all the fullness of the Deity lives in bodily form."[71] If God allows frail sinful human authors to write the books, is it not reasonable to infer a progression of some sort, at least until God revealed himself fully in the face of Christ? After all, it is only in "these last days he has spoken to us by his Son . . . the radiance of God's glory and the exact representation of his being".[72] Previously it was "through the prophets at many times and in various ways".[73] It is certainly clear from the writings that God did not obliterate the human personalities of the authors. Revelation can be held to be perfectly consistent, albeit progressive in certain respects. Nevertheless, Jesus' entire ministry, we might say, being characterised by love, mercy and forgiveness, bears no relation to the picture of Yahweh in the "offending" Old Testament chapters, save one of radical opposition. ("*I say to you, love* your enemies.") But this is surely missing the point. Aspects of Jesus' teaching are at least as severe as some of the Old Testament teaching is. He warns us to flee from the wrath to come and paints terrifying pictures of the consequences of sin. The radical difference is not in the severity but in the fact that it is now for God to dispense it, not Joshua. The Church will be drawn from all nations. Strongholds will fall, but the weapons of our warfare are not carnal.

It is interesting that to the New Testament writers the main value of the Old Testament (and a large proportion of the quotations from it) seems to be its prophetic witness to Jesus himself. "These are the Scriptures that testify about me", said Jesus.[74] There are no citations of Canaanite genocide in the Gospels (despite Deuteronomy being frequently quoted) and the very idea of such verses being included is actually quite a shocking one, such is the contrasting tenor of the writing on occasions when Jesus is reported as speaking to or about Gentiles.

For each of the five responses above, the position could be expressed something like this:

1. God is "other"—we cannot understand his plans entirely.
2. The Old Testament record of these passages is there for us to learn from; we do now understand God's compassionate purposes far more fully because of Jesus, and yet we have to accept that God does punish sin, even though he does not expect or want us to take on that role for ourselves. Moreover, severity and love are complementary in God's nature, as Christ shows.
3. There was a struggle for the supremacy of monotheism and the writers of Deuteronomy and Joshua were seeking to show Yahweh's sole power over all his created people, either by writing what they conceived to be true and right about him, or in recording acts that they conceived to be morally right.
4. The Canaanite culture had sunk to such a low ebb (for example, the practice of Molech) that blood had to be spilt if a new start was to be achieved. Given the current state of the world it would seem that neither humanity in general now nor the Jews in particular then were capable of learning lessons about corporate responsibility save *in extremis.*
5. The biblical revelation of God is consistent but progressive, and the invasion narratives do not contradict the rest of Scripture which sheds increasing light until the Incarnation shows us the true nature of God perfectly and in terms we can understand.

None of these points need invalidate the Bible's claims for itself as having a unique authority and status and origin which are ultimately divine and therefore profitable for the four purposes which Paul reminds Timothy of in his second letter quoted above. Indeed, treated in this particular way, the very passages we have been considering do all of these things. They teach, rebuke, correct and train us.

What this approach *does* invalidate is the simplistic statement that the God of the Bible is a genocidal God, since that picture will not fit any part of the rest of the Bible save these few chapters which I have shown can be approached in many different ways without losing the integrity of the Biblical record. From times even before the canon of Scripture was fixed, the Church has seen the Bible as an organic whole and Scripture has been used to interpret Scripture. Where inconsistencies occur we need scholarship to explore them rather than denial, or simple soundbite answers with heads in the sand. The benchmark for both the medieval Church and the reformers was that nothing was allowed in doctrine which was repugnant to Scripture. For Wesley the principle was that the Scriptures must be read Christocentrically: there is nothing higher than the love demonstrated by Jesus.[75] For all these times and people the inspired Bible was the foundation of all true theology and that theology did not include genocidal action as an option of the day—even when Charlemagne and others wielded the sword rather than the Word to extend the boundaries of Christendom. It is not therefore surprising that despite appalling deviations by sections of the *visible* Church, Christianity has not for most of its history pursued militaristic conquest, or genocide, or sought to impose by force its beliefs upon the world. Our faults are our own; there is far more about providing for the poor in the Old Testament than there is about destroying alien cultures. The military occupation of Bronze Age Canaan, remote at a distance of one, or two, and now three millennia from the Church throughout its history, has not been a frequent or even repeated paradigm, inspiration or example. What the Church's example *has* been we will start to see in the next chapter.

CHAPTER 3

Very Odd and Rather Beastly

One of the astounding facts about the Christian church is its origin. It would be hard to imagine a less promising start. From political and social standpoints it would have been ludicrous to predict, in AD 35 for example, that this new sect of "Christiani", as they were first known in Antioch, were anything more than chaff in the wind. And for about 250 years they were "religio illicita"—illicit—or at the least "all very odd and rather beastly", as Charles Williams summarised it in *The Descent of the Dove*.[76] For Christians today, the transformation of the first very frightened and cowed disciples into a force which fearlessly proclaimed a message that undermined and opposed both the prevailing Jewish and Roman religious systems is clear evidence of the power of the resurrection of Jesus and of God's hand at work. But for secular historians it is a problem that requires some thought and is hard to explain away.

Our concern here however is not so much with what caused such a reversal of attitudes, but with the impact that this small but steadily growing minority had on first-century society. In the apostolic age, and the generation that followed it, what were Christians known for? Were they liked or disliked, and by whom? What contribution did they make to the provinces of the Roman world where Christian communities took root? In the first instance, how were they *supposed* to be behaving according to the Scriptures they so revered, and how did the Apostles instruct them?

We know that the public reading of the Old Testament Scriptures was a standard part of Jewish and Christian practice on the Sabbath. Paul tells Timothy, "devote yourself to the public reading of Scripture", and we have seen that Paul's letters were accorded high status from very early times.[77]

We can therefore expect the content of these readings to impact on the behaviour of those who heard them. We also know that the small, tightly-knit Christian communities enforced strong discipline on themselves where scriptural injunctions were not followed. Those injunctions were aimed both at personal and public obedience. Individual hearts had to be orientated towards God, but the evidence for this was to be visible and tangible in people's lives. Had not Jesus told them that people, like plants, are known by their fruits, not just their names? And had not his younger brother James written with clever rhetorical flourish: "Someone will say, 'You have faith; I have deeds.' Show me your faith without deeds, and I will show you my faith by what I do."[78] So, "faith without deeds is dead".[79] Almost the whole of the five chapters of James's letter are filled with advice and instruction about how to live more like Christ. He variously touches on, or considers, wisdom, humility, endurance, self-control, impartiality, mercy, right speaking, ambition, honesty, modesty and patience. His conclusion focuses on prayer, as if to say that all the things he has worked through must be the result of a mind and will depending on God rather than human endeavour. It is hard not to think that in creating this picture James is reflecting on his older brother—his stories, his teaching, and example in life and in death. James is also the New Testament writer who more than any other urges his readers not to allow social status or wealth to influence how they treat each other. It seems that this teaching really impinged on the Christian community in the second-century burials in the catacombs in Rome where there is little difference between how the Church leaders are buried and how the rest are. In an age of martyrs, what distinguishes one person from the next is not their wealth, sex or social status, but courage, conviction and faithfulness—qualities accessible to us all. A far cry from Victorian graveyards with their imposing headstones afforded by the rich!

Peter, writing self-evidently at a time of terrible persecution for those he addresses, urges them to "live such good lives among the pagans that, though they accuse you of doing wrong, they may see your good deeds and glorify God" as a result.[80] Peter's concern is that the church should be different from the culture that surrounds it; they should "live (their) lives as strangers here", and do this by avoiding "all malice, and all deceit, hypocrisy, envy and slander".[81] As with Paul writing to the Romans, such a life includes submitting "to every authority instituted among men",[82] even if it means suffering for doing good, because this is the supreme example of Christ and part of the meaning of the cross. Other instructions from Peter are also unequivocal. Christians are to be sympathetic, compassionate and humble, and should repay evil with blessing. They should avoid their past behaviour of debauchery, lust, drunkenness and idolatry, but use their energies to serve others, unashamed of having to suffer simply because they are Christians. All these moral imperatives (and many more) are at the heart of what Peter has to say, not peripheral to it, and wherever he enjoins these things he brings the reader back to his rationale—namely that we must do these things because Christ has done likewise for us.

It is easy for the modern reader to miss just how extraordinary these letters are. Familiarity and context have dulled their edge. But we should be seeing them as more akin to revolutionary tracts, not as parts of the furniture so familiar that, along with Shakespeare, they are a necessity for your desert island along with your favourite discs. These letters were not written lightly or without cost, and represent an upheaval of early imperial attitudes, or attitudes natural to humanity at any period of history. Christianity was not persecuted in the first century simply because Christians would not do reverence to the image of the Emperor, but because their attitudes were successfully divisive and perhaps inevitably subversive. Those who did not join them would number amongst them those who were mightily put out by such behaviour. Paul certainly found this: "In fact, everyone who wants to live a godly life in Christ Jesus will be persecuted."[83]

But there is another reason why these documents are remarkable: they so clearly reflect the teaching of the Gospels which probably only reached their written form, as opposed to their oral form, *later* than these letters. James and Peter are harking back to their experience of Jesus, whose company they shared for an astonishing, life-changing, revolutionary three years. This was the paradigm for life that the Apostles were trying to share with the world that lived so differently.

It is often thought that Paul's letters do not have the same practical emphasis as those of Peter and James, and of course to some extent this is true. He is so concerned to argue a case, or refute error or prove a point (as his training fitted him to do), that his direction on matters of practical day-to-day living is not always as prominent as his argument. In other ways however this is a misconception. Once Paul has made his case, his concern is very much with everyday behaviour rather than theology. A glance through the later passages of his letters reveals this well enough.

The repeated theme of Paul's letters (examples can be found in Romans, One and Two Corinthians, Galatians, Ephesians, Philippians, Colossians, One Thessalonians, One Timothy, and Titus) is essentially the same as that of Peter and James: we should behave in a particular way because that is how Christ behaved, and "so that your daily life may win the respect of outsiders and so that you will not be dependent on anybody".[84] There is another "so that" in Two Corinthians where Paul says that providing service and generosity to others will enable people to "praise God for the obedience that accompanies your confession of the gospel".[85] The cascade of abstract nouns comes again and again throughout the letters: goodness, gentleness, self-control, compassion, kindness, humility, gentleness, and patience are the characteristics to practise. Not only are these the qualities we are to "put on", but we are to "put off" bitterness, rage, anger, brawling, slander and malice. "Your attitude should be the same as that of Christ Jesus,"[86] Above all, the "most excellent way" is love, because it sums up the entire law "in a single command, 'Love your neighbour as yourself.'"[87] Christians are told by Paul to "live a life worthy of the calling you have received".[88] They are to "forgive as the Lord forgave you", "not counting men's sins against them", and to "make sure nobody pays back wrong for wrong but always try to be kind to each other and everybody else"—clearly an instruction to direct kindnesses not merely towards other Christians but to *everyone*.[89]

Those who have been immoral or criminal are mandated to stop lying, getting drunk and stealing, and instead to work honestly so they can share with those in need.[90] The rich are instructed to be generous and willing to share in One Timothy, and masters are enjoined not to threaten their slaves in Ephesians and to provide them with what is "right and fair" in Colossians. All are to "consider others better than yourselves" and to look to the interests of others.[91] Prohibitions are placed on pride and revenge in Romans 12.

The fact that Paul suffered for his unremitting pursuit of these goals is too well-known to document, but we should not forget that even though "against such things there is no law",[92] those who feel threatened by this degree of counter-cultural behaviour will find ways with or without the law to exact their revenge. The fact too that it was taken, in the most virulent way, against both Paul and those who sought to emulate him (and in doing so emulate Jesus), is a tribute to the fact that the early Church impacted on lives whether people liked it or not. If there had been no change, and no impact, the authorities, religious or secular, would not have bothered. There is no point in trying to hurt a corpse.

Can any other worldview or thought system or religion claim to be so idealistic and yet so pragmatic, so spiritual and yet equally so concerned about the here and now, as this? So concerned for deep personal integrity, yet so focused on the well-being of others? I don't think so. Be perfect even as your heavenly Father is perfect. Love your neighbour as *yourself.*

If, in looking at the social concerns of the New Testament writers, I have neglected to look at the teachings of Jesus directly, it is because few have had the temerity to question the altruism of his life and teachings. The title "Man for Others" is one that few seem to argue with. The writings of the Apostles that we have looked at reflect this altruism as well as they can, albeit imperfectly. Indeed, it is a curious exercise to reflect upon the force of character, the moral leadership and courage, the willingness to serve and to suffer that the Apostles and others display in the New Testament and then to place them next to the picture of Christ that we have in the Gospels. The disparity between the portraits is startling.

But what did the overwhelmingly powerful, pagan (and seemingly invincible) world make of this tiny, irritating, predominantly lower class "Jewish" cult with their resurrected messiah, political intransigence, social cohesion, and curious, slightly alarming rituals? A number of documents give us some clues.

One of the earliest documents from the Roman world which mentions Christians is the *Annales* of Cornelius Tacitus, a historian who lived from about AD 60 to 120 and described the Neronian persecution of AD 64. His intention is to blacken Nero's character (as if he needed to) while showing little sympathy with the followers of "Christus" who "had been put to death in the reign of Tiberius by the governor Pontius Pilate".[93] Tacitus can't find much to say about Christianity save that it is a "pestilent superstition"—a rather worthless annoyance, in other words.

Gaius Suetonius (born *c.* AD 69) tells us that the Jews were making disturbances at the instigation of "Chrestus" which led to their expulsion from Rome in *c.* AD 52, merely two decades after the crucifixion.[94] The Book of Acts (18:2) seems to corroborate this, and Suetonius too calls Christians those who adhere to a "new and mischievous superstition".[95] Actually they were thought to be involved in cannibalism and incest—the combination of a series of misunderstandings about the *agape* meal where the "body" of Christ was eaten in seeming secretiveness and where the "kiss of peace" would have been offered between "brothers and sisters". Such things, says the horrified Christian writer Eusebius, are not lawful to speak or think about, nor even to believe were ever done among men.

Other factors that made Christians unpopular and suspect included the age-old prejudice against Jews (from whom at first Christians were not distinguished) who were seen as exclusive and rather traitorous; Christians' natural disinclination to join in with the prevalent moral laxity obtaining in the society of any era; their negative impact on certain businesses such as prostitution and image making (as witnessed in Acts 19); their difficulty in accepting military service; their reputation as atheists because they would not worship idols, but worshipped a common criminal who lacked the respectability of antiquity; even their hesitation in using the public baths, which as Diarmaid MacCulloch points out probably made them smelly and antisocial![96]

There was then, a huge prejudice against this new sect, and human nature, then as now, found it easier and more attractive to believe the worst of someone rather than the best. To overcome all this they would have to move mountains. And they did. Or God did.

The reality of Christian behaviour is dealt with more rationally by Pliny the Younger, governor of the province of Bithynia in Asia Minor, writing in *c.* AD 112. In his famous letter to the Emperor Trajan he says that if Christians persist in confessing to be what they claim, he sentences them to death for their "pertinacity and unshakeable obstinacy" (though not the Roman citizens) in not revering the Emperor, and not cursing Christ.[97] The fact that Pliny has to report the spread of the superstition through cities, villages, and rural areas, and its effect upon all ages and ranks, despite these draconian penalties, is a measure of how brave, determined, and certain the Christians were in their faith. Not all of course were steadfast; doubtless many gave way, but we know that those who recanted told Pliny that the sum of their guilt had been to sing to Christ as to a god, and to bind themselves not to commit adultery, or to steal, and to keep financial integrity. When he tortured two servant girls to obtain further evidence all he discovered was more "superstition". Pliny naturally thinks therefore that the sect can be eliminated and all will be put right—or at least so he maintains to his boss.

To those in power in Rome there must have been a feeling that, in Gibbon's epigram, to politicians all religions are equally useful, to the people equally true, and to the philosophers equally false. "The people" in this analysis are predictably the least cynical and least arrogant of the three groups, and the growing number of cults to which they belonged, unlike the religion of the state, frequently aimed for personal purification and for immortality (while often ending in debauchery). It is less remarked today, but older writers used to suggest that Christianity exploded into a religious atmosphere in the first century, but one which had no power to change lives in the way many were looking for. Love, order, discipline, purity, and simplicity were the hallmarks of the new religion. If those five qualities were on their own the reality, Christianity would still have made a powerful, if transient, impact on the period. But if, as Christians believe, this was the result of God's intervention in daily human life, then the rapid spread of Christian communities can be accounted for more convincingly. These are qualities that make for stable societies and harmonious living. The high standards Christians exacted of each individual in the first two centuries are evidenced not only by Paul's severe language about the unrepentant sinner at Corinth, but also by the fact that excommunication from the Church lasted for life, and, anecdotally, by the story of St John (as told by Irenaeus) who fled the baths at Ephesus when he found the heretic Cerinthus there, and feared both pollution and disaster. This may well not be true but the fact that the story circulated shows what was expected in terms of keeping oneself pure. Curiously, several heresies arose later as a protest against *leniency* in Church discipline. Those early believers were a tough lot! It was not until the Decian persecutions in the third century that sections of the Church learnt to be more merciful to their own who had strayed.

Roman authority, however, did not learn to be merciful to the Christians, and the stories of the martyrs, whose blood was the seed of the Church, is not often enough told today. Freedom from persecution was never certain from the second century onwards, when being a Christian raised charges of sedition. Public torture, imprisonment, the dismembering of "criminal" Christians by wild beasts in the arena, attacks on person and property by the mob: all became increasingly common events for Christians as the second century drew on, until at the start of the third century Tertullian could complain of the proscription: *Non licet esse uos*—"You are not allowed to exist!"[98] Through it all, the beleaguered Christian community at worst exhibited to society at large "mere obstinacy", as the stoic, and Christian persecutor, Marcus Aurelius (Emperor AD 161–180) noted to himself about them, and at best the qualities borne wonderful witness to by the aged and venerable Polycarp (the last of the Apostle John's pupils) in AD 155; he had served his master for eighty-six years, during which time "he has never done me wrong".[99] He was burned alive for his gentle faith—with timbers and faggots brought hurriedly from the workshops and public baths.

Polycarp lived at the time of Justin Martyr, one of the first "Apologists" for the faith—those who used rational discourse to defend the truth of the Christians' beliefs about their Saviour and the nature of the world God had put them in. He was ambitious. His audience included the Emperor, Antoninus Pius, and the Roman Senate. He, and men like him such as Clement of Alexandria and Origen, intended to show the educated classes that not only was Christianity not opposed to reason and education but that it was positively the most reasonable answer to the ever-recurring problems of understanding the world which each generation reshapes for itself. They saw that the revelation of God in history had been progressive, and that Socrates, Plato, and the Stoics had been instrumental in preparing the world for the revelation of God's unique Son, Jesus, the Logos, the Wisdom of God. The link between Christianity and education had begun. Yet it was only after Origen that the larger scale martyrdoms began. Christianity had become a force to be reckoned with.

But mobs don't stop killing martyrs because of reasonable persuasion. They kill them because they feel like it and reason has nothing to do with it. One of the odd paradoxes about second- and third-century Christianity is that as Christians became more reasonable (at least in the writings of their Apologists), so their opponents became more unreasonable, and the persecutions more violent and widespread. The Stoics had taught the brotherhood of humanity, and Seneca that slaves should be treated considerately, but this "religion of slaves", as it was known, was treated with increasing intolerance and ferocity in the persecutions which punctuated the peace of the third century as Roman administration and society became more disordered. It was the century of assassinations: the Emperor was more likely to be murdered than to meet a gentler fate. *Coups d'état*, border wars and civil wars meant repeated burgeoning violence, and with borders 3,000 miles apart along one dimension, and 2,000 miles on the other, it was impossible to maintain their security. Increasing taxes, and widespread flight from settlements to evade their collection, made for lawlessness, fear and violence. A natural imperial response to this was to demand increased enforcement of sacrifices in honour of the Emperor and intense suspicion of those who would not comply. This ferocity may also have been the result of the increasing number of believers among the higher classes of society who, being more influential, posed a greater threat. By AD 303, as churches were pulled down, Scriptures confiscated, and Christians systematically martyred in larger numbers than ever before, it would have been impossible to foresee that just a decade later the Emperor Constantine himself would be proclaiming at Milan equal toleration for the "Christiani" alongside all other religions. Whether it was to the betterment of the world that Church and State were soon to be allied if not identified is a question that has proved controversial ever since.

CHAPTER 4

The Not-So-Dark Ages

If we speak of "The Dark Ages" now as a historical period in which civilisation simply halted, we are the ones who are ignorant. Historians seldom use the term, but if they do, it is because there is so much we would like to know about these centuries, roughly from some point in the fifth century through to the crowning of Charlemagne as Emperor of the West in AD 800, and on perhaps as far as the tenth century. During these centuries the Church was at first a minority that had gained the favour of a fourth-century emperor and existed at that point only as an upstart minority in the eyes of established society; yet it emerged from that period as a pan-imperial power to which, in its own eyes at least, the Emperor was subject. How this happened is not our concern here, but rather the matter of what influence this change had on the lives of individuals and on society. We need therefore to consider briefly the Church's contribution in a variety of areas. Foremost, as we might have guessed from the Apologists, is the matter of education.

Clement of Alexandria (*c.* AD 150–*c.* 215) had taught that philosophy was conducive to piety and that Christians who were afraid of it were like children afraid of ghosts. Not all had agreed; Tertullian, for instance (who was, nevertheless, the first Christian to think and write in Latin and the first to use the term "Trinitas" about the Godhead). But Origen (*c.* AD 185–*c.* 254) furthered the work and was the first commentator to produce an edition of the Old Testament which laid side by side six different versions for comparison. If we conjoin this approach, and these efforts, with the complex ideas of St Paul and the Gospel of St John we can see the birth and the necessity of Christian scholarship.

It has been noted by various sociologists that the Church in the modern West is frequently strongest amongst the educated middle classes. In modern English society, where the established Church used language hundreds of years old right up till the later part of the twentieth century, and where its clergy lived in houses distinctly indicative of a certain status, and where wealth and deference seem to be part of the fabric, this is understandable enough. But there is a less immediately obvious reason for this demographic, namely that "Christianity is an education itself".[100]

The root cause of this is literacy and the fact that the *hearing* of the Bible is not enough for those captivated by its message. There is a need to read it for oneself. Missionaries have long known that the only way to enable an indigenous church to stand on its own feet is to provide the Scriptures in the language of the people. But in turn, reading is not enough either. There has to be understanding, and for that there has to be study. Once the study is underway, the reader comes under both the discipline and the authority of the teacher who holds the key to its interpretation— the Teacher who explained to the two on the Emmaus Road what was written in the Scriptures concerning himself. The earliest proclamations in the Christian Church were not about new ways of living but about certain facts that had happened in recent history. Those facts demanded a response, and the response would direct your life choices. From those choices, circumstances would arise which would reinforce them. Focus, motivation, a sense of direction, of self-worth, even the sense of a part to play in the universal outworking of the divine plan—all result from those facts and the discovery that the Bible is the written Word, God's truth and light to his benighted people.

Of course, to some extent this would be true of any of the major world religions. If you are a follower you are on a journey, and the implication of that is that a process of constant learning and revelation and adjustment to new environments and knowledge is constantly taking place. But not quite the same can be said about either a secular worldview which can be threatened by a sense of futility or self-importance, or (for instance) Islam. Western Christendom found its educational methods prevailing across the globe, not because of the sword but because it was not rote learning that was predominating so much as *understanding*, the tools for which would be used in the universities. There was never the feeling that the Scripture could not be translated without irretrievable loss—which is still the view of Muslims about the Qur'an. On the Day of Pentecost the Apostles spoke the Word in many languages. Neither was there the struggle to shape thousands of complex characters in order to sequence phrases or convey information, a process which the Chinese would be subject to.

In our age today when absolutes are so reluctantly accepted, and when truth is often subjective and ethics situational, it is too easy for opposite and contradictory ideas to be held together in a single mind, even though logic would say they cannot be. The post-modernist uses stones that fit many buildings. The early Middle Ages were not like that. Had they been, we would never have read the Athanasian Creed, or probably any other creeds, because the need and desire for their formulation would not have been there. People would have been content with something much sloppier intellectually. But as things were, statements of pinpoint precision were important in the way they are in a legal document today. Getting them wrong can lead to disaster further down the road. It was not just that God was knowable in Christ that was important, but equally, that although Jesus was a man, he was also fully God; although there was only one God, there were also three Persons in that one God; although Jesus was the Son, he was consubstantial, co-equal, and co-eternal with the Father These are paradoxes to stretch the greatest minds, but ones susceptible to intellectual enquiry. By contrast, Allah, the unknowable, the un-incarnate, cannot be defined at all, or only in the most generalised terms, because so much less can be known of him. The struggles of the early Church to define, within human limitations, the God-man (first Jew and then man, or vice-versa? He had not waived the Judaic law, yet he clashed with the lawyers who interpreted it) ensured an extraordinary level of intellectuality in the debates and writings of the Fathers, and yet the proclamation of the need for repentance for sins in order to receive the gift of the Gospel was so simple. Some structures need complicated engineering in order to make a simple architectural statement. G. K. Chesterton reminded his readers that there is only one angle at which something will stand stably, but many at which it will fall.[101] Getting it there and keeping it upright is not a simple business.

Equally, the decision about what to include in the canon of the New Testament, when it had been written over an extended period by different men in different places, was more complex than the process of simply designating certain writings holy because they emanated from a single source. These complexities might be seen as a strength or a weakness, but whichever it was they stretched the minds of those engaged in the task of describing them. It ensured that those responsible for the preservation of doctrine were highly able and highly educated. And education is the prime bequest of the early medieval church to the world. In the period we now come to look at, the Church, and especially monasticism, was the single greatest preserver in the Western world of manuscripts, literacy and study. Without the monks there would have been darkness indeed.

It should come as no surprise that a movement such as monasticism, which had its ancestry in a people called to be separate or "holy", and which had survived on the margins of acceptability through two centuries of persecution, should feel the need to be distinct in a physical sense ("monachism") when society finally and officially accepted the sect's adherents. To the man who has everything, the ability to choose to have nothing can be a liberation. Jesus had taught that camels and rich men have something in common.

Anthony, the first hermit, having heard the voice of God calling him to leave his possessions and at the same time being dissatisfied with his own personal holiness, began a way of living that was central to the expression of faith for more than a thousand years. The beginning, as Chesterton said, is the right end at which to begin and yet those thousand years are somehow forgotten today by most of us who remember only the end—the corruption of the monastic movement and the dissolution of the English monasteries in the sixteenth century. This is a sort of backward reading of history in which we see the reverse of what the movement was famous for across the Western world, as if that were its true nature, not its degenerated state. This must be partly due to the suddenness and violence of their overthrow (sensationally newsworthy, as we saw in Chapter 1) but also partly due to the general contention of this book, namely that the evil that men do has a longevity in the human mind which their good deeds do not benefit from. Indeed, the interred bones of the monkish saints, or rather their tendency to become revered relics, is still ridiculed in the press today, while the reasons for that reverence are given no column inches. In addition, the few monastic houses that survived the sixteenth century up until our own times are perceived to make so little apparent effect on society that their importance today is reckoned negligible. We shall see that nothing could be further from the truth in the early and high medieval periods. For some people it is impossible to appreciate a whole world of ideas because all they see is the corruption or degeneration of them. The libertine and the Puritan can seldom see any virtue in the other's viewpoint. Shakespeare's Sir Toby Belch put it nicely when he said to Malvolio, "Dost thou think that because thou art virtuous there shall be no more cakes and ale?"[102]

The impact that the monasteries made on society was partly because, even from the outset, as MacCulloch has shown, the "Desert Fathers" were far more part of urban and agricultural life than is often imagined.[103] Certainly, Anthony retreated increasingly far from company into the Egyptian desert, but the simple uncluttered life he led set a precedent for a particular sort of Christian living which is surely admirable in so many ways. Discipline, fasting, poverty, meditation and prayer in themselves are ingredients for well-being and make an interesting contrast to the prevailing concerns of today: gratification, indulgence, luxury, constant noise and an overwhelming submersion in the superficiality of everyday living. It is hard to see how the ideals of the earliest monks can be criticised, even if some fell short of making disciples of all nations. This is even more true when we turn to Pachomius, who began the first Christian commune (also in Egypt) of which we have any details. In addition to the practices listed above, Pachomius ensured that members worked to support themselves and that aspirants were serious. They had to be able to read and write in Coptic and to have learnt substantial portions of Scripture before being admitted. The Church was unwittingly laying educational foundations for the next thousand years.

Had the monks been the sole focus of Christian practice the whole of Christian history would have been different—but at the same time as the monastic retreat from society, or solitary and isolated living, grew in popularity, so did the political advancement of others in the Church. Bishops and emperors had different roles, but while the Emperor was at least nominally Christian, as a post-Constantine "Christian" state required, those roles also overlapped and were frequently in conflict. Who should dictate to whom? If the Emperor is a loyal servant of the Church, his bishop should be allowed to influence or direct ethical policy. If the Emperor is truly absolute however, and has to govern, he should have the final say in home and foreign policy. Matters came furiously and famously to a head at the end of the fourth century when Bishop Ambrose of Milan forced the Emperor Theodosius I to do public penance for his authorisation of a massacre in Thessalonica. The problem with this was that Ambrose himself had not been entirely praiseworthy in his own political positioning. Moreover, in making Christianity so obviously a power which could enforce certain public behaviour (Theodosius made Christianity the official state religion), the state brought about the corollary that heresy would, henceforth, be treated as treason. At that point something changed in history that would plague the Church till the eighteenth century. The flirtation of the Church with temporal and political power, which had begun as a quarrel, was now a marriage, but of partners "unequally yoked together" as St Paul described the marriage of two people with differing goals. Fortunately, Ambrose's power-play was far from the only drama that would be played out. The monastic life continued to attract all those who wanted to find a different sort of power centre in their lives.

The Rule of Basil the Great, Bishop of Caesarea (d. AD 379), added a greater degree of care and concern for members of the community along with the scheme of seven daily services for the monks around which their life revolved. But in addition to that he knew the value of writing and study—of education. (We have 300 of his letters, as well as lectures, homilies, and other anti-Arian works.) He corresponded with the heroic, five-times-exiled Athanasius in defence of the doctrine of the Trinity. This found its liturgical expression in the Nicene Creed (and the Apostles' Creed at about the same time), which was formulated at the first Council of Constantinople in AD 381, at which the heresy of Arianism was outlawed. Such things are utterly remote to the secular world today, but actually are fundamental to Christian belief and practice. M. A. Smith, in *The Church under Siege,* has suggested that Muhammad may even have derived his inaccurate views of Christianity from fringe churches, perhaps Arians, where Christ was not upheld as an equal person in the Godhead.[104] The defence of this belief, that there are three equal persons in the Godhead, means that Christians have subsequently been unashamed of the view that Jesus was perfect in his moral example and in his teaching. It has meant that the revelation of God through him has never had to be superseded and that his words are for all time. It has also meant that his sacrifice for sins can in no way be bettered, and that it is "full, perfect, and sufficient", giving hope even to the greatest of sinners. This sort of assurance has been at the heart of Christianity from the beginning, giving rise to the joyful proclamation of good news, without which there would have been none of what the Church has been noted for: its service of others based on the conviction that if God the Son died for me, he did so for all others too. They are equally the actual and potential recipients of grace, which may well be understood or received by them initially in the form of social action: help with material well-being. This is what the monasteries under the Rule of Basil initiated.

The monks' care for the sick, having its basis in the Jerusalem diaconate of the Book of Acts, and reflected in the letter of James, created in time a new institution, the hospital. Their imperative of personal charity towards the poor, "the widows and fatherless" led also to their taking over the orphanages which the Church had founded in the fourth century. They also educated boys without (surprisingly) expecting them to become monks; they took alms to the poorest, and carried out relief work via a carefully planned system. Basil dignified work by specifying the need for it not merely as an occupation, but because it is a good in itself, and because it should be a means of doing good to others. Indeed, in one sense *laborare est orare*—to labour *is* to pray, though this formulation had to wait for the Benedictines. The Rule of St Basil still obtains today in the East.

Another figure who had the same social concern as Basil was Bishop Martin of Tours (AD 316–97), in France, who founded the first monastery in the West. Having come from a pagan family and a military background, Martin was energetic in evangelising the Gauls, but accounts show him to be kindly in doing so. Our use of the word "chapel" derives from the *capellae*, as the little churches founded in Gaul were called. The name was used because Martin was said to have shared half his soldier's cloak ("capella") with a poor man in need (St Martin-in-the-Fields church in London is famous to this day for its work with the homeless, immigrants, and Amnesty International). Martin also continued the tradition of allowing his monks to engage in learning, and to make copies of Scripture.

They were literate, educated, and continued to become more so as they took painstaking trouble over their sacred task.

Asceticism, social concern and learning were the hallmarks of these early monasteries, but by far the most learned figure of the Western world, whose influence has been so great as to be incalculable, was Augustine, Bishop of Hippo in North Africa. As the Roman Empire physically and functionally came to an end in AD 410 with Alaric the Visigoth's sacking of Rome, Augustine, one-time professor of rhetoric at Milan, was engaged in bequeathing to Christendom the greatest and most influential body of theology ever written by one man. By no means everyone thanks him for this, and it is easy to focus on three aspects of his work which seem hard for many to accept today: the doctrines of predestination and original sin, and his attitude towards sex. The last, as so often in humanity, stemmed from his own inability, as a young man before his conversion, to remain continent, and from guilt—which has provided us with the first (and many would say unsurpassed) analytical autobiography exploring the emotional side of Christian experience, his *Confessions*.

But if a negative attitude towards sex means struggling with thoughts and acts which do not reach an ideal Christian purity, is that an entirely bad thing? Some will have shipwrecked on this rock, it is true, but how many may have been saved by it? Restraint, inhibition, self-disgust even, sometimes have their place, and the absence of them can sometimes lead to much greater evil and harm. Predestination too is a doctrine which has led some to despair, and has become, in popular terms, the defining characteristic of Calvinist churches. But for the Calvinist, one of the proofs of being the Elect is that the individual Christian perseveres in his calling and he cannot therefore be lazy or nonchalant about his behaviour towards God and others. As Middleton Murry pointed out in 1938, where people cease to be fearful of hell after death, they all too often have to be fearful of hell in this life—"by a Gestapo".[105] In our own century we could now multiply the example many times. This doctrine too has therefore prevented social evils as well as caused them. Augustine accepted that there were both good and evil people within the visible Church, and that only at the end of time would they be separated out, thereby making a distinction between the visible and invisible Church which later ages could usefully have remembered more often. Wolves do masquerade in sheep's clothing; spirits should be tested, not blindly followed, as St John tells us.

It is not always remembered that Augustine, in fighting the Manichaeans (he had been one himself) ensured for subsequent ages an understanding of the *goodness* of God that could have been lost had his massive intellect been employed differently. He taught that moral evil springs from free will and is the distortion or absence of good, not something willed from the beginning by God. We can therefore be more certain of God's grace, which Augustine personally felt very strongly.

His teaching of original sin (perhaps born out of that very emphasis on the goodness of God), which secular critics love to throw at Christians as being a crippling shackle on human endeavour, somehow looks more like liberty when we place alongside it current alternative explanations of human moral failure. For instance, if our genes predetermine who we are and how we behave, then we can despair of change and throw moral responsibility out of the window at the same time. Or again, if our nurturing is entirely to blame for our bad actions, then we are either left with a mystery when the best parenting and education still produces a wayward or even criminal child, or we are left with a profound (and of course irredeemable) guilty feeling that it's all our fault when our child goes wrong. If, however, we accept that there is an innate bias towards selfish and sinful behaviour, but that it can be improved by education and care, then there is an understanding and joint responsibility shared by parent and child which makes purposeful all that Christian education has been striving towards for two millennia: a self-assessment qualified by realistic humility and guided by the hope and promise of future fruition, even glory. Original sin may not be a palatable pill to swallow at first, but it fits the perceived facts of human behaviour and is the doctrine that the Church has believed from the beginning. St Paul had made clear that in Adam all had died as a result of sin, but that Christ was the second Adam, the one in whom "all shall be made alive". If we are not sinners by nature then can we not perfect ourselves by our own efforts? And if that is true, to what purpose was Christ reconciling the world to himself through the cross?

One further implication of this doctrine is its taming and control of human anger. Never has humanity lived in an age when so much is within

our control. Twenty-first-century technology has enabled us to choose
the sex of our babies, map our genes, predict and prevent many of our
diseases, and determine the time and manner of our own painless deaths.
And yet, paradoxically, the more choice we are enabled to exercise, the
more angry we seem to become as a society, when even tiny incursions
are made into what we have learned to see as our rights. The higher our
expectations are raised, the more we focus on our human rights; the
more we become frustrated when they are not met. The faster you expect
to travel, the worse it is when someone holds you up. Road rage is not
usually the mark of the pedestrian, but of the fast driver. Original sin
puts paid to certain sorts of expectation and assumption. For instance,
it is impossible for someone who holds to this doctrine to be enticed
into thinking what the advertisements love to tell us, that "because you
deserve the very best", you should buy this product. The result of this
consumerist approach to life is obvious: whenever you fail to receive or
achieve the very best (whatever you conceive that to be) you feel hard done
by; life is unfair, there's no justice in the world, and so on. If, however,
you reckon that, given humanity's failure to live up to its pretensions of
civilised behaviour and your own signal failure even to keep the standards
you set for yourself (let alone expect of others), you deserve rather less
than constant happiness, then you are much more likely to think you
are blessed or lucky. It is easier, so to speak, to enjoy the roller-coaster
adventure of apparent fortune and misfortune in which the rough has
to be taken with the smooth, and a brave face put on things when they
are tough. Self-evidently, this is a socially cohesive approach to life, and
one more likely to produce a cheerful positive attitude than any of the
alternatives. Again we see that what at first sight seems to be a formula for
misery and resentment actually turns out to be the best medicine. "The
unpopular parts of Christianity turn out when examined to be the very
props of the people", as Chesterton said in *Orthodoxy*.[106]

Augustine's greatest work, *De Civitate Dei*, in twenty-two volumes,
began with a refutation of the idea that the world had gained nothing
by adopting Christianity in place of paganism (but he took five books
to complete the argument). In fact, people had said, matters have been
worse since Christ came. In almost 800 years Rome had not been violated,
but then was sacked just fifteen years after the death of Theodosius, who

had made Christianity official! Augustine's reply is that, though worldly civilisations have achieved awesome status, the state is not, as we would say now, fit for purpose in achieving its aim of providing peace and happiness in individual lives. Rather, it has been an almost total failure. Misfortune, malice and misery trample on us: all that the state attempts in order to avert disease, poverty, crime, ignorance and war is merely a measurement of the extent of humanity's suffering. We are destroyed not so much from without as from within. The only inviolate city, the only real city of refuge, is the City of God. It is curious and also a matter of some shame that 1,600 years later the same argument has to be made against the most strident secularisers despite the evidence.

Augustine's last twelve books describe the two polities: one temporal, the other spiritual and exercising universal dominion. Whichever view we take of the history of the Church and its dealings with society at large, positive or negative, Augustine must stand centre-stage in having made it happen. If paganism had earlier crushed "poor talkative Christianity" as the Visigoths sacked Rome, not only would Augustine not have written as he did; it is unlikely he would have written anything that would have lasted at all. Classical paganism was not only morally unable to empower its adherents, it was intellectually shallow, even empty. Reading, rational argument, philosophy and debate were not important to it: in the end no one cared enough about whether it was true or not. It is singularly appropriate that when at his conversion Augustine heard what he took to be the Divine Voice in the garden, saying in Latin, "*Tolle lege*", what he was being told to do was to *read*.

Keeping manuscripts in existence, enabling and motivating people to read, sustaining the ordered conditions in which debate, rational argument and intellectual enquiry are possible were the scholarly, as opposed to spiritual, common denominators between the different monastic orders.

Unlike Augustine, Patrick was no scholar, but his extraordinary contribution to the Christendom of the Far West was the restless physical energy which kept him on the move. Whether negotiating with tribal chiefs, or preaching, or ordaining clergy, he set up small groups of believers wherever he went. His reputation was such that he was credited with appointing hundreds of bishops and being the inspiration for countless monastic houses. These would become the places where Celtic Christianity could flourish in a world of disorder, plague, famine and war, and in which civilisation survived in smaller and smaller social groupings. What is certain is that he brought Ireland into touch with Rome, introduced Latin as the language of the Church in Ireland, and brought order to existing Christian societies.

If Patrick is the patron saint of Irish and Celtic monasticism, Benedict (c. AD 480–544) is the patriarch of all Western monks, and his influence was to be even more widespread.

Through the early Middle Ages, the Benedictines, or Black Monks, were responsible for saving the civilisation of North West Europe through their hundreds of houses and thousands of monks, each in their own autonomous, independent communities but each following in their own way the Rule of St Benedict, which divided the day between "offices", or religious services, fieldwork or whatever labour was useful, and reading—of which there was about four hours. This indeed was "God's household, built on the foundations of the Apostles, prophets and Jesus Christ".[107] Worship, service of the community, work, and study of the Scriptures made for godly living. Benedict began with the foundation of twelve houses in the Abruzzi mountains north of Rome, but is most famous for the monastery on the summit of Monte Cassino, which became for centuries a chief centre for Christianity in Western Europe.

All over Latin Christendom the Benedictines modelled organised labour, agriculture, and farming of many kinds, as well as pursuing the arts and practising skilled trades. The result of course was that admiration for this way of life brought conversions. The Teutonic races, Friesland, Holland and central Germany became Christian. Through the efforts of the Benedictines Christianity was planted firmly in England too. And, as we have seen from the beginning, the *education* of the Church, and others—initially boys destined to become monks, but later those who would work in other professions—was central to the monks' contribution to society.

In about AD 680, a small boy, Beda, was admitted to the Benedictine monastery of St Peter and St Paul at Wearmouth and Jarrow to be educated. He spent the rest of his long life there, where he claimed he had always delighted to learn, teach and write. The boy was to become "the Venerable Bede", and the foremost scholar of the century: his writing practically sums up all the learning of his day, whether scientific, historical or theological. But Bede himself could not have written as he did and preserved this knowledge for us if he had not had access to the library of Abbot Benedict Biscop, who had founded the monastery. In turn Ecgbert, one of Bede's pupils, became Archbishop, and founded the Cathedral School in York, at which a certain Ealhwine was taught. This promising and clever boy is better known to history as Alcuin, who under Charlemagne was the main agent of the Carolingian Renaissance, which as we shall see, had far-reaching influence and directly touches our lives today. It is therefore the Benedictines, the Black Monks, that we have to thank for the preservation of learning both through and beyond the end of those so-called "Dark Ages", when the sky, though darkened, was peppered by innumerable pinpricks of brilliant spiritual light. The image is an appropriate one if we imagine, in every corner of Europe, the midnight oil being burnt in the scriptoria and libraries of the monasteries and reflected in the beady eyes of the monks intently poring over their precious manuscripts—Seneca, Horace, Ovid even, and not just Scripture—which without their labours would have been lost to all of us for all time.

How strange then that we remember or are reminded so little of this achievement when it has been responsible for so much that is good, and educationally and socially desirable in an age of fragmenting values.

The boy Ealhwine, or Alcuin (c. AD 735–804), did not become a monk, though he lived like one—but he did become a poet, ecclesiastic, teacher, logician, and finally in AD 796 Abbot of the monastery of St Martin at Tours. Archbishop Ecgbert had reorganised the church over which he had authority and reformed the clergy, with an emphasis on the need for learning which the saintly Bede had taught him. Alcuin became Master of the school in York (today St Peter's) and revived the curriculum of the seven Liberal Arts, which became the core of medieval learning in the universities as it had been for the earlier Romano-Christian schools. The *Trivium* (grammar, rhetoric, and dialectic, or logic) was followed by the *Quadrivium* (arithmetic, geometry, music, and astronomy). The whole curriculum took seven years to complete. Grammar consisted of reading, writing and speaking, all in Latin. Rhetoric was the process of learning the art of the spoken word, especially in debate or dialectics. The unspoken assumption today is that such early programmes of learning must have been very basic, but patronising the past is not a valid way of exploring it, and these subjects were often far from simple. It would be a good exercise for modern schoolchildren to look at some of these topics to convince them of that. If in doubt, look at Alcuin's *Propositiones ad Acuendos Juvenes* (*Problems to Sharpen the Young*) and try to solve the problem of the three jealous husbands—recreational maths and logic comparable to the mind games and "brain training" found in books and papers today.

In AD 781, King Elfwald sent Alcuin to Rome to gain confirmation of York's status as an Archbishopric. On his return journey, Alcuin met King Charles of the Franks in Parma; in AD 800, Charles would be crowned the Emperor we know as Charlemagne, the conqueror of two thirds of Europe. Charles persuaded Alcuin to join the Palace School in Aachen in AD 782, and he stayed in the job until AD 790, during which time he taught the King himself, who was keen to include the study of religion in the curriculum, and also his sons, courtiers, and clerics. Alcuin, being a Christian, tried to show Charles the folly of forcing pagans to be baptised on pain of death (his practice until this point) by convincing him that real faith is an act of the will and cannot be produced by coercion. In AD 797, Charles abolished the death penalty for refusing to believe in Christ.

But Alcuin achieved far greater things. He was responsible not only for the curriculum of the cathedral and abbey schools which under him became models of excellence, and for the education and civilisation of the supreme ruler of the age, but astonishingly also for literacy as we know it today. Continuing the tradition of monasteries everywhere, he encouraged the copying of manuscripts to ensure their survival. We think today of writing, especially typescript, as virtually indestructible, but the monks knew it was more like, in today's terms, the preservation of an endangered species. We look after rare animals in captivity in the hope that we can get them to breed; the monks looked after manuscripts instead, and their abbots got them to reproduce these by copying. Without this process, an incalculably greater number of them would have been reduced to a last priceless copy which would then have finally crumbled to dust.

Others besides those at Aachen and Tours of course had done this, but Alcuin alone insisted on the most beautiful calligraphy, the Carolingian Minuscule, which became the writing standard in Europe, so that the

Roman alphabet could be recognised across widely different parts of the continent. This script was disseminated from the scriptorium in Aachen for which Alcuin was responsible. Essential aspects of writing which we don't even consider, such as capital letters, became standard for the first time in the documents of the day. Legibility (the result of increasing regulation of how letters were formed) was also essential where documents had to be read in public, such as lectionaries or collections of Scripture to be read aloud. Minuscule was taken up in England and Ireland in the tenth century, and via the Renaissance humanists studying the Carolingian texts, found its way into the printed books of the fifteenth and sixteenth centuries, thereby becoming the basis for modern lowercase typefaces.

Latin as the *lingua franca* of Europe, Charlemagne's Renaissance, the renewal of Christendom, the preservation of fragile links with the glories of the classical world, the survival of rare copies of the New Testament made from copies dating back to Constantine, the medieval curriculum which formed the basis of study later on at the universities of Oxford and Cambridge: all these can be attributed to the monks dressed modestly in black; to Benedict, to Patrick, to others like them, nameless monks and nuns, and before them to the good news of the Gospel in the first place.

When we consider monasticism and the Church of the period in these terms, it is hard to see why a movement so powerful in its appeal, so effective in its aims, should have fallen so far from its ideals as to find itself portrayed satirically by William Langland and Geoffrey Chaucer exactly 1,000 years after Basil. In the General Prologue to *The Canterbury Tales*, dating from the 1380s, Chaucer depicts six clerics; only one of these, the Parson, is treated without some degree of satire. The Prioress is vain, pretentious, coy and inviting; the Monk is worldly, intellectually and physically lazy, indulgent and vain; the Friar is promiscuous, greedy, snobbish and venal. The Summoner is disgusting, frightening, ignorant, conniving, cynical and manipulative; the Pardoner is most of these, as well as sexually ambiguous, avaricious and hypocritical. There is no evidence that Chaucer had any axe to grind, so even given that satire makes for better reading than hagiography, we may take it that his portraits, while comic, also contain a measure of truth that his (admittedly small and courtly) reading public must have been able to recognise if the satire was to make any impact. So what had happened to the Church by the later medieval period?

In 1932 H. G. Wells gave a very useful and penetrating account of the history of religions in *The Work, Wealth and Happiness of Mankind*. To summarise his view, Wells characterises all religions at their start as transfiguring and intensely practical—but when the Master is no longer present to revive flagging zeal, compromise creeps in, attenuation takes place, and the priesthood takes on a distinctive role disallowed to the laity. Religious fervour cools and tolerance of those inside and outside the religion becomes necessary. Ultimately it becomes difficult or impossible to pick out the converted from the rest by external tests. Once society is without easy means of making this distinction between groups, the glad tidings have little appeal, and so the inattention of the majority produces indignation among the faithful, which breeds resentment from the rest, and so the religious find their backs to the wall.

Is this what happened to the medieval Church? Is it as simple as that, convincing as it sounds?

There is a good deal of truth in this picture and lessons for the Church to learn from it. Not least among them is the truth that if the Church is not distinctive, the result will be much as Wells suggests. However, I am disinclined to accept his view entirely, because it is too simplistic, and is not really an explanation of the Church's situation in the fourteenth century.

In the first instance, "the Master", in the case of Christianity, was only present in bodily form for an astonishingly brief three years. For the next 300 years the Church's growth was generally steady despite persecution. Thereafter, for 1,000 years, the monasteries grew in influence and good works. The Benedictines and others were self-reforming and put many strictures in place. Each generation faced their own temptations and had to combat growing secularity in society: the Church no longer provided the only safe haven for ordered living, and the clerics were no longer the only lawyers, statesmen and medics. Through the fourteenth century, discipline became more relaxed, there was a diminution of learning, and rivalries between communities too often replaced brotherly love. It is clear from Chaucer that the ideal was not lost sight of (he depicts it with superb economy, respect and affection in the portrait of the "pore persoun" or Parson: "first he wroghte [worked], and afterward he taughte") but the ideal was too seldom attained. The orders of Dominican and Franciscan friars, started in the thirteenth century, were two attempts to restore and maintain this ideal, and in some measure they achieved it—the former by learning; the latter by service and sharing the hardships of the poor.

It is hard to say how spiritual decline sets in—which of us can trace it accurately in ourselves, let alone another? But a large number of factors played a part, including the absence of the best leadership, reliance on wealth from tithes, and the loss of authority and self belief bequeathed by the movement of the Papacy from Rome and then the Great Schism (1378–1417) in which rival papacies undermined and attacked each other. In addition to all these things, other major factors may have been the relaxation of monastic discipline with regard to food and clothing, increased time in travel away from the monastery in order to administer the great estates given to the monks (often in different counties), the resultant financial anxieties that come with wealth, the use of increasing numbers of servants to carry out menial tasks, rival claims on the monks' allegiance by pope and king, and of course the Black Death (1348), in which up to a third or even half of Europe may have died, and which hit the monks harder even than the rest of society. The result of this plague was inevitably economic and social upheaval, culminating in England with The Peasants' Revolt of 1381. Such are the multiple complexities that give rise to the sense that we have lost our way.

One of the most damaging developments was the appointment of "commendatory abbots" (who could be anybody) who drew revenues from the great wealth of the monastic houses without performing any duties. Only Cardinal Wolsey had this shameful status in England, but it was commonplace in France and Italy. In the fifteenth century, numerous reforms were set in place throughout Europe by the different orders, but the very austerity of these produced a harshness of regulation that was not attractive either inside or outside the monasteries, thereby paving the way for the Reformation and the destruction of the old religion.

But not entirely. Monastic houses began to reappear in England as soon as the law allowed, and Patrick Leigh Fermor noted in *A Time to Keep Silence* that in 1957 there were fifteen monastic foundations in the United Kingdom, housing 1,000 monks in enclosed orders.[108] Having felt

at first hand the deep benefit of just visiting such places, he concluded
that England could hardly afford their loss.

But many were lost in the Dissolution, and the pretext, if not always
the real reason, was their corrupt state. And perhaps the single greatest
corrupting influence was the granting of indulgences, a practice born
of, and popularised during, the Crusades. The Church had originally
exacted penances from repentant members who had fallen short of what
was required, and an indulgence was a remission of this penalty in some
part. By the thirteenth century an indulgence had come to be reckoned
as freeing the sinner not only from the penalty, but also the *guilt* (in the
case of a plenary indulgence) of *all* his sins. There would therefore be
no purgatory and the sinner could go straight to heaven. Pope Urban II
offered precisely this incentive for those who went on the First Crusade,
to which we now turn.

CHAPTER 5

Crusaders and Conquistadors (The Really Dark Ages)

"This story is about ruin. Ruin and gold." So says Old Martin in the opening speech of Peter Shaffer's *The Royal Hunt of the Sun*, one of the most powerful and enduring plays of the mid-twentieth century.[109] He is talking about Spain's conquest of the Incan Empire in the 1530s in what is now South Ecuador and Northern Peru. Old Martin goes on to say that he has spent most of his life fighting "for land, treasure and the cross".

In a couple of sentences Shaffer captures not only the spirit of the conquistadors, but also of much of the Crusades. The two fit together not only thematically but also chronologically, for when one ended the other began. The turning was not from military expeditions to peaceful exploration, but simply from East to West. Where France had been the prime mover in the Crusades, Spain was the protagonist in the Americas, most infamously through Cortes and Pizarro.

The First Crusade began in 1096 and the Eighth in 1270, but Crusades continued for another two hundred years, with the Ottoman Turks as their object. The Churches of the East and West even secured a temporary union to achieve the partially successful crusade of 1443. Ten years later, however, Constantinople fell to Mehmed II and was lost to Christendom for ever. As when today a grand piece of foreign policy can be used to bury bad news, so even as late as 1500 the crusading spirit was still powerful enough to be used as an excuse for the unpopular partition of Naples in the treaty of Granada.

The motives in these conquests, both East and West, were far from pure, and Old Martin's rank order of invasion motives—land, treasure and the cross—seems to be telling, at least for the Spanish. But it is misleading to generalise. Millions of people, from the richest kings to the poorest serfs and peasants, took part in Crusades over the centuries, to retake and colonise the holy places—and the unholy. Of course, as always, we are encouraged by our contemporaries to remember the massacres perpetrated by "Christians", and not the vision of St Francis, defenceless, penniless, suing for peace and trying to convert the Sultan of Egypt, or the Franciscan mission to Morocco where the friars were martyred. Indeed, this has been the attitude prevailing since the Enlightenment.

To create a more balanced picture, we need to consider the world which gave rise to the Crusades, their causes, the conduct of them, and their results. No one can claim that the Crusades were a success, and in one sense war is always a failure. They did not achieve their intended overall aim and were an expensive, spectacular mistake in the long term; but in unforeseen ways they had remarkable results.

The World of the Crusades

In some ways it is more appropriate to place the 600 years of the deep Dark Ages more nearly between 1000 and 1600 than between 400 and 1000. That period contains the Reformation, and John Wycliffe, its "Morning Star", so the suggestion might surprise some. But the brightest lights produce the darkest shadows. According to some police, burglars love security lights.

The period stretching roughly from the Norman invasion of England through to the end of the Elizabethan period and the Tudors witnessed not only the Crusades, but the formation of the Inquisition, the torture, burning and execution of Christians by fellow Christians, the imposition of the death penalty on any Christian who became a Jew or Muslim, a variety of popes of quite staggering vileness, the rape of the New World by the conquistadors, and witch hunting. These things simply cannot be excused or passed over.

Equally, on the other hand, during this period, we first see the development of parish churches, and of pilgrimages; a new interest in preaching and mission; the growth of the miracle and mystery plays. Later, St Francis and the Franciscans brought practical help and hope to the poor by possessing nothing yet sharing everything; Thomas Aquinas and Dante wrote the most complete and sublime theology and poetry of perhaps any age; cathedral spires soared for the first time into heaven and their vaulting rang with the divine harmonies of Thomas Tallis and Palestrina; in the Sistine Chapel, Michelangelo lay on his back sixty feet in the air, painting frescoes to the glory of God in the very place where popes defiled God's name. Tyndale and Hus gave their lives in protest against vice, ignorance, depravity and lies; Sir Thomas More suffered the headsman's axe rather than allow Henry VIII to go unopposed in his self-indulgence, self-deception and rapacity; and countless ordinary people found that Jesus was indeed the light in their darkness. There is no doubting which of these two opposing sets of behaviours we hear more of today.

Intellectually, too, there was enormous development emanating from the Christian Church. Peter Abelard (1079–1142) not only lived one of the great tragic love stories of history, but also provided by his brilliant teaching the attraction that drew thousands to the first great university in Northern Europe: Paris, where the common use of Latin, and the twin methodologies of lecture and disputation used for both the training of monks and the regular clergy set the nature of university life for the centuries ahead. Abelard also taught students that to quote the Fathers was not enough if their arguments were to carry weight, by demonstrating that each theological controversy could be answered in opposite ways depending on which passage they cited. The implication was that they had to think and reason logically.

John of Salisbury (1115–1180) was the greatest social thinker since Augustine of Hippo, and the finest English scholar of the Middle Ages. Secretary to Archbishop Thomas Becket, and present at his assassination, he bequeathed to us the function of the rule of law, which distinguishes the tyrant from the virtuous ruler, who sees himself as the people's servant and subject to the law which will dictate how he rules. It thereby becomes

legitimate to remove the tyrant from office—by force if needs be: a huge step towards power being in the hands of the people.

Thomas Aquinas (1225–1274) synthesised Augustine with the rediscovered Aristotle and showed that all things in the material world are significant and not to be despised. Like John of Salisbury, he insisted that rulers derive their authority from the people, if also from God. Misuse of that authority negates it. He argued further that, by nature, all men are equal, so to heighten the inequality of their circumstances—by unfair trading for instance—is a sin. It is unjust to sell something for more than it is worth. There must be state regulation of weights and measures. Lending or borrowing money at interest can only be justified under the strictest controls. His theory of the "just war" was designed to limit war by forbidding its initiation to all except the sovereign, and then only to avenge a specific wrong. The intended good must always outweigh the harm, and the actions be the only means of producing a just outcome. Had the crusaders followed this they would have averted countless acts of unjustifiable aggression. St Francis took the theory to the heart of the Crusades when he foretold that the crusader army at Damietta would be destroyed because of its very aggression. It was.

Modern man has some difficulty in recreating the normal backdrop and ambience of the medieval and early Renaissance world. All too frequently we wrongly think of its horrors as being confined to the battlefield, or to the world of extreme poverty or remote areas of barbarism. In his essay "The Dawn of the Renaissance", J. H. Plumb paints a picture of Europe in which walled cities and splendid churches rose out of the rubble of centuries. Amongst the rubble and filth were the hovels that served as home for those who lived long enough to call it such.[110] Roman peace, trade, law and government had not been re-established and a violent world removed the security which allows for reflection, understanding and generosity of spirit.

Feudal law and the Catholic Church provided whatever cohesion and purpose could be found beyond mere survival. The religious life was seen to be the most meritorious, and in many ways the most secure, both in terms of this world and the next. It was, however, unattainable by the majority who had neither the education nor the leisure to pursue it. War, disease, famine and grinding poverty all presented constant threats to any

long-term plans or schemes of personal improvement. Life for most was a terrible and never-ending battle against the odds; the hope of paradise a distant glimmer on the other side of the grave. It is hard to imagine a society so strikingly different from our own, at least in Europe. By contrast, today in the West laws guarantee our basic freedoms, work is balanced by holiday, and war and famine for the vast majority are solely virtual experiences, not visceral ones. The word "poverty" no longer means the same as it did in the eleventh century. Citizens think of their rights before their duties, and paradise is offered to us in every shop window. For most people, whatever lies beyond the grave, it is not something to discuss, because if we hope for paradise at all, it has got to arrive long before that.

In the world of the Crusades, men, instead of being slaves to their possessions, had slaves *as* their possessions; slavery was the unfading backdrop to all commercial enterprises, and one of the most lucrative. For everyone, slave or free, to work on the land, as most did, was to fight with your bare hands and with primitive tools against nature's unquenchable desire to take back what had been won so laboriously from it before it interred intruding man beneath its endless wastes.

Even the greatest of Italian achievements, intellectually and culturally, were completed in times of appalling violence between and within the city states. The centuries of the Crusades may have witnessed in Italy the brushwork of Giotto and the cantos of Dante, but the struggle for secular power in the Italian towns led men to butcher, burn and disembowel their rivals, to exterminate whole families in vendettas, to publicly hang, encage or otherwise torture those with whom they feuded. *Romeo and Juliet,* one of the best known love stories of the sixteenth century as well as today, found its source in the much adapted story of one such city state feud. In Northern Europe too we have thirteenth-century records of the commonplace nature of slaughter, maiming and torture, of the enslavement of children, the frequent torching of crops and the burning of houses.

Into such a world the Crusades were born, triumphed briefly, faltered and finally died.

The Concept and Causes of the Crusades

Historians of a more recent and very different war, that which began in 1914, tell us that for many who joined up in that hot August, the prospect of a fight was not unattractive. Their lives were monotonous and cramped by work, with little prospect of advancement, adventure, excitement, leisure or a comfortable old age. How much more must this have been the case for the poor of Europe in the eleventh and twelfth centuries? They knew nothing of distance, geography, climate, politics or peoples but they knew that mother Church should not be violated by unbelievers and that if the Pope himself was offering the absolution of all their sins, as well as the ultimate prize of eternal bliss just for taking part in the First Crusade, it was too good an offer to neglect. Moreover, it meant that what you did on the Crusade no longer really mattered in terms of your acceptance before God. The Pope had it covered. And of course it was not just what Charles Williams calls "the multitudes of the uncomprehending good" that went.[111] The papal offer was just as attractive to the rogue and ne'er-do-well, the petty criminal or deviant, as it was to the solid burghers of the towns. Seldom can any army have been quite such a mixture. Some of the knights, however, were professional soldiers. As the Carolingian Empire had collapsed, bishops in Southern France came together to proclaim a peace and commission groups of knights to enforce it. Thus it arose that the military were found in support of the Church working as peace keepers. As with the United Nations today, on occasion this would require a response involving violence, particularly in frontier areas where a permanent force was required. The Order of the Temple, the Templars, grew out of this. They escorted pilgrims to Jerusalem through dangerous regions. Being successful, they were popular and other groups emulated them. Perhaps this was one way in which the notion of warfare against those whom the Church was supposed to love gained acceptability. The Pope then made it meritorious. Link this with the idea that Christendom was not the whole world (an awareness that had been growing for at least a century before the First Crusade) and it brings together mission and the use of force.

Some popes and abbots (famously St Bernard) preached and wrote that military conquest and religious conversion went hand in hand. Error, they said, had to be rooted out, the intransigent destroyed and Christendom expanded by conquest. This is so similar to how we think of fundamentalist Islam today as to be quite shocking. So powerful is the impression left by these wars that it is easy to forget that not everyone approved of their continuance. John Wycliffe, "the Morning Star" in the fourteenth century in England, was writing that a militarised church was expressly the reverse of what the New Testament demanded of Christ's followers.

Though each Crusade arose as a response to different circumstances the causes of the First are plain enough. Weak government in the eleventh century had caused Byzantium to neglect its army. The Normans in Italy and the Seljuk Turks in the Near East laid prostrate swathes of the Eastern Empire. These new invaders of Palestine made access to the holy places less easy and thereby drew attention to the fact that they were under new ownership. In 1071 they had defeated the Byzantine army and the Emperor Alexius Comnenus asked Pope Urban II for help. Urban wanted access to the holy places and also saw a victory in Jerusalem as strengthening his hand against rivals and enemies; he was very willing to help.

Once the invitation, challenge and rewards had been offered by Urban, all varieties of men could see heaven in prospect: there was trade for the avaricious Italian merchants; lands for territorial barons and knights; holy relics for greedy clerics; the prospect of a change of scene for those under the heel of feudalism. There must of course have been some with loftier motives and perhaps most had some view that they were doing the will of God, but from the conduct of the wars it does not look as if it was the first priority of the majority.

The Conduct of the Crusades

When we look at how the Crusades were conducted, it is hard to believe that their leaders were motivated solely by love of neighbour and a desire to spread good news. The bad news is that the First Crusade (1096) may have raised the cross over Jerusalem, but it also slaughtered the city's inhabitants. Even before the armies reached Palestine they had plundered,

ill-treated and massacred hundreds of Jews in Europe at Worms. The
Second Crusade, sent to recapture Edessa (one of the four Latin states
created in the Near East as a result of the First Crusade, lost to the Turks
in 1144) was marked by dissension, bribery and absolute failure after
only four days of besieging Damascus. The Third Crusade (1189) was a
response to further Muslim attacks on Christians and the fact that Saladin
had retaken Jerusalem two years earlier. However, Richard I of England
and Philip II of France quarrelled disastrously and so had insufficient
manpower or motive to succeed in capturing the city. The Fourth and most
infamous Crusade (1202–1204) was so compromised by politics, lack of
men, ships and purpose that it was diverted to Constantinople and ended
with the sack of that city which was the heart of Eastern Christendom.
Christian now fought Christian in what by many is considered to be the
most shameful episode of the medieval Church. The terrible Crusade
against the Albigensians, unlike the others, took place not only in the heart
of Europe but was conducted from the start against heretics rather than
the infidel (as we shall see in Chapter 6). It was at least in part politically
motivated. The princes of Southern France had gained almost complete
independence from their theoretical sovereign, and this, along with the
fact that the Spanish princes were on the move nearby against the Saracens,
was making those in the North nervous. The heretical Cathars around
Albi (in the critical area of Southern France) had the support of noble
families with fortresses in impregnable places. Action needed to be taken
to preserve the sovereign's power, and it was—with dreadful indifference
not only to life but to allegiance as well. From start to finish unnecessary
bloodshed stained every Crusade. But there again, the evil that men do . . .

The twenty-first century, however, has forgotten to consider numerous
points. First, the areas of Palestine, Asia Minor and Egypt were not in
some inalienable sense territorially Muslim. Long before the prophet
Muhammad's followers invaded, they were the heartlands of Christianity
for three hundred years, but were conquered by the sword in the period
of great Islamic expansion in the seventh century. By the time of the First
Crusade, half of the world's Christian population was under Islamic rule.
Second, Saladin consistently waged war against other Muslims until he
took Jerusalem. Third, though we hear about the barbarity of the Crusades
towards Muslims, we do not hear about the barbarism and brutality of

Islamic conquests reaching through the Mediterranean areas towards the heart of Europe until stopped at Tours in 732 by Charles Martel, whose 15,000 Frankish infantry routed 60,000 Arabs on horseback. It is also true that prior to the Crusades, Christians had been persecuted in Egypt and Palestine and the Church of the Holy Sepulchre in Jerusalem destroyed by Al-Hakim. Many at the time thought this a Jewish plot. Fourth, though Christians are required to apologise for the Crusades, and have done so repeatedly, we seldom hear of the representatives of Islam apologising for their predecessors' misdeeds in North Africa and Spain. Indeed, perhaps it is not unfair to remind people today that Muhammad himself was a general who fought twenty-seven battles in nine wars during his twenty years as a military leader. Fifth, Peter Frankopan, Director of the Centre for Byzantine Research at Oxford, has suggested that the First Crusade was not a religious war at all but a targeted military expedition against the cities of Nicaea and Antioch in response to a request from the Emperor of Byzantium.[112] Jerusalem was just the prize in a purely political struggle.

We should perhaps remember that a great role reversal, in religious terms, has taken place in our own times. The greatest massacres of the twentieth century were perpetrated by atheistical regimes, not Christian ones, under the rule of Soviet Communism, Maoist China and Nazi Germany, and how often do we hear mentioned by Muslim leaders the fact that it was "Christian" countries (America and Britain) who saved the Kosovan Muslims from genocide?

Perhaps the only campaign of this terrible period which is capable of eliciting our sympathy, whichever viewpoint we take, is the Children's Crusade of 1212. In this pitiable pilgrimage, utterly misconceived and led by sincerely deluded teenagers (though with purer motives than their predecessors), none of the children even reached Palestine, imagining as they did that the sea would part before them as it had before Moses. Ignominious death, slavery or shame were their terrible and inevitable fates as the predators of the day took advantage of these naive bravehearts.

The Results of the Crusades

How we view the outcome of the Crusades a thousand years after they started depends, as with everything, on where we stand. But not everything can be a matter of opinion and the following results seem universally accepted.

One of the most immediate results was commercial. Tens of thousands of soldiers and hangers-on travelling back and forth through Europe and the Levant not only spent money but opened up by familiarity and frequent passage many routes for trade. They also brought with them, and heard from others, tales of wealth and opportunity, people and places, hitherto unknown to them. Horses, weapons, maps, compasses, ships, food and clothes are just some of the obvious areas both of increased exchange and new development. As trade developed so did towns and cities, especially the Italian cities. By 1600 wealthy Venice was known as the "city of sin"; as Iago slyly tells Othello, "in Venice they do let heaven see the pranks / They dare not show their husbands."[113] Such is the irony of this worldly result of the Crusades that it is hard not to think of Jesus' comments about the impossibility of serving both God and Mammon. When we try to serve both we are liable for disappointment if not a rude shock. Where cities produced wealth there was an obvious source of taxes and as the costs of the Crusades continued to mount, systematic taxation was required.

Another result, tragic in its long-term consequences, was the increased bitterness between the Eastern and Western wings of the Church. What had begun as an opportunity for Christendom to come together in a joint enterprise ended in a division which has not yet been healed. The Sack of Constantinople by Western forces shows up more than any other event the true nature and motivation of this undisciplined army. If they could not have Jerusalem, Byzantium was the next best thing: if you are a looter at heart then it is the size of the loot that interests you, not to whom it belongs.

Thirdly, the papacy was weakened. Papal association with the ravages and thefts of an uncontrolled army, failed ambitions, quarrelsome princes and internecine warfare, took their toll on its authority.

But there were more hidden and ironic effects too which served to lessen the prestige of the pontiffs and ultimately the Catholic Church. The

Crusades had been possible because a theocratic government called on its faithful to flock to the banners of war and sacrifice their worldly security in the name of Christ. However, that appeal produced social dislocation on a grand scale, an awareness of other worlds and other ways of doing things that would contribute to the decline of the old feudal order and the unquestioning acceptance of its hierarchies. The fact that there existed a wider world so unlike anything Western Europeans had known was a shock that rippled far beyond the thousands that went and returned. Added to this unsettling but mundane knowledge were the heady tastes of intellectual excitement such as the mathematics, history, geography and poetry which filtered out from the Islamic world.

Only the Franciscans, peaceful and spiritual in their intentions and actions, made ground for the kingdom of God, so that by 1350 Christian bishops were established from Persia to Peking, even though that expansion was short-lived. It was not a lesson that much of the Church would learn properly until the eighteenth and nineteenth centuries—though there is an interesting passage in the essays of Francis Bacon (published in 1625) where he writes that we may not "propagate religion by wars, or by sanguinary persecutions".[114] He goes on to note, with characteristic insight and economy, that those who like to do such things "were commonly interested therein themselves for their own ends".[115]

With all historical studies there is revision and reappraisal but the Crusades especially have evoked strongly contrasting feelings over the last hundred years.

In 1910 *Encyclopaedia Britannica* was published in its eleventh and famously scholarly edition. It concluded an entry of some 30,000 words on the Crusades with the words:

> The ages were not dark in which Christianity could gather itself together in a common cause, and carry the flag of its faith to the grave of its Redeemer; nor can we but give thanks for their memory, even if for us religion is of the spirit, and Jerusalem in the heart of every man who believes in Christ.

The paragraph had begun: "When all is said, the Crusades remain a wonderful and perpetually astonishing act in the great drama of human life."[116] Needless to say, the fifteenth edition (2002) does not include any of these words or sentiments.

In 1936, H. A. L. Fisher concluded his chapter on the Crusades by calling them a movement of "adventure and piety, curiosity and greed", reminding us that their result was not to bring Christ nearer to man but to found the Venetian trade empire in the Levant.[117] In the 1950s, Sir Steven Runciman, in his great three-volume history of the Crusades, concluded that the wars were no more than acting out human intolerance in the name of God.[118]

All three of these opinions are variously true except for the element of Runciman's reductionism. There was devotion, there were high ideals and loyalty, there was courage and the defence of the right—and not only by the Franciscans. A medieval chivalric inscription in Chartres Cathedral asks that a knight should always be "disposing his heart to goodness" so as never to misuse his sword. Jonathan Riley-Smith, in his 2012 book *The Knights Hospitaller in the Levant, c. 1070–1309*, sees those taking part in the First Crusade as being motivated by love of God and neighbour and the Hospitallers as those who had a heart for the poor.[119] Ideals cherished in men's hearts do emerge in their actions and Christian ideals were not absent from men's hearts in those centuries, but in battle ordinary people have to make extraordinary decisions. Which of us know whether we would acquiesce, resist, or entirely succumb to evil? Wilfred Owen writing in "Spring Offensive" remembers the "superhuman inhumanities / Long-famous glories, immemorial shames" perpetrated by decent men in the "hell's upsurge" that constituted battle.[120] We are sometimes too glib in our ready condemnation of those who lived in very different worlds from our own.

Some Conclusions

The seeds of the failure of the Crusades came from within and were implicit in the very concept. The word "crusade" is a gloss on their first title which was "armed pilgrimage", surely a contradiction in terms. Had they been truly "crusades", a word deriving from *crux*, the Latin for "cross", they might have achieved a very different result. The cross, being a torture instrument, is a symbol of passive suffering, the very reverse of armed militancy. Were these warriors deceived by others or by themselves that they thought force was the way of Christ? Perhaps neither. They wanted to fight or grow rich or escape hardship, and any excuse to pursue their own ends suited them well enough.

If they had not fought the Muslims they would have found others to fight (as they did) and as the conquistadors did in a later century.

"Holy war" of any kind has long been a source of controversy and embarrassment to the Christian Church, and has raised its head again in our time over the wars with Iraq where the theory of the "just war" was dusted off by politicians and scrutinised by journalists. C. S. Lewis was prescient when he said, "Large areas of 'the World' will not hear us till we have publicly disowned much of our past."[121] Apologies have been, and continue to be, made by the Church, if not by politicians, but the apologies are worthless unless we can be seen to be understanding our faith in such a way that repetition is unthinkable even if there is, as some have wanted to put it, a "clash of civilisations".

Perhaps the first reassurance that we can give ourselves, and offer others, is that the intervening centuries of both church and social history preclude the repetition of conditions that made holy war a possibility. In the high Middle Ages the Church was the most powerful institution in the Western world. It stretched across the boundaries of Christian kingdoms and empires. The Pope could humiliate even the Emperor himself, though not always get his own way. Equally, ruling political leaders were frequently in high office in the Church: princes were bishops and vice versa. Prior to the Reformation, in the West, the Catholic Church was the sole arbitrator of whether a man's soul would be saved or not from an eternity of torment, and frequently his body from temporal pains. Today the Church does not have any such powers: the Reformation, the Enlightenment, Victorian agnosticism, Darwinism, Marxism, post-modernism, pluralism and militant atheism stand between us and the Crusades. Such a barrier is impenetrable. An irreversible historical process debars us from re-entry to a medieval Europe of that kind. There are no Christian theocracies, save the Vatican, and that has to operate through non-theocratic states. Islamic states however have not been through that same historical process. It would be completely unjust to suggest that the actions of a few fundamentalist Christian churches, such as burning copies of the Qur'an, or taking militant anti-abortion action are in any way comparable to the actions of fundamental Islamists in terms of the threat they pose. No state in the world today sponsors or supports such actions by Christians, nor are they supported by widespread popular opinion. Indeed, the reverse. They have earned opprobrium on all sides, including from the White House and Downing Street.

The second point worth noting when it comes to the fear of history repeating itself is that the late eleventh century was a period of loss of control for the Church. The monasteries no longer enjoyed their largely exclusive right to an almost absolute control of education. As secular forces gained power in the professions and took these out of Church hands, the fear of weakening, diluting and polluting the faith made for aggressive stances to prevent the changes in the air from settling on the ground. In the thirteenth century Muslims were deported or exiled from places where they were considered too strong. In Spain and elsewhere, sexual and even some social relations were forbidden between Muslims and Christians. Today the Church is no longer monolithic, has no military resources, is part of a pluralist society which is highly mobile, both through space and cyberspace, and has to work hard to make its voice heard in the marketplace of opinions. The press and media are dominated by liberal secularism; clerical preaching cannot now exact a fraction of the attention it did before the arrival of mass communications.

The Christian's task now is more like that of the early Church: to pass out good news to one person at a time in a society that is jaded by its own affluence, confused by its plurality, and curiously discontented with its ceaseless activity. Such a situation should give Christians hope, but we nevertheless have to speak out in this new arena in which, twenty centuries after the first Christians made their presence felt, the odds are fairer: we can use the same tools of communication as our assailants in most countries. Or at least, we ought to be able to—though some would like to prevent this, and others in their thinking serve the same end, even if without any ill-will.

Mary Warnock, leading British moral philosopher and controversialist (when it comes to ethics), comes near to this when she argues in her book *Dishonest to God* (2010) that religious and theological issues should have no place in questions of public morality and that valuing religion as the essential basis of morality is a mistake with far-reaching consequences. There is certainly some danger in doing so but we also need to consider the dangers of not doing so. To believe "It is the right thing to do because it is the Christian way", or even "Without religion there would be no basis for morality", and fearing these watchwords as a rallying cry in public debate, is very different from excluding eminent or expert people from being heard objectively in the public debate *because* they have views necessarily informed by their religion.

In the UK we have often seen that approach. Take the case of politician Ruth Kelly. Kelly, in her various posts including Secretary of State for Education and Skills, and Minister for Women, was criticised as someone who allowed her Roman Catholic views and membership of Opus Dei to influence her policy decisions on matters such as the proposed trust schools, stem-cell research, equality issues and abortion. Effectively, Kelly was hounded from office by the force of these criticisms and resigned from being an MP in May 2010. More recently, in September 2014, Labour frontbenchers criticised the appointment of Nicky Morgan to the post of Minister for Women and Equalities on the grounds of her opposing the re-definition of marriage. When Tim Farron was elected leader of the Liberal Democrats in July 2015, a leader in *The Times* dubbed him illiberal[122] and Radio 4 and *Channel 4 News* focused on his prayer life and views on homosexuality rather than his politics.[123] Ultimately, to go down that line takes us to the thought police and discrimination of the grossest and most blatant kind—the very thing that the liberal West most deplores. Government would in that case be solely by atheists and policy would naturally conform to their worldview and their agenda. It could not be otherwise because what we think about matters of ethical controversy cannot but be the result in part of our religious beliefs or lack of them. Everything from the immigration laws, to ethical banking to the treatment of prisoners is at the heart of the Judeo-Christian message as evidenced in the Old Testament prophetic tradition, the Sermon on the Mount and Jesus' action in overturning the tables of the moneychangers in the Temple. If it were not so, Christianity, Islam, Judaism and Buddhism would not be able to impinge on this world in their teachings at all.

In October 2012 the Health Secretary, Jeremy Hunt, was taken to task by some commentators because his views in favour of an earlier legal limit to abortion were deemed to derive from his Christian faith and an MP who also spoke in the same vein at the same time had his views discounted when the journalist reporting them found out he was a Catholic. This is surely irrational. If the level of the debate is to come down to "I can ignore your view because you only think like that because of your Christian faith" then the obvious response is "And you only think as you do because of your lack of it" which gets us nowhere. We all have aesthetic, emotional and ideological prejudices but arguments should stand or fall by their intellectual validity, their rationality, and not according to the perceived group membership of their proponents.

Towards the end of *Dishonest to God*, Warnock writes:

> It is argued by the militant atheists that religion has done enormous harm by its bigotry and moral imperialism. I would agree that, without going back to the Crusades or the Inquisition, one can lay immense suffering at the door of the Catholic Church, with its insistence on the evil of contraception and the consequences for the control of AIDS ... and no one can deny the atrocities committed in the name of the fundamentalist branches of Islam. But in these and similar cases, it is not religion itself that is to blame, but the belief that religion can provide unassailable moral truth and, above all, that it has the authority to enforce what its morality dictates. This is what does the damage and has always done so.[124]

Leaving aside the reference to contraception and AIDS, it would be hard to argue with Warnock. She is being as fair as she can be to religion in making a distinction between the religion itself and the practices of its adherents. She goes on to mention, however, unassailability and enforcement, so let us look at these two things. Is Christianity "unassailable" either in its historicity or its moral truth? Is it invulnerable, not open to any hostile attack? The answer from history is self-evidently, no—at least since the Enlightenment (that very word is an implied assault on the "darkness" of the previous Christian centuries). From the eighteenth century onwards there has been a steady stream of powerfully destructive criticism aimed at the Church—the historicity of the Gospels, the impact of its dogma, the practices of its clergy, the imperialism of its missions. Even in the medieval period it was the subject of satire by poets, as we have seen. In that age, however, the Church, knowing itself to be the most powerful institution, not only lost its way but deceived others into thinking it had not. The coincidence of power with religion, of religion with politics, where religion *dictated* the politics without effective opposition, has always been a snare to the Church and unhelpful to its cause. We might even say that the measure of the Church's spiritual effectiveness is in inverse proportion to its political power. Christianity was not designed to work as a political force in its own right. The question then arises as to what role the Church does have when issues of public morality become the focus of political attention. The answer must surely be: salt. Christians have been told that they must be, indeed are, the salt of the earth: a sprinkling which is not only flavoursome, but *an irritant* as well as a preservative from corruption. The picture is one of an influence working against the natural tendency of the main body, which will slow down or even reverse the way things tend to work, but only by being consumed in the process.

The homeless Nazarene carpenter told his disciples to take next to nothing for the journey and to be wary of riches. He warned that they would have to appear before the authorities but gave no instructions about being those authorities. The first critics who derisively called Christianity a religion of slaves spoke truer than they knew. The idea that all power tends to corrupt is one that Christians have to be especially aware of. Christianity works best from the bottom up, not from the top down. It is an essential part of its nature that it is a seed not a structure; it works best underground, in the secret places of the earth. It is not a roof to protect the soil but has to grow out of that soil and to take its chance in the open air and the elements. When the Church feels *unassailable* in its authority, it displays the arrogance it has liked to feel distant from—and also condemned in others. Religion should never be "unassailable".

Warnock's related point is that the worst damage is done when the Church sees itself as an enforcer, which it clearly did through part of the medieval and Renaissance periods. It seems to be part of human nature to end up using powers which we create for ourselves or which we are handed. When the Church hands temporal power back to the state, or is deliberately separated from it as in the US, it has a greater chance of spiritual growth. The Church there, having no established governmental role, has kept its hold better on the nation, and its politicians, than the established Church in the UK.

How big a step then is it from believing we have the "unassailable moral truth" to imposing it on others? Dangerously, the answer may be "not very big", which is why it is of the utmost importance that Christians and Christianity remain "assailable"; open to criticism, rebuke, scrutiny and satire. This is something which present-day Islam finds very difficult to accept, a fact of which few dare to be openly critical. Any sense that no criticism may be stated or even implied tends to make the privileged party self righteous, having a God-given superiority, which can rapidly spill over into demands that others not only respect their views, but also adopt them, if they are to be counted among the civilised and enjoy the same privileges and rewards. As it was wittily put, "A reformer is someone who insists on *his* conscience being your guide." Cardinal Cormac Murphy O'Connor argues that (as in America) religion and democracy must allow each other space and that to banish religion from public debate in the name of freedom and democracy is actually to threaten those very things.[125] We have seen Islamophobia in Britain and Europe because there is the feeling that Islam is outside the realm of public criticism, even discussion. Minarets, burkhas, the strictures of the Qur'an, Muslim homophobia, are not points of easy conversation in cafes and bars. Such absolutism in a religion is surely born of fear. There is no need for such where all is open to analysis and debate. It is when we are afraid that we do not like to open up, and our fears are often disguised to ourselves as hatreds—it makes us feel stronger. Christianity, by contrast, is today placed under the fiercest scrutiny in matters such as the wearing of a cross at work, the adoption of children into a Christian family, the rules on the use of double rooms at Christian hotels and the wrong actions of Catholic priests towards children. All these have produced a voluble public debate and much criticism, but we have no need to fear it.

It is not only the current practice of the Church, or some of its members, that is subjected to the bright lights of the interrogator. So remote is Christianity from being "unassailable" that militant atheists such as Christopher Hitchens and Richard Dawkins have enjoyed proclaiming their views on every aspect of religion on prime time TV and radio broadcasts. In 2010 Hitchens debated on radio the value of religion with Tony Blair, the former Prime Minister. He urged that the world would be a better place if there were no religious fanatics. Blair sensibly replied that if we got rid of religion, would we be sure of getting rid of fanatics? It does not take a religion to make someone feel that they must impose their views or policies on others. Communists, fascists and potentates of every kind have felt and done the same. Not only where religion has been involved have men's ulterior motives been secular and selfish—the search for land or power or gold. It is egocentricity that produces intolerance; the religion of Jesus was the opposite: "deny yourself" and serve others. He who would be greatest must be least of all. Love must be demonstrated in service. The unforgettable action of Jesus, at the most heightened and intense moment of his teaching in the last week of his life, was that of washing the feet of his own followers. Equally, when at the start of his ministry Jesus was tempted in the wilderness, and shown in an instant the kingdoms of the world, the Devil told him, "I will give you all their authority and splendour, for it has been given to me."[126] How much more must Jesus have felt and experienced that at the end as a victim of the Roman and Jewish legal systems. If the Church had understood the account of the wilderness temptations better—that even the Devil's lie had, as so often, a subtle and misleading truth in it (namely that trying to wrest power from devilish hands would be attractive, but turn out ultimately to be a disaster)—the history of the world would have been different. A few verses later Luke pointedly tells us that Jesus returned from the wilderness not with that sort of power but "in the power (*dunamei*) of the Spirit".[127] A different sort of *dynamite* or *dynamic* altogether.

There is nothing in the New Testament which would suggest that we should impose our views or practices on others. The pattern shown and recommended to the disciples by Christ was that they should proclaim the kingdom and move on. When Peter teaches the early Church to make a defence of their beliefs, it is to be a verbal one spoken with gentleness and respect, reverencing Christ as Lord.[128] Had not Jesus told him to put away his sword at the moment of his own arrest, and then healed the wound Peter had so impulsively inflicted? The hallmarks of Christian behaviour, as we saw in Chapter 2, are obedience to legitimate government, love of others, service and humility—in public and in private. Christians have to forgive if they are to have hope of forgiveness themselves. It is not intolerance but tolerance that is at the heart of the New Testament. Jesus tells the disciples that the peacemakers are the blessed ones; James tells the early Church that heavenly wisdom is peace-loving, considerate and submissive; Paul tells the Roman Church to make every effort to do what leads to peace and tells the Philippians to emulate Christ's humility at the cross and consider others better than themselves. Interestingly, Arnold Toynbee wrote that humanity's greatest progress in the nineteenth and twentieth centuries was in the area of tolerance, but, we might add, if it had not been for the Church's insistence on the authority of Scriptures like these, the rest of society would not have followed the Church in those two centuries (if not the previous ones vitiated by political power) in making strides towards a fairer, more tolerant world.

Note on the Conquistadors

As the crusading spirit became enervated in the East, some of those who went westward could not but feel that to take Christendom to new lands was a new crusade which would reinforce the re-conquest of Spain and its removal from Islamic hands. In an age of constant war and conquest, when every power felt itself to be capable of overcoming another, the Spanish conquests in Mexico and Peru in particular stand out from the rest. They are extraordinary because the meeting of the Old World and the

New yielded stories never told before. For Europeans, there were stories of human sacrifice, cannibalism, sun worship and unimaginable quantities of gold and jewels. The old stories were those of slavery, treachery, and impossible odds against overwhelming foes. But these too captured the imagination and became legends—and in those legends the Church played a part. For the New World, their stories grew out of (to us) the most mundane and everyday matters: guns and coins, cows and horses, goats and guard dogs. Such things had never been seen by Native American peoples before. Could the gods have come back to earth?

In 1519, Hernan Cortes, with no more than 400 Spanish soldiers and the aid of the city of Tlaxcala, conquered the Aztec capital Tenochtitlan (under Mexico City today), ostensibly for Spain and the Emperor. The young, recently crowned Charles V could see the Habsburgs ruling not just a Catholic Europe but a Catholic world. That world had to be Christianised by one means or another and the cruelties of the Aztecs put them beyond the reach of even the Divine Mercy unless they could be taught the error of their ways. The sheer scale of the Aztec systems of human sacrifice required the public slaughter and mutilation of thousands of victims, all carefully and ritualistically prepared prior to having their hearts torn out, in order that the sun should rise, crops grow, and the world continue. The spectacle, or its aftermath, appalled even the most bloody of Spanish soldiers. And of course it appalled the faithful, who saw the reverse of their own belief that God had offered himself in place of any other sacrifice. Here was not just heresy, but an *inversion* of the truth. Such horrors could not continue on the now Catholic and Spanish soil. Which nations today would accept such evil practices?

For the soldiers, for Cortes and the administration, to subdue Aztecs to the Europeans' will meant also to Christianise, for in conversion would not these savages be transformed automatically into the most loyal subjects of the holy Emperor himself? It was similar too for the Catholic priests, though not all. How else could these aliens, these subhuman creatures be transformed save by force of arms? Once their opposition to the invader was stifled they might learn that their gods were mere powerless golden idols, and slowly learn true worship of the One God. For the conquistadors, in an ironic and unconscious exchange, those mere golden idols became their gods as they coerced the Native Americans to accept ours. Francisco

Pizarro's religion was gold, not Christianity, and no mere moral scruples such as promise-keeping could be allowed to stand in the way of his one and only god.

Pizarro (1471–1541), illegitimate and largely illiterate, is infamous for his treachery and greed in his conquest of the Incas with only three ships, 180 men and thirty-seven horses; but the force of his character is apparent in his winning over the Emperor Charles V to his cause. His huge physical vitality and endurance were matched only by his brutality and Machiavellianism. Gaining and holding on to power by any means when there was gold to be had as a result was his overwhelming purpose. His understanding of the Christianity he pretended to, represented by being in league with a Catholic priest, seems to have been negligible. The friars and priests who colluded with Pizarro were also responsible for, and guilty of, ending the Inca civilisation.

Mercifully, not every member of the Spanish Church colluded with such murderous intentions and actions. Missionaries to the Canaries had already spoken out against the enslavement of native peoples. The Christian monarchs Ferdinand and Isabella of Castile had forbidden it by 1500, and many friars continued to speak out against it. The most prominent of these was a former plantation owner turned Dominican, Bartholeme de Las Casas.

Las Casas was the first to protest against the Spanish military atrocities in the West Indies. He wrote eyewitness accounts of the horrors perpetrated upon every manifestation of native humanity in his book *A Short Account of the Destruction of the Indies* (1542).[129] Las Casas was acting not only in accord with his calling but with the support of the Laws of Burgos (1512) which, as a result of Dominican outrage at the way the native labourers were abused, had declared that Indians should not be enslaved, that work should have limits, and that conversion was not to be coerced. Sadly the laws had little effect at such distance from Spain in an environment which only the most greedy or disaffected would choose, and in which only the most ruthless survive. His mistaken attempt to save the natives by the importation of African labour to take their place (an idea he bitterly regretted when he later saw their treatment) must be one of the great ironies in the history of slavery. Back in Spain, at the University of Salamanca, another Dominican friar, Francisco de Vitoria, boldly discredited the idea

CRUSADERS AND CONQUISTADORS (THE REALLY DARK AGES)   87

of any crusade in America where no wrong had been done by the native peoples to any Christian person or cause, prior to their country being invaded. Papal rights over a newly discovered country could no longer be taken for granted, it could be inferred; other countries have sovereign rights too. But Christians were slow to learn key lessons whatever laws were made and intellectuals wrote about. New World savagery met all too often with equal savagery at least from the soldiery, and where a founding church disallows indigenous clergy (a decree to this effect was passed in 1555), it can have little hope of taking root in a foreign culture.

In our next chapter we shall see that in this darkest of ages it did not take human sacrifice and cannibalism in the New World to provoke the wrath of Church authorities which had become the power in the land. Mere theological debate was enough to spark off the fires of hell all over Europe.

Postscript

What is it in humanity that brings the worst and the best out of us at the same time in history, and even in individual lives? It is not only possible, but manifestly evident through history, that learning, culture, and cruelty may often co-exist not only in the same state, such as the Byzantine or the Nazi, but in the same person. Byzantium was the apogee of European culture, but heretics were branded on their foreheads with red hot irons. Mary I could read and write Latin and Greek and studied the sciences as well as being a musical and beautiful young woman. Nevertheless, in the pursuit of her cause, in her brief five-year reign, she executed (mostly by burning) about 280 Christians of different persuasion from her own. She also forced Archbishop Cranmer to watch the death of Bishops Ridley and Latimer at the stake in Oxford. The Nazi Joseph Goebbels wrote a doctoral thesis on eighteenth-century romantic drama and also wrote novels and plays, but his egomania was almost unparalleled even in the Third Reich, and he was the architect of the Jewish pogroms and a complete devotee of Adolf Hitler. By way of contrast, Dietrich Bonhoeffer preferred to hang rather than compromise with such a man. Richard Wurmbrand danced with joy in the dark and airless underground cells of Soviet Communism because he was counted worthy to suffer for the Name.

Such extraordinary elevation and degradation within humanity, quite unparalleled anywhere else in the animal kingdom, has always seemed to me a strong argument for the unique and spiritual nature of *homo sapiens*. We are indeed "sapiens" but also bad almost beyond imagining. Rowan Williams, in *The Lion's World*, quotes C. S. Lewis's *Prince Caspian*, where Caspian has to be reminded of the fact that he comes of the lineage of Lord Adam and Lady Eve, "and that is both honour enough to erect the head of the poorest beggar, and shame enough to bow the shoulders of the greatest emperor on earth".[130] No non-religious thought system does justice to the extremes of which we are capable. Evil is not so much a problem of Christian theology as a demonstration of its truth. It is reasonable to expect devastating evil to be operative in a world in which irredeemably wicked forces are at work, as theology claims they are. Conversely, if God is the source of goodness, we should expect to see elements of the mystery of the human spirit that leave us dumbstruck with awe and humility— as they frequently do. Currently however society has chosen to reject any language that does justice to this mystery, as Robinson has noted. Conveniently, our ability to use language nonsensically has flourished.

Perhaps this simultaneous flourishing of both the best and worst in human nature is an inevitability rather than a coincidence. If Augustine was right that evil is not just an absence of goodness, but is goodness derailed or warped, then the very force that propelled all that positive energy will not be lost but turned with equal vigour back on itself and others. *Hamartia*, the Greek word for error or fatal flaw, and related to the verb for "to miss the mark", a concept emphatic in the Greek tragedies, did not stop the arrow flying but redirected it off course. It would hit a mark but not the right one. All goodness therefore is dangerous. The greater the good, the greater the possibility of evil, of disaster. Satan had been the brightest of angels. Even if goodness stays good, it will be opposed by forces that by nature, and by its very presence, it will diminish. Conflict will result—both of principle and of practice. This was, and is, the heart of the opposition between Islam and Christianity: each believes the other has a profoundly wrong view of God and to allow it space in people's minds can be seen as dishonouring to the Deity. The same principle sadly applied to the wars between Christians in the past. Roman Catholic and Protestant alike saw their duty as being at least ready either to exact or pay the ultimate price for their convictions. To do less would be hardly better than apostasy for them. If we put this view of human nature alongside a highly principled, but highly intolerant stance, and then place it in the world of the later Middle Ages, I believe it is possible to understand a little of why these centuries contain such dark and shameful passages. Nothing however, can excuse or condone them.

CHAPTER 6

Inquisitors, Heretics and Witches

In leaving the Middle Ages behind we instinctively feel that a more humane society would, or should, have taken its place. The term "medieval" is after all used now of practices or perceptions that are not only long discarded, but of which we are scornful or dismissive. Things are "positively medieval" when they fall far below present-day standards in some respect. The world in which the Inquisition operated spans both the medieval and Renaissance worlds, the institution having been started in 1232, with the Spanish Inquisition being set up in 1479 by Ferdinand and Isabella and only finally suppressed in 1820.

As with the period of the Crusades, we need to set the Inquisition in context if we are to avoid misunderstanding the evils it gave rise to. Essentially, the Inquisition was an ecclesiastical court set up to investigate heresy and to persecute it on a juridical basis. It was to punish people who stepped out of line. How it did that, and how it zealously overstepped the mark itself are the things that have given it notoriety.

The concept of punishment has been a central feature of all societies from the most primitive times and has changed crucially both in theory and method as those societies changed. What we know of primitive societies suggests that punishment then was left to the individual and that it bore no necessary relation to the gravity of the offence: it was vindictive. For the ancient Hebrews however we know from the Books of the Law that the *Lex talionis*, the eye for an eye principle of proportionate punishment, was central, though interestingly there were many clauses of mitigation taking into account the circumstances of the offender—an idea not really reconsidered until the eighteenth century in England, and one which was still being developed in the nineteenth and twentieth centuries. Prior to this, the state had not been concerned with the dignity of the individual, his rationality or lack of it, or the degree of his responsibility. "Justice" was for the maintaining of public order; retribution and deterrence were supreme above reformation of character or rehabilitation into society.

Curiously, the Inquisition, for all its appalling abuses, did begin with the idea of reformation and rehabilitation. For the best part of a thousand years the Church had mostly kept to the teachings of the early Christian fathers who had disapproved of physical penalties. It was only after the thirteenth-century Catharist heresy, which threatened not only religious life but society at large with its belief that material creation was evil, and that Christ was merely an angel with a phantom body, that the Church in general allowed the infliction of physical pain rather than excommunication. To say it was a mistake is needless; our need rather is to try to imagine that sort of pain in their world rather than ours—if we are to understand it. After all, the modern world has devoted as much time, energy and scientific ability to the eradication of pain as it has to anything other than the generation of money. We have failed to eradicate the last enemy, death, and so have done the next best thing—created a world as free of pain as we can. Pain is an evil to us and it is commonly thought that no one deserves it. We not only protect the law-abiding from pain but also the criminal; not only the naughty child, but many forms of animal life. The deliberate infliction of the mildest pain (other than in medical procedures) in any corner of western society is liable to be a criminal offence. Hospitals are commonly expected to be able to render pain down to levels unimaginably comfortable by the standards of previous ages.

The pre-modern world had next to no means of alleviating pain and so lived with it, often for prolonged periods. Disability, accident, mutilation, disease, physical aggression, punishment, and even surgery mostly involved chronic pain. Up until the second half of the nineteenth century, death rates in hospitals could be as high as 90 per cent—from gangrene, septicaemia, blood poisoning or other infection. There were no effective anaesthetics. Amputations were carried out in a matter of seconds by the best surgeons, while patients bit on a piece of leather. The novelist Fanny Burney wrote an account of her mastectomy in 1811, graphically describing the sensations of "the dreadful steel" cutting through her breast while she was fully conscious. Surprisingly, she lived on until 1840, dying at the great age of eighty-eight. For most of history pain has been an inevitable part of daily life for most people and of course death was frequently preceded by pain and was a household experience. A death at home meant laying out the body at home, keeping vigil by it, and paying your respects. Such traditions continued into the twentieth century.

Living in a world where frequent high levels of pain were commonplace seems to have conditioned people's view of its use in punishment. The fact that this appears to be socially engineered and can alter very quickly is evident from the way social attitudes towards corporal punishment in schools changed over a mere decade or two in the late twentieth century. Though the use of the birch in British prisons was abolished in 1948, the use of the "slipper" and cane continued until 1987 when corporal punishment was outlawed in state secondary schools.

A decade or so before that, the use of the cane, in some cases by a senior pupil on a junior, without reference to teachers responsible was common enough, and neither those who administered it nor even many of those who suffered it thought very much about its use. It was the way things were, and always had been. There seemed no particular reason to change it. Twenty years later social attitudes had changed so markedly that its use was unthinkable irrespective of its illegality.

Prior to the Enlightenment, and the establishment of prisons as places of detention for a fixed term, punishments were likely to be physical if they were not fines, confiscation of property or exile. It is of interest to list something of the variety of these corporal punishments. Today many of them would be considered torture, but then they fell far short of the horrors of the torture chamber. What is hard for us to grasp is both the barbarity of the punishments and the fact that this was frequently a public spectacle—something to look forward to for those not emotionally or otherwise attached to the victim.

The pillory and the stocks were mild punishments for minor offences but today the combination of such stress positions with public humiliation would be classed as torture. A comparatively merciful punishment was beheading, but to watch such an event now would be seen as traumatising in the extreme. Yet the last such act in France was in 1977—though seen presumably only by the executioner and officials. It is hard to believe that Henry VIII passed a law in 1531 which allowed prisoners to be boiled alive; that branding with red hot irons was only abolished in 1829; that burning at the stake was only abolished in Britain in 1790, and flogging in 1881. Of course, for the crime of treason in earlier centuries, the traitor was "hanged, drawn and quartered", an expression which has lost the force of the terror it was designed to inspire among the onlookers. The utter degradation of what happened in the privacy of the torture chambers of kings and princes is not a fit subject for this book, but the inventiveness of the cruelties surpasses a normal imagination.

This, then, was the judicial backdrop to people's lives, and it did not especially horrify or appal them, since the witnessing of public punishments was, it seems, one of their pleasures, and of course a means by which the authorities could deter future miscreants. Even the schoolboy knew no escape. If he struggled or sought to evade the birch, it was recommended that three or four of the strongest scholars should hold him fast while the schoolmaster beat him, according to *The Grammar Schoole*, published in 1612.[131]

What then are we to make of the Inquisition's notorious punishments and why was it both feared and yet accepted? We cannot understand that, without realising for ourselves how an age so different from our own perceived not just pain and punishment, but heresy.

It is ironic that the word "heresy" is the English equivalent of the Greek word which the Septuagint employs meaning "free choice". We recognise the term as being used mainly in a time when any such choice of conscience was far from free, but rather very costly. Today the term is hardly used at all by most Christians, but has become useful in a light-hearted, often secular, allusion to ideas that are not mainstream, or are slightly subversive of conventional views. Whichever century we allude to however, the heretic is always the person with the opposing view; never ourselves. In the earliest days the word was used of Christianity itself by its opponents in Acts 24:14. Paul uses it when speaking of "the works of the flesh" in Galatians 5:20 and Luke of the Sadducees in Acts 5:17. Fierce condemnation of heretics is found in the letters of John and the second letter of Peter. We have already seen in Chapter 4 how fiercely the heretical Arians in the post-apostolic age were opposed and why this mattered.

Wilful departure from orthodoxy, or the creed recognised and accepted as public doctrine, has been "anathema" from the beginning. But from the Reformation onwards there was no longer any sense, even in the West, in which Catholic doctrine was catholic, or universally held. Obvious examples are the dogmas of the papacy—the Immaculate Conception and Infallibility from the Reformed point of view, and in Roman Catholic minds from the Council of Trent onwards, all the distinctive doctrines of Protestantism. In the late medieval world it was the duty of the state to co-operate with the Church in order to maintain both right living and right thinking, so the civil authorities were bound to punish those whom the Church considered to hold dangerous views.

The question then arises as to why those views about such matters as religious doctrine (essentially abstractions) should be seen as dangerous to society. Charles Taylor, in his extremely detailed analysis of how society changed in terms of its secularisation between 1500 and the present day, makes the point that in the sixteenth century it was God who guaranteed the triumph of good in the world.[132] The idea that public good could be achieved by anything less than a proper understanding of God was remote. Where there were aspirations towards better conduct, stronger communities and less lawbreaking, these were always interpreted in terms of God's actions towards people and vice-versa. Evil is evil precisely because it wreaks malevolent ends and saps our will to resist temptations away from public order and commonwealth. The boundaries of influence, says Taylor, were porous: there were no barriers between areas of life which might be brought under the control of the Devil or God. Today, for instance, we attribute depression or other diseases to body chemistry or hormone malfunction and so on, but pre-modern man would be told that his melancholy came from black bile which was a part of him and could not be separated out and dealt with. Taylor describes the modern concept as creating a buffered view which makes for a very different existential experience. The "porous" self however was subject to all kinds of cosmic forces, spirits and demons, and thus, as we shall see, gave rise both to witchcraft itself and the fear and persecution of it. Equally of course, heresy, the distortion of God's true picture, was a result of evil influences, and it was imagined by the orthodox in the early days of the Reformation that these distortions would be temporary. Preventing their growth was essential if the whole nature of life were not to be spoilt by this false picture. The modern idea of the pursuit of fear, or of the spiritually unorthodox for its own sake, in which, either by physical or spiritual adventuring beyond the edge of safety, mankind seeks out excitement as an antidote to ennui would have been unthinkable for the sixteenth century save for the tiniest number of those on the verge of insanity or those who turned to witchcraft for quite different reasons. Where you are continuously terrified by the real possibility of possession, torment or extinction, you do not go looking for it. When our everyday lives are so shielded from these things that they are no longer part of normal expectation or frequent possibility, we find the need to re-create them for ourselves in film, TV and computer games. The evidence is that the latter, at any rate, are addictive and the former an extremely major part of our weekly entertainment. This says something about human nature: if we are not subject to violence or perpetrating it ourselves, we need to experience it vicariously. Through one institution or another, through one medium or another, we need to bring violent conflict into our lives and we derive something powerful from witnessing it or imagining we do.

Such a view of human nature at first sight may look entirely disadvantageous in terms of social progress. Terror is hardly conducive to personal development. But we need to remember that not only was there, in Taylor's terms, another sort of "buffer"—a bulwark between the person and the pit, namely the Church and the Gospel—but that an holistic approach to disease, depression, and disaster, as opposed to the approach that treats our bodies as units independent of mind, is something that alternative medicine has been advocating for many years. "Keep taking the tablets" is not always the solution, but too many of us have been taught to think that the physical entirely controls the psychological. Worshipping the relics of a saint or drinking holy water or visiting a site of miraculous healing may not be scientifically creditable but if it renews hope, and a sense of purpose, and provides an awareness that the mind affects the body as profoundly as the body affects the mind then we reach a conclusion that many counsellors and psychologists would be pleased with. A "porous" world, open to good and bad influences is one that both pagans and Christians can share and one that has distinctive social advantages as well as dangers. The roots of sin may lie deep within the good and even thrive within it, but to eradicate them would mean the eradication of all the good which such forces as the Reformation and Counter-Reformation brought to us. The line between idealism and sadism, as MacCulloch reminds us, is a fine one, and the original aim of the Inquisition was in the first place to change society for the better, not merely punish it for its sins.[133] The Dominican inquisitors were pastors and there was a pastoral element to their work.

Nevertheless, heresy was something the inquisitors were charged with erasing: it had split the world in two; it had given a foothold to the Devil; it was a disease that was both infectious and contagious; it knew no national boundaries and could exist and spread undetected if preventative measures were not taken, if its carriers were not sought out and destroyed. It would therefore be easy for certain sorts of people to become paranoid about it. We have seen the same in the twentieth century with McCarthyism in the United States, and in Russia the paranoia of Stalinism. The persecution of heresy has by no means been the preserve of the Christian Church. It has happened in the other major world religions and in states with no religion—China, Burma and Russia. Essentially, the desire to root out heresy is a desire for control, for purity, for security in the knowledge that the world is, or could be, as those in power want it to be.

To be fair, we have to ask the question, would the world have been better off at this period had there been no religion, no monotheism, no theological pretexts behind which to hide megalomaniac tendencies?

Probably not, for two reasons. The first is that powerful men love to dominate others and will always find a pretext to justify such behaviour: racial purity, the needs of the state, the will of the people, historical destiny, and yes, the will of God. But a minimum of classical education reveals that vicious wars were fought long before and beyond the influence of monotheism. Whatever the corrupt and powerful do, they will find a means of justifying it, for they too have some sense of morality, albeit hideously warped. The second reason is that without religion, as we constantly need reminding, that sense of moral compass, of being required to follow the Golden Rule, to be honest and to be just would have been absent, dormant or just less strong than Christendom demanded of people's social behaviour. The glue in society, the awareness that revenge or limitless selfishness was not the only or best way to live would be weaker. Yes, good and educated pagans had known this and acted on it but their transmission of that knowledge had never reached the masses. Where the gods are fickle men will follow; where they are absent men forget their own fragility. Hubris produced catastrophe in the Greek tragedies.

In 1480, when the Spanish Inquisition began to operate, the kingdoms of Aragon and Castile were newly united. Their Christian monarchs, Ferdinand and Isabella, knew that their territories were full of *conversos*, or converted Jews, and "Moriscos", or Moors converted from Islam. But were they really converted? After all, there was every social and financial reason for them to want to appear to be so, and therefore every possibility that in reality they were not. Should there be too many such people would that not be a threat to the monarchy, the unity of the country? How could it be possible for genuine Jews or Muslims to pay anything more than lip service to a Christian king? Centuries of war against Islam made Christians suspicious of Muslims and gave the people a militancy in defence of their faith. In places where you need to conform in order to achieve high office, there is always suspicion about motives, and some jealousy of those one-time "outsiders" who are appointed. Between 1481 and 1488, inquisitors were responsible for delivering 700 "heretics" to the stake. Twelve years later, in 1500, Isabella required all Granada's Muslims to convert to Christianity. The government's policy (and the Inquisition was its tool) was demonstrably designed therefore to crush any potential rival civilisations as threats to unity and order. This was effectively a reversion to forced conversions, a retrograde step by some 600 years and more, and a better example could hardly be found of failing to understand that the heart of the Gospel is that the individual must turn *freely* to Christ. If further evidence were needed that this was a racial and political tool it is that the Spanish Inquisition frequently regarded heresy as hereditary, or familial, as much as they saw it to be a matter of individual conscience. If a family or village was on the wrong side of the historic divide, they were fair game (there are features here similar to the tribal area divisions of Northern Ireland which masquerade under religious labels). This work of political separation went on to reach a climax in 1609 when 300,000 Moriscos were expelled from Spain altogether.

Despite all this, various modern studies surprisingly have found that the methods and punishments of the Inquisition were not quite what

The Black Legend stories have bequeathed to us, though the reality is that terrible tortures did take place. However, many *autos da fe*, the infamous public humiliation of the victims, did not involve any burning or capital punishment. In 1972, Henningsen and Contreras made a study of almost 45,000 summaries of trial records between 1540 and 1700, revealing that though the 1480s were terribly punitive, for most of this time capital punishment was exercised on less than 2 per cent of those examined: on average five people per year.[134] Their study also found that from 1540 the Holy Office was mainly concerned with minor heresies such as wrong sexual behaviour, superstition, and blasphemy. Henry Kamen, in his radically revised view, puts the total figure of executions between 1540 and 1700 as less than 500. In *The Spanish Inquisition: A Historical Revision*, he refers to research which also estimates that in nineteen tribunals throughout the period 1540–1700 no more than 2 per cent of those examined were executed, which works out at only three people per year under the jurisdiction of Spain.[135] He concedes, however, the difficulty of estimating accurately the total number of those executed or tortured. His final chapter, "Inventing the Inquisition", reveals how the mythology about the Inquisition grew—as well as showing that much of Spain would see an inquisitor only once every ten years, if that. Compare Kamen's figure of lives lost in 160 years with the fact that in England, over a period of 33 years (1570–1603), 127 Catholic priests were executed. The figures per year are not so different. Both states recognised that dissidence in religion was a threat to the Crown. In 1570, Elizabeth had been "tried" in Rome, found guilty, excommunicated and deposed. Later, a sort of "fatwah", as we would now say, was issued against her life. Little wonder then that in 1581 an act was passed in England declaring that converts to Rome would be seen as traitors. It was in the middle of the twentieth century that we hanged Lord Haw-Haw, not for his actions, but for his words—because of the threat they had constituted in time of war. In the "porous" society of Elizabethan England such threats did not have to be public to be dangerous. Both a civil war and a Spanish war were horrors that Elizabethans in England did not want to contemplate. Shakespeare reinforces that revulsion in his history plays, which promote "the Tudor myth", designed to preclude any possibility of another civil war like the Wars of the Roses. The surprise is not that Elizabeth gave the order for the execution of Mary, Queen of Scots, but that she kept her off the throne, yet alive for seventeen years, despite the threat that she constituted.

Some historians have also revised their view of the Inquisition's use of torture, providing a figure of about 10 per cent or less of cases being tortured for the Granada tribunal (1573–1577) and for Seville (1606–11). Its methods too were not distinctively its own but those of the secular courts, and though today it seems inexcusable, torture was commonplace throughout Europe. A physician attended on behalf of the Inquisition and the process was designed to extract information and not to do lasting physical damage (though of course it did, and abuses of the code must have been regular). Tortures used at the same time and at later dates in the Far East were, however, infinitely worse and designed to kill in the most painful ways possible (today Amnesty considers that one third of the world's states employ torturers). Kamen concludes that the Inquisition's impact on Spain's civil liberties was, overall, slight. Its purpose was also to inform and educate and this it seems to have done with considerable success.

We may conclude then that the Inquisition was in line with most medieval courts and certainly no worse than them. This, however, still leaves us with the issue that the Holy Office tried only crimes of heresy and these are "thought crimes". Such a policy runs quite counter to a modern liberal democracy in which a theist (T) and an atheist (A) might argue as follows:

> T: The Inquisition tried only heresy.
> A: Yes, thought crime: needless. It would
> be better not to have heresy, then there
> would be no need for an Inquisition.
> T: If we had no heresy, we would have no religion
> and if we had no religion then we would have
> no ideas about origins or purpose or destiny.
> A: Yes we would. Darwin has supplied them.
> T: Well, not strictly. Darwin talked about mechanisms
> rather than purpose or absence of it.
> A: Well, now we can see with hindsight that totalitarian
> religion was a disaster, even if we concede that

> modern non-fundamentalist religion does provide
> comfort to some individuals, and cohesiveness
> in some societies or social groupings.
> T: Agreed; Christianity at any rate was (as we have
> been saying from the start) not designed to be
> used as a control mechanism for those in power.
> When it is, it is corrupted and very dangerous.

Any leader holding a strong worldview, wanting his people to benefit from the structures he has imposed or maintained for their good is bound to be put out by dissent since it works against his definitions of life, liberty, and the pursuit of happiness. The cost to everyone else is, as Lord David Cecil says in his book *Library Looking-Glass*, that Torquemada, the first Grand Inquisitor, Robespierre and Hitler represent those who have made mankind suffer the most, precisely because of their strong faith.[136] Their faiths, however, though in utterly different models or blueprints for society, had this in common: it was centred on themselves—that they alone had the sole vision capable of saving society. When your self-assurance is of that order of magnitude, any behaviour, criminal or otherwise, becomes justified and therefore a virtue in the pursuit of the ideal. However, as Lord Cecil said, when we think we have the power to establish heaven on earth we are more likely to create a hell. But the seventeenth century's wars of religion did not create a secular society which was characterised by peace. Moreover, the wars of the twentieth century were even more terribly destructive and had no religious causation.

The causes of the horrors of the sixteenth century in Europe go further than this. Whether we think of it as a metaphor or the literal truth, Jesus' teaching about the seven devils is profound. If you cause one devil to flee, he taught, seven will come and take its place unless you fill the void with something better. That something has to be "a still more excellent way": it has to be the way of love: love of neighbour, love of enemy, love of God "because he first loved us". The Spanish Inquisition and all who tortured their enemies, substituting a mere idea, a way of seeing the world, for the presence of God the Holy Spirit, were bound to open themselves to the forces of hell, rather than the Kingdom of Heaven. And having those forces in them, they expected and needed to find them in others—but they seemed also to instinctively sense a spiritual inadequacy which they were loath to recognise in themselves, and thus projected on to others. The two strands of Jesus' teaching contained in the parables about the speck of dust in another's eye, and the farmer with wheat and weeds in his fields, are utterly pertinent.

When we conjoin such psychological forces with political ones, it is almost surprising that the Inquisitions did not do more damage than they did. Civilisation had to be protected, but one reason that civilisation had emerged from barbarism in the first place was the impact of Christian doctrine in restraining violence among communities. In an age of such absolute belief of every kind, to dissent from that doctrine seemed little less than an act of war. To defend the doctrines was therefore seen as a direct contribution to the preservation of society and civilisation. To argue that we would have been better served without *any* doctrines is simply to argue that human nature ought to be different from what it is. Men fight for their corner, be it territorial, intellectual or spiritual, and that corner has to be defined in order to be defended. The only way out of the cycle of atrocities and reprisals is to love your enemies and do good to them that hate you.

It was a cruel age. We have spoken of the physicality of legal punishments, but our understanding of this needs to be broader. Attitudes to the pain of others and of animals were generally coarse in the medieval and Renaissance world, as a glance at some eyewitness accounts from *The Faber Book of Reportage* makes clear.[137] One of the most striking and horrific passages is an account written by Edmund Scot in about 1602 detailing the multiple torture methods and slow deaths suffered by Chinese "thieves" suspected by English merchants. Three points are of particular interest. First, these tortures, of the most terrible and lingering kind, were designed solely to inflict pain and not to extract information which the torturers already had. Second, there was no religious motive, and third, the writer, who was also the torturer, felt no shame, guilt or any sense of impropriety or cruelty about what he was doing.

Another account from the same date shows the impact of Elizabethan policy in Ireland against those in rebellion. "No spectacle was more frequent" than to see heaps of emaciated bodies in ditches, their mouths discoloured green by the eating of nettles and docks in their attempt to avoid starvation. Others attempted to survive by cannibalism—including children, who were recorded as eating their mother's body bit by bit from the feet upwards over a period of three weeks. One more example of cruelty to humans will suffice. A century later, in 1702, John Bion was chaplain aboard one of the French galleys which employed five slaves to every oar and in all carried 300 slaves aboard. Subject to the lash on their naked backs throughout the day, they were tormented at night by lice which infested every inch of their sparse clothing (two shirts were issued per year). When not chained to the oar they were allocated an eighteen-inch wide plank as bed space. Deserters from the army were condemned to the galleys for life, but others were there too: "criminals" who because of their poverty had been forced to buy salt illegally in a neighbouring province, and of course, Protestants, unwilling to sell their souls for the whole world.

If this was how humanity was treated it will be no surprise that the animal kingdom was seen by many simply as a resource to be exploited—for the sating of whatever appetite was uppermost. An account of bull-baiting in London in 1710 by Zacharias Uffenbach describes a typical Monday evening in a courtyard surrounded by high benches for the spectators of the opening spectacle, namely a young bull tied to an iron ring being baited by as many as thirty dogs in succession which the bull proceeds to gore. This was followed by similar treatment for a bear and a "common little ass" with an ape clinging to its back for fear of falling off during the assault. It caused huge delight for the English but did little to entertain the visiting Uffenbach.

Witchcraft

It was not mere accident that gave rise to the high incidence of witch-finding in the sixteenth and seventeenth centuries, an activity that had not greatly troubled the Middle Ages. A loss of authority in the church, suffered as a result of rival popes fighting each other and the Pope later being seen as Antichrist by the reformers, meant that other sources of authority could now be countenanced. Moreover, blame for the Church being in such a divided state had to be lodged somewhere. The Devil, the father of lies, was suddenly not only a plausible enemy but a useful one. He gave a chance to the aggressive and the guilty, as well as the insecure and the anxious, to serve their own ends.

These centuries were also, however, the age of print and the age of discovery—both territorial and intellectual. Ships, telescopes, compasses, printed books and charts were enabling the educated and better-off to reach out across new and untouched worlds. And because the real limits to discovery are only set from within, some would overreach into magic and the occult. The type has been preserved for us in Christopher Marlowe's *Doctor Faustus*. There is so much to be known, and so little time in which to know it, that students of every age are tempted to take shortcuts, and the ultimate shortcut is not plagiarism but necromancy and magic: the journey which promises to take you to a source of knowledge beyond time itself, but at a cost. Shakespeare's Banquo had it right when he warned Macbeth after meeting the witches:

> The instruments of darkness tell us truths;
> Win us with honest trifles, to betray us
> In deepest consequence.[138]

Macbeth, like Faustus, pays not just with his life but with his soul.

The practice of the dark arts—witchcraft, sorcery—was by definition hard to see, harder to fathom. Though the witch might cast spells, the means of doing so were often innocent enough (cooking pots and needles) and the likelihood of witnesses slight. In the most difficult cases, those who could testify would be solely the witch and her victim. The witch would hardly accuse herself so the victim's testimony becomes the sole means of establishing guilt. In an age which allowed torture it could become preferable for the accused to plead guilty rather than continue under excruciating duress. Any sign of scepticism about witchcraft was tantamount to scepticism about the Devil and therefore heretical and subject to the same penalties as heretics.

We have already seen how the Spanish Inquisition dealt with heresy as a response to the need for national identity threatened by secret non-believers or misbelievers. Where such heresies existed, they were seen to be diabolical because the Devil is the ultimate enemy of true belief—but the unwitting mistake made by such courts was that such emphasis on the diabolical created its own devilish temptations. Certain sorts of people would find in it a particular fascination—as they do today. The invisible world, as envisaged by Reverend Hale in Arthur Miller's *The Crucible*,[139] with its secrecy, codes, illegitimacy, brotherhood, seeming power and results, was a heady mix to try, especially for those on the fringes and excluded from the usual rewards of social living. No wonder then that the majority of "witches" were women, often older, often uneducated and often rural. The same set of reasons appealed to those who would destroy them, these unseen canker sores bent on destroying the happiness of the righteous. By 1563, therefore, witchcraft in England had become a crime to be tried in a court, and by 1604 was a capital offence. In 1590, James I had written a book on the subject suggesting ways of identifying witches, and their "familiars"—animals which doubled as devil and an instrument of the witches' work. War had broken out, and one of the prime requirements of the soldier in time of war is the ability to identify the enemy, for this not only lessens the chance of sudden attack but helps to control fear. And fear itself creates a lot of enemies.

Nowhere has this been more true in modern times than during the McCarthy era in America in the late 1940s and early 1950s when the House Un-American Activities Committee had powers to investigate anything or anyone who seemingly posed a threat to the safety of the state. Their focus was Communism rather than diabolism. Miller, perhaps the greatest American playwright of the twentieth century, wrote *The Crucible* at the height of this era and was himself later summoned to answer questions before the Committee. His play is the best depiction in modern literature of the absurdity, paranoia, and injustice that characteristically accompanied most of the witch trials of the seventeenth century. The witch hunts in the play have strong parallels with those of the McCarthy era.

The Salem witch episode of 1692 (on which the play is based) occurred when a group of adolescent girls, after dabbling in the supernatural, exhibited signs of "possession", and accused scores of townsfolk of bewitching them. Twenty people were executed. Twenty years later compensation was awarded to victims still alive, and the excommunications were rescinded. This has long been seen as one of the most awful chapters in American history, but Europe has fared no better. Hundreds of witches were hanged in England, the last being Old Mother Osborne in 1751. The bloodiest of judges sent hundreds to their death on his own account. Miller, in a sort of Shavian preface to the play, gives an extremely penetrating account of the causes of the witch hunt which the play goes on to illustrate. He reminds the reader of the unique circumstances of the town of Salem in Massachusetts in the 1690s and draws a picture of a group of intensely religious people whose families and forebears had accepted voluntary exile to the edge of the world rather than live in the corrupting atmosphere of English Church and state in the earlier seventeenth century. Their lives were almost unrelentingly laborious, having to fight for every ear of corn they harvested and unrelieved save by the Sabbath which was equally disciplined. The continent they inherited was imagined to be the last preserve of the Devil—dark, unknown, untamed and thickly forested. Within the forests were the barbarian tribes who had murdered the settlers' forebears. In Europe of the day there was social disorder and political instability (the Glorious Revolution in 1688), which were also both signs of devilish activity. Their leaders had to be autocratic and theocratic to ensure order, but also because their ideology was the justification for their sufferings and sense of persecution. Such a sense leads to meting out harsh justice.

Miller is careful to say that the social results of such a worldview cut both ways. The sense of purpose, discipline and dedication which justified the hard work meant that the community survived in a way that the more commercial Jamestown did not. But the theocracy was based on exclusion and prohibition which reached the point at which its repressive order became too heavy for the diminishing dangers that originally warranted it. An instinctive recognition of the changing balance allowed resentments to issue in revenge and pent-up hatreds to emerge under the guise of godliness. What the playwright does not deal with adequately, or allow for fully, is that the Devil was indeed present in Salem—just not in the way that its inhabitants imagined. Yes, Miller sees that the girls' symptoms of "possession" were probably psychosomatic, but fails to see, or to suggest, that this itself was used diabolically. If we allow that a force of evil is operating in the world (as I earlier argued), then for the Devil to do it this way, using the moralistic judges, the religious townsfolk, and the Christian law to achieve the required destruction, rather than the usual and obvious lawbreakers, must have been a peculiarly satisfying and diabolical turn of events, and makes of course for great drama (Shakespeare does something similar in *Othello* when he enables Iago to see that it is the very goodness of Desdemona that will bring about her downfall). Nevertheless, the stand of the central characters, Elizabeth and John Proctor, against terrible wickedness simply in the name of goodness, truth and honesty is a heart-wrenching example of truly Christian self-sacrifice and courage.

To what extent could any of the circumstances of the town of Salem be a microcosm of a wider and less intensely painted canvas of the social conditions in Europe rather earlier?

We have been looking at some of the darkest places in these terrifying centuries, but surely there must have been brighter spots to inhabit? Fortunately there were, and it will be a relief to look at them briefly.

One of the remarkable features of this period of Christian history, but one that is seldom remarked upon by Christians and, needless to say, unnoticed by detractors, is the fact that the desire for social justice, for less inequality and greater adherence to biblical teaching as we have seen it in earlier chapters, was shared by some in every quarter of the Church, whether among reformers or among Catholics. Thomas More's *Utopia* (1516), like the whole genre of books it gave rise to, was not so much the depiction of a perfect world as a satirical joke at the expense of the present one. More drew attention to the lack of holiness among the clergy, the grinding lives of the poor, and the lies told about war. Hugh Latimer (later martyred) defended the peasantry against the landowners; Luther and Calvin (strange to mention such giants simply by way of reference to secondary matters) in turning the world upside down again made each "Protestant" conscious of his worth, his individuality, his relation to God, and his political power. No longer were the Pope, his cardinals and clergy the only means of determining the rightness of your conduct, or the meaning of your existence, or even your place in society. The concept of a "Protestant work Ethic" may be derided by some but Calvin's support for trade and business made the "bourgeoisie" (as they became) a force to be reckoned with. Calvin also was quite clear that society has an obligation "to provide for the poor and redress their needs", thereby removing the occasion of beggary. Such is the impact of recognising the image of God in our neighbours. A man could now take pride in his ability to escape his social circles by hard work, prayer and the grace of God. Capitalism is a far from perfect system, but as was said of democracy, it seems less bad than the alternatives.

S. G. Evans, in his book *The Social Hope of the Christian Church*, reminds us that the Anabaptists, led among others by Thomas Munzer in Germany, believed God's kingdom was intended for *earth* and that in it there would be no room for wealth, poverty or class when it arrived.[140] Interestingly this is a view being expressed more widely among Christians today than at any time previously in my lifetime. Others preaching and working for a better, fairer society were figures as diverse as Lancelot Andrewes, Bishop of Winchester, speaking out against usury, and Archbishop Laud against enclosures. The Diggers and Levellers, from a very different stratum of society, produced pamphlets decrying private property altogether, thereby giving the most dispossessed a focus and hope in their deprivations.

One of the best-selling books of all time in English came out of this period. John Bunyan's *The Pilgrim's Progress* was started in prison in the 1670s. In it he tells an unforgettable story: the individual's journey towards his God, guided by the Bible and an inner voice, after the burden of sin has rolled from his back at the Cross. Translated into 200 languages and never out of print for 350 years, the number of copies sold bears testimony to its power and the sense that the individual under the hand of God is master of his own destiny. This is a message of amazing power: Christian is empowered to forge his own way, not to be just a passive receiver of such sacraments that the Church might choose to grant him, not to be someone who has to do what he is told by others in the Church (who indeed, in the person of Formalist or Hypocrisy in the story might or would mislead him) but to be one who chooses freely to obey a quite different sort of authority: his lord and master Jesus, the Christ, as revealed in the Bible and in his heart. The social impact of this cannot be exaggerated and of course has been explored often. Nothing could ever be the same again once the doctrines of the Reformation had taken hold in the way that *The Pilgrim's Progress* illustrates that they did. Nonconformity in religion was much bigger than thinking about a different set of abstractions. It meant basing your life on a whole new set of premises. If we value democracy, we have to value those who would not conform to the religious system, from Luther to Bunyan and beyond. This is true too of John Wesley in the next century.

Charles Williams, in discussing this often bleak period of religious history, traces the shadowy growth of something he calls "the quality of disbelief".[141] Though pre-existent through all of Christian history, this first emerged politically, he suggests, in Elizabeth of England and Henry of Navarre, finding polished expression in the pages of Montaigne, the sixteenth-century French intellectual, sceptic and essayist. Perhaps, he thinks, it was born of exhaustion; perhaps of revolt or revulsion at religious conflict, but Williams finds this thread consistent (surprisingly) with sanctity, and orthodox (even more surprisingly) in terms of the Creed. Montaigne's passion for questioning everything, his doubt about the validity of his own opinions and his fear of religious fanaticism made him the supremely humane figure of his time. But equally, as Sarah Bakewell points out in her biography of him, he has little or nothing to say on most Christian ideas. Despite advocating complete obedience to all Christian teachings, Montaigne lived and died, she concludes, a secular yet joyful man.[142]

Contemporary with Montaigne was the Englishman Sir Francis Bacon, philosopher, essayist and statesman—to many the greatest and most original of his time. Bacon, like Montaigne, could sit sufficiently detached to see that extremity could be avoided "if the points fundamental, and of substance, in religion, were truly discerned and distinguished from points not merely of faith but of opinion".[143] In another place he feels quite able to reprove equally both the bishops and the puritans for their shortcomings.

But essentially, Montaigne, says Williams, reminds us that faith is an *hypothesis*—Christians might say a glorious one, and one for which the evidence is more convincing than any other, thereby acknowledging that there must be others with a rival claim to truth—and that intolerance and certitude, and the cruelty that results from them, are not part of that hypothesis but only part of the anger and obstinacy and egotism that men indulge in everywhere. The whole of Williams' chapter "The Quality of Disbelief" is bright with spiritual illumination, love, clarity of mind and deep faith. Would that it were read more. It is in understanding "disbelief" in this sense that Susan Hill, another Christian novelist, cites the paradox of George Savile, the Marquis of Halifax, who believed men had to be saved by their "want" or lack of faith.[144] The intolerances born of too much faith, or rather too much faith in things Christians have no right to put faith in at all, were all too evident in the fifteenth and sixteenth centuries, as they are again today.

Today, of course, intolerance is not just the preserve of certain parts of the Church but is a mark of the New Atheism too, as A. McGrath and others have pointed out. To argue that any position other than your own is irrational, and that religion has brought no social benefits, is a view so blinkered as to remind one of the worst dogmatism of the seventeenth century. A "quality of disbelief" (in the right sense) is needed by some *atheists*—as well as an awareness too that we tend to believe our positions more strongly at the end of an argument than at the beginning, as Williams notes. The more strident we are, the more fiercely we believe afterwards— but this is more about egotism than truth.

Nothing has been said so far about the cultural impact of the Church during this period of unrivalled creativity, but it is beyond the scope of this book to try to demonstrate the almost incalculable impact of Christianity on literature, art, architecture, music, sculpture and painting as a civilising force—without rival—from the late Middle Ages until the late nineteenth century. More mundanely, bathetically, streets, place names, even public houses, reflect our Christian heritage along with our parish churches.

Much has been made since the 2011 anniversary of the 400-year influence of the King James or Authorised Version of the Bible (KJV), published in 1611. The degree to which this Bible, along with the *Book of Common Prayer*, informs our language is so strong as to be unquestionable. The Bodleian Library in Oxford lent its weight to the quatercentenary celebrations by publishing *Manifold Greatness*, written mostly by senior Oxford academics, on the making of the King James Bible.[145] The book identifies the scholarly precision of the translation and the astonishing range of Hebrew, Christian and Pagan texts brought to bear by the committees and used in establishing the best meaning. The chapters on "Afterlives" and the KJV's impact on America give a scholarly overview of its influence on literature and politics. Melvin Bragg takes up the theme in *The Book of Books*, reckoning the KJV to be without parallel or match, and wonders why the Church of England has abandoned it.[146]

It might be argued, however, that the geniuses in each of the areas of human creativity listed earlier would have existed anyway and easily found something entirely different from the Bible (KJV or otherwise) but equally uplifting to be creative about. I think this is a mistaken view. C. S. Lewis has an interesting essay ("The Literary Impact of the Authorised Version") in which he demonstrates that Bunyan's *style* would have been little different if the Authorised Version had never been written.[147] However, in terms of *content,* of course, the concepts on which he bases his plot could not have existed without the Old and New Testaments, and of course it was those concepts, their content, message and contention—of both Bunyan and the Bible—which appealed to people. There was no story to equal it in terms of imaginative range, sublimity, depravity, shock, irony and tragedy. It is a story that, while filling the heavens, also illuminates the whole earth. A story of blood, self-sacrifice, humility, grandeur, courage, dignity and hope—as well as one of pride, greed, and failure—and success grasped in the closing moments of apparent tragedy. There was, and is, no story to rival it. If the creative geniuses of the past had not had this to feast on, the material they would have used could only have been inferior.

CHAPTER 7

Cromwell, Commonwealth and Restoration

Society is never static in its attitudes and beliefs. As we move down the axis of time we also move in relation to another axis: that of moral absolutes, or at least definite statements of belief or doctrines. Whether we move towards or away from an absolute will depend on innumerable factors, but one of them will always be the actions and beliefs of the preceding generation. In a drama, the playwright knows that intense emotional excitement cannot be sustained indefinitely: there must be periods of relief, of quietude, prior to any further call on our emotions. The first part of the eighteenth century looks like one of those periods, a calm between two high points of religious fervour: Puritanism and the Evangelical Revival. But of course it is far more complex and interesting than that.

The attitude of many today, in keeping with our cynical age, is to laugh at the Puritans, not least for the fact that they could not laugh at themselves. Even in their own day this was a popular attitude to strike, and for those who were humbugs or self-righteous it was an appropriate response. Shakespeare lampoons them marvellously in *Twelfth Night*, where the hypocritical Malvolio, on attempting to break up some late night revelry and fun, is utterly discomfited by Sir Toby Belch: "Dost thou think, because thou art virtuous, there shall be no more cakes and ale?"[148] Sir Toby knew perfectly well, of course, that Malvolio was *not* virtuous. Maria the waiting-gentlewoman knows too: "The devil a puritan that he is, or anything, constantly, but a time-pleaser."[149]

Malvolio is a revealing portrait of those (seeming) Puritans who used their freedom from Church authority as a means of furthering a purely selfish individualism and egotism under the guise of obedience to the Divine Will, thus investing themselves with divine authority. Intelligent

Christianity recognises this—as William Law (who was to greatly influence John Wesley) did in remarking that religion in the hands of "the mere natural man" always makes him the worse for it. Genuine Puritans, however, were a quite different order of person. Originally a nickname, but one that stuck, the term "Puritan" (first coined in the 1560s) described those who, at cost to themselves, sought greater simplicity of worship than the Church of England provided, and greater strictness in behaviour and morality than the Church of England demanded. Naturally, such people were derided. They did not fit in.

Laughing at the Puritans is only one modern response. The other is to hate them. But it is not for their scholarship, rigour, intensity, and conviction, though such qualities are often not easy to live with. Rather, it is for their absoluteness, their inflexibility, in some cases their unbending fatalism that they are today remembered unsympathetically. Yet as former Chief Rabbi Jonathan Sacks reminds us in his book *The Great Partnership*, it was the Puritans who created the ideas and covenants that produced for us the liberty that underlies all others: freedom of conscience.[150] We should remember too that it was a Puritan, the poet John Milton, who in 1644 wrote *Areopagitica* and in it gave us the first proper and full defence of of "unlicenc'd printing" or freedom from censorship in print.

Nowhere does the absoluteness of the Puritans raise its head in the mind of the general public so forcibly as in the figure of Oliver Cromwell, Lord Protector. Such is the power of history that Antonia Fraser noted in her 1973 study that Cromwell's statue in St Ives was still frequently being daubed with red paint to illustrate his guilt, such was the passion that his name evoked during "The Troubles" at least.[151] His treatment of the Irish whom his troops put to the sword at Drogheda and Wexford and his settlement of that country is still seen as a root cause of so many of its subsequent troubles. We shall see that this is yet another example, perhaps one of the most salient, not only of the principle that the evil that men do lives after them, but that it goes on growing as the years pass, thereby falsifying or unbalancing their true historical significance.

That Cromwell, besides being a military genius, was essentially a humane, kindly, unself-important man is something that his more modern biographers find hard to deny. The evidence for this in his family life, letters, speeches and the recollections of observers is inescapable. His conversion was preceded by a long period of mental and spiritual anguish, and followed by a great outpouring of gratitude to God for the grace which had been shown him, the greatest of sinners as he perceived himself. The fact that he was an Independent in churchmanship, rather than Presbyterian, laying emphasis on the right of each church congregation to be autonomous (hence why they were later called "Congregationalists") entirely fits with his views on the toleration of other Christian believers. Independents saw church authority as inhering in each local church congregation and free of external human control in order that the will of God might be more fully obeyed. Needless to say, this puts a huge demand for godliness on each church member, for without that there would be rapid collapse in the absence of other sanctions and controls. But this godliness is what Cromwell expected from himself and others—both in the army and in parliament. Being denied it, the structures he hoped to make permanent were doomed to fail.

John Buchan, in his brilliantly readable biography of Cromwell, described by A. L. Rowse as "essentially right",[152] says simply at one point: "Oliver remained humble". But Buchan also draws superbly, not only the picture of a soul humbled before the awe-inspiring majesty of God, but a picture of the age and the particular circumstances of Cromwell's behaviour in Ireland. He does not excuse it but shows it to be out of character: "In Ireland he was false to his own creed." It was "the chief blot on his fame" which he himself knew, for he sought to justify it afterwards. Buchan quotes Cromwell's own description of events at Drogheda in which he takes full responsibility for the massacre: "I forbade them to spare any that were in arms in the town."[153] The actions and orders are merciless, part of a war full of bitter hatreds, something we instinctively deplore, but in judging we must not lose sight of how things were in the middle of seventeenth-century Europe, or judge without reflecting on times then and now. Certainly, in the European wars of the later sixteenth century, a soldier in battle was not expected to show any sort of restraint, but rather be beside himself, berserk, not accountable, as Sarah Bakewell points out in her biography of Montaigne.[154]

Yes, Cromwell was extremely intolerant in Ireland, but at the time any toleration in important matters, of those opposed to you in practical affairs, politically or religiously, was an almost revolutionary novelty. "The notion of tolerating more than one kind of religion within the borders of a state was alien to the thought of the time", G. M. Trevelyan tells us.[155] And it was the belief of the politicians as much as the priests. In the twentieth century, Fascism and Communism were considered threats real enough to fight against and die for. In 1650 Papism was a political force, a seedbed for the re-establishing of the Stuarts, which threatened the loss of very real freedoms: of speech, of action, of belief. Since all things were lawful against such a heretic nation as England the extirpation of that threat by the English armies was essential. The prospect of the young King landing in Scotland and being joined by forces from Ireland was too great to allow. Modern Western governments have been taking pre-emptive action against armed fundamentalist Islamist groups concertedly since the destruction of the Twin Towers in 2001. England in 1650 was far more vulnerable to the forces marshalled against it than it had been for many years before or since. Cromwell could not afford to leave the struggling republic with its back door open.

Moreover, Cromwell suffered from the blindness that all suffered at the time: the inability to see that the Irish were an equal race. We have already seen how they suffered under Elizabeth's policies. That gentlest of poets, Edmund Spenser, despite seeing their pitiful condition, "goes on to urge that Essex should harden his heart, and reduce other parts of the land to the same condition".[156] The Cromwellian Settlement, though more the work of Fleetwood than Cromwell, made matters even worse in its confiscation of lands, prohibition of Catholic rites and priests, its relocation of thousands of peasants.

In all this horror we must not lose sight of "cometh the hour, cometh the man". Cromwell arose from the Fens to meet a crisis unlike any other in English history. No ordinary man would meet such a challenge. He was, in Buchan's phrase, "the creature of emergencies",[157] but longed for the day when government could be by the general will rather than his own and when all classes might have a partnership in the duties and rights of the polity. He also longed for toleration. His speech to the Rump Parliament is a measure of his magnanimity and desire:

> [T]ruth . . . will teach you to be as just towards an unbeliever
> as towards a believer; and it's our duty to do so. . . . And if

the poorest Christian, the most mistaken Christian, shall
desire to live peaceably and quietly under you—I say, if any
shall desire but to lead a life in godliness and honestly, let
him be protected.[158]

It was the "godliness" in men which led Cromwell to desire their protection.
His passionate desire that men should tolerate each other was founded on
the deeper ground that God tolerates us even though we are fallen sinful
creatures. Issues of class, even of doctrine, Cromwell would not allow to
obscure this central fact. But self-interest is what always does obscure it
and he knew that the Rump Parliament was dominated by self-interested
parties. Dismissing the Rump, therefore, if it was an act of intolerance,
was only one insofar as it aimed to do away with intolerance, much as his
attitude towards Papism was intolerant. How can one tolerate those who
tolerate no one save themselves and their kind and whose avowed intent
is to coerce you to conform to their beliefs and way of life or suffer in
consequence? To remove such a threat is an understandable aim, and the
twenty-first-century West is presently involved in that endeavour across
the globe. What then, of the gospel's injunction to turn the other cheek?
It is certainly a Christ-like principle, but there is no reason to suppose
Christ intended it to characterise states in their dealings with one another.
Absolute pacifism can be honourable and brave, but when it means others
will be slaughtered in their thousands or millions, or forced to live contrary
to their conscience, that principle can hardly apply. Cromwell's words,
"Bethink you that you may be mistaken",[159] find much resonance in an age
of growing and irrational fundamentalist violence; they reveal Cromwell
as a man ahead of his times by many years, but held back, not by his own
lack of tolerance, but that of others. Middleton Murry thought he came
as near to loving his adversaries as any great ruler of men had done.
Trevelyan called him "an early Apostle of the principle of Toleration".[160]

Antonia Fraser, in Cromwell: Our Chief of Men, paints a comparable
picture in a number of respects.[161] She sees his religious conviction as
entirely authentic, and his personal tolerance of other views, along with
his recommendation (to Major General Crawford) that he should show
toleration to "men of different minds from yourself", as largely in advance
of his day. She shows that for the ordinary people, if not priests, Cromwell's

actions as well as his words confirm that he did not think it his duty to enquire into their thoughts if they were honest and peaceable.[162] In a terribly cruel age when Puritans had their ears cropped, and faces branded for printing pamphlets, Cromwell, she suggests, was not a Macbeth, who being steeped in blood so far, considered that "Returning were as tedious as go o'er".[163] Rather, after the bloodshed at Drogheda (an action not at all in contravention of seventeenth-century military codes), his terms for other surrenders were mild by the standards of the day. Folk memory based on the great events of those days, however, does not record his courtesy to women and children, his clemency to many prisoners and the weak, and his friendship to both men and women, for it served no political or social purpose to do so in a country that continued to be treated by the English for hundreds of years mostly with disdain and shocking indifference to its suffering. According to Antonia Fraser, Cromwell "lost his self-control at Drogheda", yet although this was quite contrary to his usual "careful mercy as a soldier" the event has echoed down history and besmirched his name ever since.[164] People do not forget such events. Or rather, we frequently choose not to.

It would be useful to understand better such a black and white dichotomy as Cromwell's distinction between the innocent and guilty, between those who must be oppressed or savagely slaughtered, and those who may be left in peace. Is this another instance of the damage religion does to society, as some would suggest? I think not. In Cromwell we see a man on the verge of a rediscovery—the knowledge that men could disagree over the profoundest issues of behaviour and belief, and yet co-exist. Such a realisation had been made in Transylvania, Warsaw, and a remote part of Switzerland a hundred years earlier, but they were not visions which Western Europe could yet appropriate.[165] Cromwell perhaps struggled to see it, but could not fully apply his vision of what his recorded statements suggest he instinctively felt on many occasions. But who *could* have achieved such a thing? What figure in history could have balanced perfectly all these: the desire for freedom from tyranny, the need to protect national sovereignty, the moral imperative of governing unselfishly, and the control of the most effective fighting force in England since the Roman invasion? If we say that Cromwell might have done better had he not been so "religious" and consequently less adamant in his desire to extinguish Irish opposition, we are talking nonsense. Cromwell without the driving force of his faith would not have been Cromwell—at least not the genius we know. He might not have led an army to Drogheda which killed its thousands, but no more would he have moved England forward from a system of tyrannical monarchy that was no longer endurable or sustainable, or fought for justice for the poor. A Fenland farmer perhaps, but nothing much more.

John Morrill, Cambridge professor of British and Irish history, in his 2007 study of Cromwell (a "distillation" of more than forty years study of him) reveals a figure whose openness and lack of duplicity "usually appeals and just sometimes appals", and towards whom historians for the last half-century have been increasingly sympathetic.[166] Whether dealing with military or theological opponents he was generous—as in his surrender terms for Exeter and Oxford and his refusal to pry into men's consciences. His law reforms in Ireland he made to benefit the poor; his horror of purely religious persecution ensured that only one priest was executed while he was Protector—and that was because the man would not take the way of escape provided; his toleration of dissent allowed for the readmission of the Jews to English shores and the 1657 general order that Quakers should be discharged from confinement. His desire for equity and social justice however was costly and made him many enemies. He recognised that sectarianism made wounds "wider than they are".[167]

Tom Reilly, an Irish columnist born in Drogheda, in his *Cromwell: An Honourable Enemy* (1999) has gone even further in exonerating Cromwell. Not only does he contend, as I have, that the modern mind is "extremely ill-equipped"[168] to comprehend the seventeenth century, and that the subjugation of weaker nations by stronger was normal and continual across the globe at the time, but also that Cromwell the "heinous monster" of popular imagination is a "profound perversion of the facts"[169] based on misconstruing primary sources, the re-writing of his campaigns by post-Restoration Royalists, the nineteenth-century rediscovery of Irish folklore, prejudice, and finally, indoctrination in schools. He reminds us again that seventeenth-century Catholicism was as much a political movement as it was a religious belief.

Even before Cromwell's reputation was partially rescued by modern biographers, the 1911 Encyclopedia Britannica concluded: "In general the toleration enjoyed under Cromwell was probably far larger than at any period since religion became the contending ground of political parties, and certainly greater than under his immediate successors."[170]

The Civil War and then the Restoration in England, as well as the Wars of Religion in seventeenth-century Europe, began to exhaust people's tolerance of intolerance. England after all had been, according to its monarchs for the last 150 years, successively Roman Catholic, Protestant, Roman Catholic, Protestant, Anglican, Presbyterian, Anglican, and again Roman Catholic. A lot of ordinary people might have asked, had they the leisure or education to look back, just when these monarchs were going to make their minds up. For the more informed, the growing recognition that hypotheses other than one's own about the nature of things not only existed but might have their own validity inevitably distanced many from holding the extreme views of an earlier age. The urgent appeals of Cromwell, the argumentation of Milton, the emotional intensity of Donne's sermons and *Holy Sonnets* became modes of expression and belief that the urbanity of the eighteenth century sought to deride and found distasteful. Protestant and Catholic had quarrelled, snarled and fought and the outcome had been the "Glorious Revolution" of 1688. The new monarch, William of Orange, was not someone to whom theological issues mattered that much. But being Dutch his occupation of the throne did away with the threat of a Catholicism unwelcome to most—and he would at least, as MacCulloch wryly remarks, be a good gardener.

For most, a bloodless coup was far better than a bloody one in the name of religion, and the anguish that accompanied it when considering the fate of others "outside the fold". But there were other factors besides political threats which led to the fact that God was no longer a constant and primary factor in the everyday decisions of those with the luxury of making any. Northern Europe was becoming more prosperous. The combination of new methods of farming, as well as new manufacturing techniques, along with increasing overseas trade, brought not only wealth, but leisure time in which to spend it. No longer was life for many merely a matter of staving off famine, for a variety of pleasures opened up which would distract from introspection and prayer. Pride in personal or national status also became a factor to a degree not previously countenanced as being consistent with faith. Was it these things that led men to push God further away and so slip into a convenient and comfortable Deism, or did the writers and thinkers who expressed that view do so irrespective of their political, social and economic circumstances? Were they the cause or the effect? Whatever the case, the French philosopher Rene Descartes (1596–1650) had already laid the groundwork for an "Age of Reason" in his attempt to eradicate any metaphysical assumptions from his reasoning: "I think, therefore I am"[171] was his famous starting-point, rather than "God *made* me, therefore I am." John Locke (1632–1704), who was hugely influenced by Descartes, argued for toleration of those with different views while making *reasonableness* the criterion by which we judge whether Christianity is acceptable or not. As he says in Chapter XVIII of *An Essay Concerning Human Understanding*, "Traditional Revelation may make us know Propositions knowable also by Reason, but not with the same Certainty that Reason doth . . . it still belongs to reason to judge of the truth of its being a revelation."[172] Interestingly however, even he would not allow religious liberty to atheists and Roman Catholics on the grounds of them being a danger to the state (an interesting observation when we think back to the role of the Inquisition earlier discussed). David Hume (1711–1776) was in turn much influenced by Locke, and with him the foundations of modern scepticism were laid. For Hume, even the plainest facts of reality cannot be established through reason alone; our observations of the world are our only valid source of knowledge and truth. This entails that most metaphysical conclusions have no good claim on our credence; in particular, reason cannot be used to prove the existence of God. Fidelity and allegiance, a sense of moral obligation, derive from "the general interests or necessities of society" rather than God, Hume tells us in his essay "Of the Original Contract".[173] Morality is pragmatic.

While philosophers were handling such abstract ideas, rather more concrete minds were looking critically at the Bible. It was not just that the Gospels were subjected to rational criticism; it was rather that rationality was the criterion to which the Gospels were expected to adhere. Anything in them either beyond or contrary to reason was deemed by the severest critics to be superstition; not worthy of the minimal belief that a fashionable gentleman would admit to. It is not so different from some of the New Atheist writers of today who make reason and science the sole judge of truth, and who refuse to admit that there can be any discovery of truth beyond or outside those two things.

Altogether therefore, whether the influences were intellectual or material, people at the end of the seventeenth and start of the eighteenth centuries began to lose the sense of the Divine as a living reality. This included the leaders of the Church. Those who would have led better had been removed, and too many of those who were left were self-serving. At a time when governments were ceasing to care about religious issues (Charles Williams says the Revocation of the Edict of Nantes in 1685 was the last time a government acted dramatically to show that religious belief really mattered)[174] and when Voltaire described the Church in France as "L'infame"—an infamy fit to be destroyed—the English Church was at its weakest and most vulnerable. Thousands of the most committed and faithful Christians had already sailed for America after the initial voyage by the *Mayflower* in 1620. Then the anti-Puritan purges after the Restoration in 1660 had resulted in a series of Acts through Parliament (the Clarendon Code) which compelled clergy and schoolmasters to declare their loyalty to the Crown, required adherence to the revised *Book of Common Prayer* (1662), stifled debate, and made illegal any act of Dissenting worship involving more than five people. As a result of the Act of Uniformity in 1662, one in five, or about two thousand, clergy were expelled from their livings. Many were learned, devout and peaceable (later in the century the faithful High Churchmen would lose their livings too). Such clergy were even forbidden, under threat of imprisonment, to approach within five miles of any parish within which they had previously preached. Men of conviction, of conscience, of character, were silenced and ostracised. Those who took their place or gained preferment were content to be the voice and servant of the state rather than of God—or could not distinguish the two voices. Indeed, by the Corporation Act of 1661 all persons holding state office had to be a communicant member of the Church of England. Thus Dissenters lost their voice in the public arena (when in 1772 the Commons attempted to repeal this legislation, the Bishops shamelessly defeated the move in the House of Lords). It is hardly surprising that the Bishops did not want anti-episcopal Dissenters exercising influence in high office when an archbishop could earn £11,000 per annum, and some bishops £5,000, while a parish priest half starved on £30 or £40 a year. Nor is it surprising that under these conditions Pluralism and Absenteeism were widespread: poverty as well as wealth can drive corruption and the collapse of values. From the pulpit the inevitable followed: platitudes. Where there is no conviction, formality must fill the gap, and dryness, dogma and boredom become general practice. It is hard to take people to a place you have not been yourself in the spiritual realm. In this way a deplorable lethargy had overcome the Church in the space of a couple of generations since the Restoration. In *A History of England*, Professor Keith Fieling makes clear that it had stopped thinking of itself as divine in foundation, separated out by apostolic succession, tradition and revelation.[175] But some eighteenth-century writers like William Law still show us the Church of his day was not entirely dead, though most of it was unutterably dull, "having a form of godliness but denying its power" which St Paul interestingly links with the love of money, pride and conceit, among other things.[176]

The result of these Acts, attitudes and developments in belief was that by the end of the first quarter of the eighteenth century the Church of England was purged, not of its dross, but of its gold. It was the production of godliness reversed. The refiner's fire had separated out the finer of the two elements and discarded it in favour of baser stuff. No wonder the Established Church did not welcome and was not ready for the phenomenon of John Wesley.

CHAPTER 8

Midnight Streets and Revolution

One of the lesser-known paintings of William Hogarth (1697–1764) is entitled *The Sleeping Congregation*. In it, the artist famous for his depiction of the horrors of *Gin Lane, The Rake's Progress* and *The Harlot's Progress* turns his brush, almost his scalpel, on the Church. He shows us a myopic and repellent-looking preacher reading his sermon to a congregation in the various stages of extreme boredom and sleep, while beneath the pulpit his concupiscent clerk eyes up a voluptuous *décolleté* young woman who has fallen asleep in studying *The Service of Matrimony*. On Sunday 28 August 1748, John Wesley recorded in his Journal that in St Paul's "a considerable part of the congregation are asleep, or talking, or looking about, not minding a word the preacher says".[177] He could be describing the Hogarth painting.

Hogarth captures the spirit of the age as no other artist has. To the modern eye almost all his satirical paintings are compelling but unattractive: they were intended to reveal the grotesque and depraved nature of life that a brutal, ignorant and corrupt century had created for itself. They do exactly that. To hang them anywhere but a gallery seems extraordinary, but in a gallery they do remind us of an age of horror and depravity, and of cruelty too. One group of his paintings is called *The Four Stages of Cruelty*—affecting the animal world as well as humanity.

As God receded from the minds of so many in the first half of the eighteenth century, society abandoned the restraints and ideals of previous ages and while the Church slept, hell broke loose. The new-found economic prosperity produced not only beautifully proportioned Georgian architecture, extravagant fashions of dress and formal gardens, but also other ways of spending money: gambling houses, drinking dens and brothels. Meanwhile, prisons and hospitals were places of nightmare. Public executions were commonplace of course, but more degraded than in the days when men's souls were still of some account; the lives of those who lived in the ever growing slums in the towns and cities, around the mines, and later the factories, and who avoided the gibbet, had become frighteningly bestial. The worlds of the rich and the very poor were so deeply separated in every respect that it simply cannot have been possible for people such as Mr and Mrs Andrews, as painted by Gainsborough overlooking their manicured estate, or for Lord Burlington, arbiter of taste, designer and owner of the Palladian Chiswick House in London (completed just as John Wesley was being ordained deacon in 1725), to have any conception of the horror of the slums. Whether they would have cared if they had an idea, I don't know.

At the time, three out of four children in London died before their fifth birthday; a child as young as ten could be hanged, as could anybody who, for instance, snatched fruit from the hand of a purchaser and made off with it. Even at the end of the century no one had put into words the social conditions more concisely and powerfully than the poet William Blake. Try unpacking the last verse of his four stanza poem "London" to realise its economy in expressing the inescapable plight of the poor, their living conditions ("midnight streets") and the hypocrisy of the rich ("Marriage hearse"):

> But most thro' midnight streets I hear
> How the youthful Harlot's curse
> Blasts the new born infant's tear,
> And blights with plagues the Marriage hearse.

It was into this sort of inequitable world that John Wesley was born and in which he grew up.

The life of John Wesley has been told many times in print and his impact on society well documented—if one knows where to look. Yet today, both within the Church and outside it, how many could recount even the central facts of his life and achievements? I suspect precious few—even among Christians, and the cause of this is obvious enough: he is the subject of few sermons, though within the Methodist Church "Aldersgate Sunday" is the day set aside to give thanks for his life. Evangelicals and Anglicans are not sure how to own him: for the former his life is not part of the process of Biblical exposition much favoured by them; for the latter he is not part of Church tradition or hagiography. For all Christians, however, there is the Biblical precedent of Hebrews 11—the celebration of past heroes of faith, and if Wesley is not one of those it is hard to think who might be.

Despite this seeming neglect by the Church, Wesley can lay claim, along with Wilberforce (whom he encouraged even in the last week of his life) to be among the very greatest of Englishmen. His impact on the way subsequent generations lived and live is enormous, as we shall see, but school history syllabuses and historians of the eighteenth century prefer to examine the politics of Pitt, the madness of King George, the gossip of Walpole, or the strategy of Marlborough rather than the extraordinary doings and significance of John Wesley. Reading or writing about such a selfless life can put us out of sorts with ourselves, as we have seen before. Augustine Birrell, amongst other beautifully-written essays, has one on Wesley in which he remarks that the story of the infant's narrow escape from the fire at Epworth Rectory, "as a brand plucked out of the burning", was once as well known to schoolchildren as the story of King Alfred and the cakes.[178] A century after Birrell wrote, the Epworth story is known by next to no school children, I would hazard.

I would also contend that to look back at eighteenth- and nineteenth-century social history is to look at change brought about in large measure by a figure whom society rejected then (and in many cases positively loathed) and neglects now. Of course Wesley was not the only person, or even the first, to preach radical Christianity to his generation, but he was the person whose gifts were especially used to bring about lasting and widespread change across the British Isles. The organisation of his work and the geographical extent of it, as well as his sheer longevity and unflagging endurance contributed much to this but was far from the whole story. We have his voluminous *Journal* in addition to record this for us. A good example might be his entry for 4 January 1785. Deep in that winter Wesley could see that the poor needed clothes as much as food, "So on this, and the following four days, I walked through the town, and begged two hundred pounds, in order to clothe them that needed it most. But it was hard work, as most of the streets were filled with melting snow, which often lay ankle deep."[179] Wesley at the time was nearly eighty-two years old. He was ill after the effort but recovered quickly. The fact that he could raise two hundred pounds in such a short space of time merely by begging for it is a mark of his stature and the respect in which he was held by this date. Much of the social and religious transformation of the nineteenth century can be traced to the work of John Wesley in the eighteenth.

He nearly didn't make it. House fires were common in days when winters were cold, dark and candle-lit; when cooking was done over a range or open fire; when people and furnishings were gathered around it for warmth. In February 1709, when the little boy John was five, his father's rectory was burnt to the ground—as Birrell has reminded us. It was a narrow escape for the younger children. But the age was such that a child's life often hung by a thread anyway. John was one of nineteen siblings, of whom thirteen would die young or very young (eight in infancy). They came from stock that was used to hardship. John's grandfather had been ejected from his living by the Act of 1662 and he had also been imprisoned in 1661 for refusing to use the *Book of Common Prayer*. Samuel Wesley, John's father, had been confined for debt and his home was twice burned.

Besides being resilient, the Wesleys were also an able family. The grandfather was highly gifted in oriental languages at Oxford, gaining the notice of the Vice-Chancellor; his son, Samuel, also educated at Oxford, published both verse and prose, including work on both the Old and New Testaments. Samuel's sons Charles and John went respectively to Westminster and Charterhouse for their schooling, and then on to Christ Church Oxford: John in 1720 and Charles in 1726. Charles was noted for his physical bravery and John for his wit and good humour—along with a love of riding and tennis, as well as skill in swimming. He became a lecturer in Greek and was elected Fellow of Lincoln College. Thus the two brothers had shared an upbringing that had bred and nurtured fortitude and resilience, and enjoyed physical, intellectual, poetical and literary gifts (Charles' unsurpassed creativity in hymn writing we shall come to later). Even before they set out as "Methodists" (another nickname that stuck) they were far from ordinary people in terms of the cards they had been handed. They had every reason to see themselves in positions of considerable worldly wealth and power: few doors would have been closed to them. God, however, had other plans: door after door was to be shut in John's face.

John Wesley's *Journal* is one of the great literary artefacts of the eighteenth century—and it was a century rich in prose writers. In its four large volumes Wesley kept a meticulous account of his days from his embarkation for Georgia in October 1735 until the year of his death, 1791. It recounts dramatic events, made all the more so by its very understatement. The abridged version, edited by Curnock, usefully prunes the account down to some 170,000 words and is prefaced by Wesley's letter to a Mr Morgan, about The Holy Club (a nickname that did *not* stick). This was a group, formed by the Wesleys, who met to study Scripture and the classics and engage in charitable work, which John admits in the letter became "a common topic of mirth" and ridicule at Oxford for its "enthusiasm", desire for reform, and "methodism" in its meetings and aims. But as Wesley points out in the letter, they were accused of practices "to which we were ourselves utter strangers".[180] Their little company took the fight to their opponents (shades of things to come) and asked them whether or not it were good to feed the hungry, visit the sick and those in prison; whether it were good to be methodical and industrious in order to be more learned and virtuous; whether in being good persuaders of others they should be good scholars, and so on. The whole extremely long and logical letter foreshadows Wesley's social and educational concerns in an extraordinary way and the predominant emphasis in it is that those who are concerned to follow Christ "who went about doing good" should follow his example in the most tangible and practical ways.[181] The letter is dated 18 October 1732. In it, one of the great hallmarks of the Evangelical Revival, and of Methodism in particular, its reform of society, seems to have found expression almost fully formed—though the letter was written six years before what Wesley saw as his conversion. As J. R. H. Moorman says in his book *A History of the Church in England*: "In the end the Church was saved not by its natural leaders but by a handful of individuals who dedicated themselves and all that they had to the salvation of *society*."[182]

Exactly three years later, in October 1735, Charles and John with two friends embarked on the good ship *Simmonds*, anchored off Gravesend, and set sail for Georgia. By any standards the reportage of events on board in the pages of the Journal for those sixteen weeks of the voyage is riveting, not just in the matter-of-fact way each day's events are told but in the insight they give us to the dangers of such a voyage and one man's use of it.

On Saturday 17 January, a huge storm engulfed the ship, "from stem to stern", burst through the windows of the state cabin and drenched the occupants, including John Wesley. After four hours of rising tempest he slept, uncertain "whether I should wake alive and much ashamed of my unwillingness to die". Six days later another storm hit the ship so that Wesley was "stunned", being thrown over by the weight of water hitting him. The noise, vibration, and movement created by the violence of the assaults upon the ship, the splitting of the foresail and the darkness of the skies, are all memorably related. In the third storm Wesley noticed the Moravians—their humility, their service of other passengers, their fearlessness. Even their women and children showed no signs of fear, and in reality were not afraid, such was their faith. This deeply impressed Wesley, who felt that his personal knowledge of Christ's saving power was much inferior to theirs.[183]

The other fascinating aspect of the journey is the self-discipline of Wesley in an age that was so profligate, self-indulgent and undisciplined among so many of his class. The friends' timetable was to "use private prayer" from four till five in the morning, and then read the Bible together from five till seven. After breakfast at seven, public prayers were held at eight, and from nine until noon Wesley "usually learned German" while Charles wrote sermons. At noon the friends met to review their learning and they dined at one o'clock. Until four o'clock they read to those children and adults they "had taken in charge". Evening prayers were held at four, and from five till six o'clock private prayer resumed. Six till seven, Wesley read to others again, and at seven o'clock he joined "the Germans" (Moravians) in their service. At eight the four friends met again to encourage one another, after which they went to bed "where neither the roaring of the sea, nor the motion of the ship, could take away the refreshing sleep which God gave us".[184] Though attention is not frequently drawn to it, this timetable begins to give us a sense, not only of the dedication, but also of the energy and strength of will that characterised this man who would change the face of England and thereby, in following generations, the Empire.

While on board, Wesley not only learned German, and spoke it to the Moravians, but also used his French and Italian to talk to passengers. By April 1737 he was learning Spanish—to use with his "Jewish parishioners".

On Thursday 5 February 1736, the ship cast anchor in the Savannah River, "an agreeable prospect", and they went ashore next day and knelt to give thanks. By 7 March Wesley had begun his ministry and the following Sunday he administered Holy Communion to eighteen people. By June he was facing opposition to his sermons and baptismal practices in various townships where the feeling against him was "indefatigably diligent" and "extremely zealous".[185] His life was threatened many times. But spiritual difficulties were far from his only hardship. As he travelled this hardly discovered country his guides repeatedly got lost, and for a man of less grit and physical endurance the results would have been serious. Wesley describes lying many nights in the open air under heavy dew, and on one occasion, wading through a cypress swamp breast deep. A mile later, with the time past sunset, and their tinder refusing to light, they lay down on the ground which was as wet as their clothes, with the result that they were frozen to the ground. "However, I slept till six in the morning", he reminds himself, reaching his destination not before evening.[186] That is an appreciable feat which few of us today would wish to emulate. By August of that year Wesley was involved in multiple court appearances and would leave Georgia by the end of the year, repelled by the settlers' view of him as "the new, illegal authority which was usurped over their consciences", as the charge described him.[187] He saw out just one year and nine months, considering himself a failure having neither won the loyalty of the white settlers nor having had opportunity to preach to the natives. As he looked back in later life he realised the mistakes he had made—of legalism and of too great an emphasis on the sacraments, which had made him deeply unpopular. He had however, importantly, preached to many black slaves, thereby gaining first hand knowledge of their plight and fuelling his life-long opposition to slavery.

On 1 February 1738 he landed back in England at Deal. A certain Mr George Whitefield had, unbeknown to him, sailed out just the day before. Neither man knew each other.

Despite his toughness and bravery, it was characteristic of the man's humility that he thought his fear of death an indication that he had only a "summer religion" that did not survive danger well. He felt unconverted and that it had taken "a journey to the ends of the earth", as he wrote on his return, to teach him that. He longed, as he wrote, for "The richness which is of God by faith", and to be "reconciled to the favour of God". He felt he lacked the faith "which St Paul recommends to all the world, especially in his Epistle to the Romans . . . 'I live not; but Christ liveth in me.'"[188] He wanted the love of God to be shed abroad in his heart, and he did not have to wait long. He had after all served a long and hard apprenticeship since his formation of the persecuted Holy Club.

Sometimes it is only by understanding the cause that we can understand a result, and in this case the cause was his burning desire to be righteous before God, to be free of sin, and able to act as his heart told him he should. The result was that he realised others could experience the same extraordinary liberation and so find a quality and purpose in life and community, and a love for others, quite unlike anything else.

The moment of Wesley's "conversion" (as he would see it) at a Moravian meeting in Aldersgate Street is probably the best known thing about him among many Christians. On 24 May 1738 he went "very unwillingly" to this group at which Luther's "Preface to the Epistle to the Romans" was being read:

> About a quarter before nine, while he was describing the change which God works in the heart by faith in Christ, I felt my heart strangely warmed. I felt I did trust in Christ, Christ alone, for salvation: and an assurance was given me that he had taken away my sins, even mine, and saved me from the law of sin and death.[189]

At this point it is worth stepping aside to reflect on the unique contribution this particular Epistle of Paul, his letter to the Romans, has had upon the Church, not just because of its revolutionary power over Wesley, but also because it seems to be seminal in the meta-narrative of the Church's history and in the lives of Augustine, Luther, Wesley and Karl Barth, as well as countless others. Each of these great men was to serve the Church at times of deep crisis—first when Rome was overrun by barbarians, then at a time of terrible Papal corruption, then when Deism was prevailing over faith, and finally during the period of the two World Wars. The Journal makes apparent that the nature of Wesley's experience, and therefore the nature of what he passed on to England emanated at root from this document.

Romans is of course Paul's greatest letter, and the passages that Wesley was struggling with are contained within chapters 6 to 8, which constitute a revelatory climax. In the year AD 386, the young professor of rhetoric at Milan heard a voice as he sat weeping in the garden of a friend, telling him to read. He picked up *Romans* and "at once a clear light flooded my heart and all the darkness of doubt disappeared."[190] Augustine's influence on history as a result of that moment is beyond computation.

Martin Luther, in 1515, was teaching Romans and yet longed to understand it himself. When he finally did, he said, "I felt myself to be born again and that I had gone through doors opening on Paradise. All of Scripture took on a new meaning . . . a portal to Heaven."[191] Wesley felt likewise.

So without Romans we would not have the creeds of the Church as they are. Without Romans, we would not have had the Reformation as it was, and without Romans we would not have had Wesley and the Evangelical Revival as it was, unless through God's intervention by other means. In the twentieth century, Barth's book on Romans had a nuclear effect on contemporary theology. In Romans, the fact of sin and God's way of redeeming it are dealt with in chapters 1–3, the meaning of "saving faith" and the two worlds we live in (sin and grace) occupy chapters 4 and 5, while 5 and 6 show us our freedom as Christians from both the penalty of sin and its power. Such logicality must have appealed to Wesley's formidably logical mind (even Southey is impressed by this in his disparaging biography), but in his *experience* he could not get beyond chapter 7, where Paul's anguished cry rings out: "the good which I would, I do not; but the evil which I would not, that I do"—the text that Wesley cites in the Journal.[192] This struggle between nature and grace had continued in him for over ten years, but at that meeting on 24 May the scales fell from his eyes: "an assurance was given me" and the meaning of justification by *faith* sank in at last.[193] He was a new man. He was able to share finally in Paul's thunderbolt at the start of Chapter 8, that there is "no condemnation"—an emphatic negative in the Greek text which a classical don such as Wesley would recognise at once.

Wesley had discovered in his own experience one of the great statements of Christian theology that separates it out from the other religious systems of the world. Whether we think of Judaism or Islam, of Hinduism, Paganism or Animism, there is always the need to placate God or the gods to avoid punishment, that is, condemnation. For Paul to say therefore, for the first time in history, that as a result of God "sending his own Son in the likeness of sinful man to be a sin offering" there was *no* punishment for those "in Christ Jesus" was revolutionary.[194] The impact of the realisation upon Wesley was certainly just that. His brother Charles expressed it exactly in one of his most famous hymns:

> He breaks the *power* of *cancelled* sin,
> he sets the prisoner free.[195]

In a single line, he captures the idea of both the power and the penalty of sin being removed from a believer. The unrestrained joy of the rest of the hymn's verses show us today something of what the Established Church of the day found difficult about Methodism.

Almost immediately Wesley decided to visit Germany, the Moravians and Count Zinzendorf, whose communities he found hugely rewarding and a confirmation of what he was learning: namely, that it was possible to behave in a way fully consistent with a Bible-believing Christian profession without the need to go to the New World. The three months he spent in Germany were an important time of consolidation and preparation. When he returned to England his energy in preaching had this focus—that God changed lives and hearts radically where people allowed Him to. That is an unpopular message amongst those who are self-satisfied, but music to the ears of those who are excluded or suffering. Wesley would therefore inevitably find himself preaching to the poor. No "enthusiast" was welcome in the circles of the complacently proud; they were far too unsettling. Church after church is listed in the Journal as banning him from further preachments.

The word "enthusiasm" has changed its meaning so markedly since the times we are discussing that we need to consider what it was that his contemporaries found so distasteful and shocking about it. What they meant by the word is more nearly akin to what we mean by fanaticism. But of course, whether something or someone seems fanatical depends on where we are standing at the time. The more remote someone's experience or ability is from us, the more extraordinary and outstanding it seems to be. The person who has little sense of balance and no head for heights will see the rock climber's fingertip ascents as utterly impossible while the steeplejack or tree surgeon may not. The Established Church was for the most part so distant from any personal experience of God that those who demonstrably enjoyed it must have been either frightening or seen as frauds. This explains to some extent Bishop Butler's offensive remark (alleged) to Wesley, who was operating in his diocese: "Sir, the pretending to extraordinary revelation and gifts of the Holy Ghost, is a horrid thing, a very horrid thing."[196]

It is difficult, however, to see how else, other than by visible manifestations, the impact of the field preaching by Wesley, Whitefield and others would result. Here at last was a member of the educated classes, an ordained minister of God, telling folk who were horribly deprived of any sense of significance in the world, and of any appreciable comfort, that they were loved and cherished by God himself, and that their every care, their every need mattered to Him. They were also told that their sins mattered just as much—so much so that God in the person of Christ had done something breathtaking (literally) about it; something so shocking, so far-reaching, and so compassionate that it lit up the darkest hovels and the darkest hearts with power to transform them both. Nothing like this had been heard in their lifetime.

Visions and voices, repentance and rapture, the horror of sin and the joy of forgiveness were all integral to the experience of those willing to listen to this entirely new development in the English Church, at least since anyone could remember. God had come out to meet them. There was laughing and weeping—something entirely improper in a church! The Father had run out to meet the Prodigal, and had embraced him. "Enthusiasm" was no pretence, either by Wesley or those he moved to repentance, but the ingenuous response of a spiritually starved nation without the need or sophistication to pretend otherwise. However, the older brother in the parable who had done the right thing and stayed at home was mightily put out. George Whitefield's invitation in 1739 to John Wesley to adopt his method of preaching, in the fields (at first so strange to a man of Wesley's background), was the essential accompaniment to the Aldersgate Street moment and the two coalesced to create a revolution in English social history.

A very full account of how this happened is to be found in J. W. Bready's study, *England: Before and After Wesley*, and anyone looking at the impact of Methodism is indebted to him.[197] Much more recently, MacCulloch, who has no particular religious viewpoint to peddle in this regard, sees the growth and effect of Methodism as astonishing. Having started from nothing, as it were, within a single lifetime, the Methodist Church found itself the spiritual home of half a million Christians (in a population of ten million) and the majority of those were from among the least privileged.

At the start of this chapter I mentioned Hogarth's depiction of a congregation asleep while the preacher droned on. His failure to catch their attention from the pulpit was all the more culpable in a world in which governments and Crown paid so little heed to those who were suffering. It is, therefore, hardly surprising that the clergy, seen as a class, were unpopular and the subject of satire: they said one thing and did another. Many were seen as time-servers and sycophants, opportunists who spent more time in tittle-tattle than in pastoral work, or who disguised the one as the other. The conditions under which the poor had to live not only remained deplorable and unameliorated by the Church, but the poor were hardly welcome *at* the church, or in the pews, many of which they were physically excluded from. So, let us see a little more of the social conditions they endured, and after that, what, if anything, the Methodists and Evangelicals did about them.

Gambling may have been a pastime for the rich, but alcohol was a distraction available to all classes. The first half of the eighteenth century has been dubbed "The Gin Age", for by 1750 the consumption of spirits had risen to 11,000,000 gallons a year, ten times what it had been fifty years earlier. Distilling had been encouraged by successive governments and it was inexpensive to do, but there was no regulation and cheap additives were often used in the process. It was a penny a pint to buy. In St Giles in London (the scene of the Hogarth painting *Gin Lane*), one in four houses was used as a gin shop. Theft, prostitution, syphilis, child abuse and neglect inevitably followed and accompanied the addiction so many fell into. One woman is recorded as strangling her two-year-old and throwing the body into a Bethnal Green ditch, in order to sell the clothes given to the child in the workhouse, that she might buy gin. Wesley visited the area in the winter of 1777, finding within it "such poverty as few can conceive" and finding even more distress in another area than "in the prison of Newgate".[198] Several attempts to legislate against the distilling which contributed to this wretchedness drove it "underground" and created smuggling rings and further criminality. It was only in 1751 that the Gin Act was passed and consumption declined sharply.

As we see in any modern recession, poverty and unemployment increase the crime rate, and one way of dealing with this is to pass draconian penal legislation, which was also seen as a way of controlling the mass of working people in cities no longer owing loyalty to rural employers. Crimes for which you could be hanged therefore increased fourfold during the century, rising to two hundred. In addition to the ones mentioned earlier, these included arson, cattle stealing, swearing false oaths, and impersonation. Multiple hangings were conducted in public every six weeks or so in many towns and cities, the bodies being left on the gibbet as a deterrent to others. These executions fulfilled the role of the modern carnival and were an eagerly-awaited spectacle where a crowd could enjoy the day out, interact with the victims on show, drink and lift purses. Those who were not hanged might be transported. 50,000 were sent to the American colonies to work on sugar and cotton plantations—sometimes by judges who were sending them to work on their own plantations to supplement the slaves there. Public burnings also took place, as did the use of pillory, branding, whipping and flogging in public—against both men and women.

Prison conditions too were unspeakably vile. It is possible still to visit the crumbling and disused Bodmin Prison in Cornwall, which gives an idea of the darkness, damp, filth and horror of the places: bare stone-built vaulted cells, some underground, without human comfort, relief or distraction of any kind, save perhaps a pile of dirty straw in the corner. At the end of the tour, the visitor walks past or under the gallows which is still in place. As Wesley said of the French prisoners in 1759 who did not suffer the gallows, they died incarcerated "like rotten sheep".[199]

Naval service was also something which Britain's huge number of merchant seamen, and at times others, had to endure if they were caught by the press gangs (who operated both in ports and inland towns), did not have exemption and were between eighteen and fifty-five. Pay and conditions aboard navy ships were much inferior to those aboard merchant vessels, even leaving aside the horrors of naval warfare. When men were pressed from the disease-ridden jails of the day, they brought terrible infections on board which spread rapidly. Men and women were also abducted from the prisons to serve out their terms alongside the slaves in the colonies. Their mortality rate on the ships was the same as that of the slaves.

The greatest injustice and cruelty of all, of course, was the practice of slavery and the slave trade. This has rightly been the focus of so much interest that there is little need to repeat its horrors here. The terror of the raiding party descending upon the African village; the prolonged misery, torture and fear of the unknown in the ship's hold where so many died; and the blank despair as all hope was lost in being sold for life to an owner who regarded you as inhuman property. A watery death was preferable for many, if they had opportunity to seize it. As always, those involved in carrying out the trade were also dehumanised, though in a different way.

Historically, alcohol and Methodism have been at best uneasy bedfellows. A movement which was born in "The Gin Age" and witnessed the degradation that engulfed so many of the poor (those to whom Wesley was mostly called) could hardly be otherwise. Bready produces extensive evidence in support of his claim that Wesley was not only deeply opposed to the liquor trade, but a highly effective part of bringing it under control. He cites his sermon "The Use of Money", which is very clear in saying that to sell "spirituous liquors" is to damage the health of your neighbour, and as such is completely illegitimate and incompatible with Christian behaviour. Those who do so, he says, are "poisoners general" and pitiless murderers who drive others to hell. They are "men of blood".[200] The immoderate language is something of a shock to those used to the more nuanced pronunciations from modern pulpits.

This opposition to the liquor trade and the drinking of liquor became a standard part of Methodism and the prohibition of all such drinking and the buying and selling of liquor was expressly stated in the "Rules of the Society", to be obeyed by any who wanted to "evidence their desire for salvation". All Wesley's local preachers were enjoined not to touch intoxicating drink on any account. Wesley's *Primitive Physic*, a little piece of medical self-help, which was reprinted nearly forty times, warned that alcohol was not the panacea that many thought it to be. Bready mentions that in 1773 Wesley asked the question why food was so dear, in his *Thoughts on the Present Scarcity of Provisions*, and concluded that since nearly half the wheat of the kingdom was consumed in the creation of strong drink which was destroying both the lives and morals of the nation, it would be better to abolish the legal manufacture and sale of it altogether.[201] (The problem of lives being destroyed by alcohol obviously remains with us today, many medics considering it far worse even than smoking or drug abuse.) On 6 September 1784, Wesley also wrote to the Prime Minister, William Pitt (himself a victim of alcohol), asking him to make distilling a felony, saying it would be the greatest service done to the country in a hundred years.

It would be unfair and untrue to say that Methodism was the sole cause of the reduction in alcohol consumption and its evils. Hogarth's work, measures by government, and the incidence of bad grain harvests pushing up prices all played significant parts. But there can be little doubt that this uncompromising, continuous opposition to the misuse of alcohol, which cascaded down to local preachers and so out to the very people most vulnerable to this very cheap form of escape from drudgery and despair, saved lives and resulted in the famous Temperance Societies in the next century, giving people a community in which to sustain their refusal to take the easy route out of their suffering into drunken oblivion. In America, by 1833, Total Abstinence members numbered over one million. William Booth, founder of The Salvation Army, which has helped countless victims of alcohol, was an ordained Methodist minister.

In the matter then of the arrest and reversal of the social decline created by alcohol misuse in the first half of the eighteenth century and beyond, Wesley, it may be said, played a key part.

Prisons and the penal code were also a concern of Methodism. Taking his cue from the parable of the sheep and goats, in which the King says to the righteous, "I was in prison and you came to visit me", Wesley visited prisoners in their hideous jails, calling Marshalsea Prison "such a picture of hell upon earth!" after his visit on 3 February 1753, as recorded in the Journal. The following week he went back: "I found some in their cells underground". They were, he says, "half starved both with cold and hunger" though busily employed if they were able even to crawl, prompting Wesley to challenge the "devilishly false" lie that they were "poor, only because they were idle".[202] This action, along with this view, was far, far ahead of his times in its understanding and compassion. In the same week he visited the sick, appalled that the pagans in Georgia looked after their people so much better than the English. His unblinkered view that any sickness they suffered had derived from gluttony and drunkenness learned from "the *Christians*", and the ironic exclamation that it would be better that the English should be "honest heathens" from the point of view of health and well-being, is one that would be met with disbelief by his detractors.

Wesley also visited Newgate Prison on many occasions and wrote about it in the Journal. Despite being rebuffed by the turnkeys Wesley was at last admitted and was often sent for by the inmates, who heard him gladly, frequently being deeply affected by his preaching the love of Christ and the fact that "God is not willing that anyone should perish" (a text from Peter's second letter). When a certain Alderman Beecher forbade his further ministry there, Wesley cited him to "answer for these souls" in his entry for 2 April 1740.[203] Two years later, in September 1742, he was still banned, but upon trying to see a particular murderer again there was a sudden reversal and the doors were thrown open to him. "It was not long before the rest of the felons flocked round", he wrote, "to whom I spoke strong words concerning the Friend of sinners which they received with as great signs of amazement as if it had been a voice from heaven."[204]

Visiting Newgate and other prisons must have been a frightening prospect, or would have been to a lesser man. Apart from the violent nature of many of the offenders, disease was rife; its impact on the Navy as a result of pressed men from the prisons joining the crews has already been mentioned, and Wesley mentions disease in an entry from November 1748: "the gaol distemper (a kind of pestilential fever) raged much among the prisoners" during a visit by another incredibly brave and generous soul, Sarah Peters, who went alone among the men with material and spiritual aid.[205] Bready says that in May 1750, a judge, jury and others all died of jail fever which they contracted in court from a group of filthy prisoners who had been confined for a long time. It must also have been frightening to visit Bedlam, the hospital-prison for the mentally ill. But Wesley was asked for by an inmate and so he went—only to have his visit cut short by the authorities. As he wrote rather wryly on 22 March 1750, "We are forbid to go to Newgate for fear of making them wicked; and to Bedlam, for fear of making them mad."[206] No man lacking a sense of humour could have written that.

All prisons were truly terrible places, as I have suggested, but not only in their diseased and stinking premises. It was also that major prisons like Newgate had so many who were condemned to hang. In 1785, on Boxing Day, Wesley preached in Newgate to the condemned men. Forty-seven were under sentence of death, twenty of whom were to die on the same day before a week was out. Wesley was highly sensitive to the fate of these men and only his love and concern for them could have driven him to speak to them in such dreadful circumstances. He felt that "while they were coming in, there was something very awful in the clink of their chains".[207]

Most people who know anything about Wesley probably know that he claimed the world as his parish, and he therefore felt no less compassion for French prisoners of war who were confined at Knowle in December 1759, at that time a settlement a mile from Bristol. He preached on the text "Thou shalt not oppress a stranger" from the Book of Exodus. The twenty-four pounds taken in the collection for them (what a fantastic sum for those days!) was used to buy linen and wool which was made up into "shirts, waistcoats and breeches".[208] Bristol and then London also contributed to the fund for their relief.

By 1761 Newgate in Bristol had been transformed to a place where work was allowed, encouraged and paid for; where Sunday services were held; and where medical treatment was given to the sick. Wesley, in writing to the *London Chronicle*, urged other prison-keepers to transform their prisons likewise. In a footnote, Bready points to the fact that the prison was run by a Mr Dagge, who was one of the early converts of the Revival, converted by the ministry of George Whitefield.

It is these sorts of footnote to history that the Evangelical Revival is full of, where work transforming the life and social fabric of Britain was carried out by men and women constrained to act as a direct result of their Christian beliefs, which inspired a self-sacrificing love of neighbours and of enemies.

The prison reformer, John Howard, could hardly be called a footnote, however. He was a Christian friend and admirer of John Wesley and the feeling was mutual. Wesley saw him as one of the greatest men of his day. The story of Howard's life reads now like a far-fetched Romantic, or rather Gothic, three-volume novel. Book One: born to privilege and wealth, but suffering ill-health, John makes an extraordinary marriage to a widow thirty years his senior who dies soon after. This is followed by travel abroad, capture at sea by the French, merciless incarceration and selfless work for his fellow captives to redeem them. Book Two: John re-marries, does charitable work in building schools, and essays further travels abroad. Book Three: Prison Reformer. For the rest of his life our hero devotes himself by the most extraordinary measures to the reform of the kingdom's prisons, and later hospitals. He demands that jailers be paid rather than exacting bribes to live; that uncharged and innocent prisoners be released; that cells should be whitewashed, cleaned and ventilated; that infirmaries be provided for the unwell, along with medical attention; that clothing be provided when needed; that underground dungeons be used only as a last resort; and that every jailer in the land should know the regulations.

Howard meets with great success in these endeavours. All these measures are brought about rapidly after his report to the House of Commons in 1774, based on his findings around the country. The following year he visits prisons in France, the Low Countries, and Germany, gaining access to the foulest places, with the notable exception of the infamous Bastille in Paris, to which not even he can gain access. The result of further tours, and an account of them in 1777, is that Parliament drafts a bill which for the first time aims at the reformation of prisoners by means of properly organised work and Christian teaching.

In his sixties, undaunted by age, our hero undertakes further arduous voyages, even as far as Constantinople, the very edge of European civilisation, in order to research the prevention of plague and other contagions. He needs to know for himself what it was to be quarantined in a *lazaretto*, or quarantine house for the poorest sick. He therefore deliberately boards a foul ship, suffers an attack by pirates whom he fends off with great bravery, and ends up imprisoned in a *lazaretto* in Venice, subject to every possible illness. While there he receives the tragic news that his wayward son has gone mad. He returns home to deal with the crisis, but then embarks on a final journey to Russia, to research military hospitals. He reaches Moscow, but on his journey south heeds a call from a young woman suffering from camp fever. He attends her, but contracts the disease, and dies far from home. By the end he has travelled 50,000 miles to the ends of the earth in the cause of prisoners, spent £30,000 of his own money on that cause, and made four tours of the United Kingdom's prisons, often rising at 3 a.m. in order to achieve the day's work.

I tell the story partly because it is irresistible, seemingly fictional in its sensation, fascinating, but also because what Howard found in England, let alone France, was what he, and other Evangelicals and "Enthusiasts" gave their lives to put an end to: jails in the cellars of public houses; chains, strait-jackets and spiked iron collars; debauchery and prostitution; men, women and children penned in together; open town sewers flowing through dungeons; starvation and endemic disease.

Prisons may yet not be satisfactory but we owe their reformation in the eighteenth century to the Wesleys, John Howard, and their friends and followers. As a measure of the importance of this, when Winston Churchill was Home Secretary he told the Commons that the treatment of criminals was one of the best tests of a country's civilisation.[209]

The reform of the penal code took longer and was the primary concern of a later generation. But in this too, evangelicals, owing their faith under God to Wesley and Methodism, played a significant role. Elizabeth Fry, a Quaker for whom Bible reading was central to her manifesto, caught the imagination of a nation through her work in Newgate. Such compassion can only have served to draw attention to the injustice of a system that landed so many of its weak and poor in that place, and to the need for humanising change that would preclude sending them to such a hell-hole. William Wilberforce frequently spoke out against hanging and other unjust or cruel punishments in parliamentary debates and was a supporter of Bentham's plans for penal reform.

Reform in the navy was also overdue. R. C. Blake, who has written on the social detail of eighteenth-century naval history, has traced much of the improvement in sailors' living conditions at sea to the work of

Admiral Sir Charles Middleton, another who was converted as a young man through the ministry of George Whitefield. Middleton, who became Controller of the Navy and then First Lord of the Admiralty, re-wrote navy regulations, demanded better pastoral and spiritual oversight of the crews, encouraged godly chaplains to join the service, and in an age of war, mutiny and riot, transformed the experience of thousands of sailors. Richard Blake's superb book shows up that by the end of the war with Napoleon, as many as eighty different ships were holding prayer meetings which included both officers and men together—surely an extraordinary fact.[210] It was two Methodists who formed the Naval and Military Bible Society which supported the work on board by the provision of Bibles. A Baptist pastor (and former seafarer), known as "Bo'sun Smith", provided Sailors' Homes ashore when their normal resorts would have been vicious. The impact of all these reforms, both on and off shore, would have been considerable. Whitefield, and by extension, Wesley (who abhorred war and attacked the usage of press-gangs), were the original catalysts for this change. Blake also shows that Middleton's wife first took him to hear Whitefield preach; she encouraged him to take up the cause of abolition in parliament, and the two of them introduced the young Wilberforce to their friend and rector James Ramsay, who had been a naval surgeon, became a pioneer Abolitionist, and was able to furnish Wilberforce with first-hand examples of the horrors of the Atlantic trade and plantation slavery. MacCulloch, interestingly, considers that study of our armed forces has frequently been overlooked as a means of spreading the gospel during the Evangelical Revival.[211] Richard Blake's research in fact corrects that omission for this period.

Because Wesley is often seen mistakenly as a conservative in politics as a result of his stance over the American colonies, it is important to re-assert that in his opposition to slavery he was as uncompromising as with other evils. The Journal entry for 12 February 1772 reads:

> I read a book, published by an honest Quaker, on that execrable sum of all villainies, commonly called the Slave Trade. I read of nothing like it in the heathen world, whether ancient or modern.[212]

His *Thoughts Upon Slavery*, published two years later is, as Evans calls it in *The Social Hope of the Christian Church*, "a formidable indictment of the system".[213] Wesley allows for no excuses for slavery, least of all economic necessity—the justification offered by MPs and slave owners alike. Evans quotes at length a passage in which Wesley concludes: "It is impossible that it should be *necessary* for any reasonable creature to violate all the laws of justice, mercy, and truth."[214] This reminder to all, from the most influential and revered religious leader of his day, of their shared humanity with the slaves, and the judgment of God awaiting us all, was a powerful constraint on all people of conscience. In the last week of his life he wrote to Wilberforce: "Go on in the name of God . . . till even American slavery, the vilest that ever saw the sun, shall vanish away before it."[215]

On all the issues discussed here, and many others, Wesley stood out against the prevailing opinion of those in power. He told others to do so in his books and his sermons. His self-discipline and organisational powers, glimpsed earlier when aboard a ship bound for Georgia, set the tone for others and led him to accomplish unparalleled things. He rode, on average, 8,000 miles a year, writing many of his books in the saddle. He certainly covered at least 225,000 miles all told, and perhaps as many as 400,000. His published works extend to thirty-two volumes and he preached 40,000 sermons, often three or four a day. He continued speaking and writing about the gospel right into the last week of his life. His own frugality and generosity were undoubted. Bready noted that he never spent more than twelve shillings a week on himself. Though his income increased greatly through his publications, he gave the royalties away and never increased his own comforts, thereby living out his dictum that one should work all one can, to save all one can, in order to give all one can. Cross calls his piety and charity uncontestable and applauds his enormous capacity for leadership and organisation. Evans calls him one of "the great individuals of English history". The novelist Kate O'Brien wrote of him as a man who "transformed the lives and hearts of millions".[216]

Despite the fact that his preaching inspired "cries of desire, joy and love on every side", as he noted on 3 April 1740,[217] Wesley was also a rationalist with an academic mind who argued his case when necessary. Several writers tell us that the literary giant Dr Johnson enjoyed conversation with him.

There is one further effect we should note as the result of this remarkable man's life and work. Unlike the Church of England, Methodism encouraged its people to be active in the governance of their chapels and churches. They became used to the idea that their view would count in a decision making process. They had to learn to debate and to listen to argument and counter-argument. The link between Methodism and the rise of the trade unions (and the early Labour Party) was not a coincidence—as Evans says. Wesley also wrote for his people extensively in language they could follow and take to heart. As at other periods of history, Christianity suddenly became an educative force again. The converted thousands urgently needed to read—both the Bible and books of Christian advice and devotion. Wesley put huge energy into creating the Book Room, The Christian Library series, editing and book distribution. R. H. Tawney went as far as to say that democracy probably owed more to Nonconformity than any other movement, in his famous 1926 book *Religion and the Rise of Capitalism*. Melvin Bragg, in *The Book of Books*, traces the rise of democracy from the publication of the King James Bible, through Cromwell's "Putney debates", to Methodism and beyond.[218]

In each of these cases it was the Christian Church, not secularity, which reformed society in the direction of democracy. Elie Halevy, the great French historian, thought the Revival the greatest influence working against the bloodshed of an English equivalent to the French Revolution.[219] The kingdom of God, we are told in the parable, is like leaven (yeast) which, hidden in three measures of meal, will transform the whole. Methodism acted in the same way. In place of frivolity and debauchery, "a wave of seriousness and earnestness" spread through England, Moorman tells us.[220] As MacCulloch says, this lasted until the 1960s. He also says that if there ever were such a thing as the Protestant work ethic, it came out of Methodism and the Evangelical Revival rather than the Reformation.[221] A proper interest was taken in the poor which alleviated their condition; it filled their stomachs with food and their hearts with hope—both for this world and the next. They were unified materially and morally by their fellowship and care for each other, intellectually by their absolute belief in the authority of a single book, and emotionally by their singing of an outpouring of new hymns which expressed their feelings. Bready cites a host of nineteenth-century historians who consider that Methodism and the Evangelical Revival eventually changed the whole tone of English society—greatly for the better. He also quotes two British Prime Ministers: Lloyd George, who thought that Wales owed to Wesley more than any other individual, and Baldwin, who thought that historians could not explain the advances of nineteenth-century England until they could explain Wesley. He said the same of twentieth-century America.

So the evidence is that, whether listening to Birrell in 1908, who considered that "no other man did such a life's work for England",[222] or to Bready in 1938, who when looking for a single volume by Wesley in King's College London library could find none despite finding all the other eighteenth-century writers well represented, or reading school history syllabuses today, Wesley was, and is, neglected. In 2012 *The Times* ran a popular "fifteen minute" History of England feature which in its columns on the eighteenth century found space to mention the Scottish philosopher Francis Hutcheson, the Luddites and Mary Shelley, among others, but failed to mention Wesley or the Evangelical Revival in any shape or form. Given the huge significance of the Revival to England and the world, there has been, and still is, a dearth of examination, teaching, and *popular* understanding of Wesley. Yet *The Cambridge Modern History* emphatically states that Wesley, with his impact on the religious revival of his times, was more important in influence and range of achievement than any other great man of the century.[223]

There is an argument therefore to be made that here it is not simply a matter of the evil that men do outlasting them, but a case where there is *no* evil, and much good; and yet people fail to (or perhaps choose not to) remark on it and celebrate it. This is not simply a question of noticing only the broken or out-of-place in an otherwise orderly garden, but more the problem of an attitude of mind which learns to expect as the required minimum standard, and take for granted, something which may have taken untold time, effort or expense to achieve. The Wesleys, John Howard, George Whitefield and others like them gave their entire lives for others. Their neglect in the twenty-first century may be nothing other than we should expect, but it is utterly unjust when lesser figures are remembered and celebrated.

The Social Impact of Song and Charles Wesley's Hymns: An Aside

It is a characteristic of the Christian Church that it makes music in praise of God. This is not as central in other major world religions and it says something fundamental about the nature of Christian faith and its distinctiveness from others. It was a central part of Biblical Judaism too, of course, because one of the things that both religions have in common is that they are celebratory of the great deeds of God. From the earliest times, even before the psalms of David, the Jews celebrated in song their deliverance in the Exodus and subsequent events, as well their annual feasts and festivals. They knew they were chosen, special, blessed and guided so their response was to sing, "Praise him upon the loud cymbals." One of the most poignant moments in the Psalms is the lament of the exiles in Psalm 137 that they cannot sing: "how *can* we sing the Lord's song in a *foreign* land?" Instead, they laid down their lyres and wept.

There is a neglected but significant verse in the Gospels, where Matthew tells us that between the Last Supper and Jesus' agony in Gethsemane, before the disciples followed their Master to the Mount of Olives, they sang a hymn.[224] In all likelihood, this was one of the Passover psalms, which are full of praise to God for his mighty deeds and goodness. Yet they sang it at a time of extreme inner turmoil and consternation. They also sang it, Matthew tells us, before Passover was ended, rather than at the end as would be normal: the Early Church then was to make this practice their own in the new institution of the Lord's Supper, and not jettison it along with the celebration of Passover. Singing was certainly part of the earliest Christian practice: Paul tells both the Ephesians and Colossians that they should sing "psalms and hymns and spiritual songs" out of gratitude to God when they meet together. When Paul and Silas were in the stocks in prison after being flogged in Philippi, they were singing hymns just at the point when they were dramatically rescued. Pliny the Younger wrote in the second century that the Christians "meet at daybreak to sing a hymn". In fact, in every period of the Church (save perhaps among some Puritans), from the plainsong of the monasteries onward, song has been important. It was said of Martin Luther by one of his opponents that he had conquered them by his songs. The same might be said of the Methodists. Conversely, it might be said that when the Church loses its voice, it loses its way. It is no surprise therefore that with the Evangelical Revival came an outpouring of song. Its social effects were significant.

How many hymns Charles Wesley wrote seems indeterminate. Cross says 5,500; Moorman 6,500; MacCulloch, nearly 9,000![225] Whichever the number, it beggars belief. On average, throughout his very long ministry, that means he must have written from two to four hymns a *week*. The productions of "Brother Charles" were not so much a response to the Muse, but more a disciplined—though joyful—method of teaching an unchurched people vital truths. Both brothers knew that a community that sang together would also learn together, and their intention in writing, arranging and distributing the hymns was plainly theological. To know Wesley's hymns is to be theologically, or at least Biblically, educated. Only one of the twenty-seven books of the New Testament is not represented, and only four of the thirty-nine in the Old Testament, according to B. L. Manning's study of them.[226] That range of reference gave the Societies a grounding in doctrine, through which their intellectual status, and therefore political understanding and participation, was able to grow.

Collecting and publishing hymns had begun in John's ministry way back in Georgia in 1737, and culminated after many different editions with the *Large Hymn-Book* of 1780. In his striking Preface to this, John makes clear what they were hoping to achieve. The book, he writes, "is large enough to contain all the important truths of our most holy religion . . . and to prove them both by Scripture and reason: and this is done in regular order".[227] The hymn book, then, was a powerful adjunct to the sermons; it was designed to teach the people not only the basis of their faith as revealed in the Bible, but also a sort of apologetics: namely, that faith was *reasonable*. In the "Age of Reason", when Methodism was dismissed as "enthusiasm", that would have been an important element in the teaching of new converts, as it is today in a different sort of rationalist age.

But John Wesley was a supreme organiser and the hymns therefore were "carefully ranged under proper heads", as he tells us, "according to the experience of real Christians". Absent are the now familiar Church Year headings or divisions into the Persons of the Trinity; instead there is the spiritual biography of the "real" Christian, beginning with the exhortation to sinners to return to God, followed by hymns about why they should do so. Next, the hymns reflect the sinner praying for repentance, and after that the sinner convicted of his sins. The hymns move on towards the experience of believers in increasing stages of maturity. The book therefore becomes, as John says, "a little body of experimental and practical divinity."[228]

The 1933 *Methodist Hymn Book* abandoned this order (good though the 1933 book is), as did the 1983 edition, its successor. But there is a lot to be said for the Wesleys' arrangement, especially considering that Methodism was a movement and was finding new converts with astonishing rapidity. The newer book has about 150 Charles Wesley hymns in it; the earlier one about 240. What has been lost as a result of the abandonment of the original structure, as well as the reduction in the number of Wesley hymns, is precisely the organised educative element which was such a strong feature in the early days of the movement. Men and women who knew their Bible had common ground from which to proclaim their beliefs, carry out their duties as citizens, and defend their rights. That is a powerful political recipe. Politics and religion may not be the same—as William Blake liked to think—but it is hard to stop them overlapping.

The social impact of Methodism was therefore created at least in part by their hymn-singing. This is not the place to conduct a critical analysis of the verse in the hymns, and as John's 1779 Preface says, "the spirit of piety" is "of infinitely more moment than the Spirit of Poetry".[229] Nevertheless, the hymns are often beautifully crafted, without doggerel, cant or bombast. As John says in praising his brother's compositions, they express purity, strength and elegance in their use of English. That is very fair comment. And of course, because they are metrical (but with many varieties of metre) and because they rhyme, they are memorable—especially to an age more used to exercising memory than we are. To that end they were also often sung to familiar tunes.

Music releases emotions. It also allows us to draw refreshment and new life from springs deeper than reason, while not supplanting or eradicating it. Some think that the hymns are too full of the blood, wounds and suffering of Christ (things which a poor, abused and labouring people could relate to), but surely, the overwhelming impression left by Charles Wesley's hymns is one of joy. A joy so consuming that it requires a thousand tongues to sing it; a joy so great that the reality of it cannot be encompassed: "How *can* it be/ That Thou, my God, should die for *me*?" Redemption, forgiveness, hope, love, and all but ineffable joy well out of so many of the greatest of them. Such a force of shared emotion has a noticeable effect on a community and counters the wretchedness of circumstance. Unlike the Babylonian exiles in Psalm 137, the Methodists had learned to sing the Lord's song *even though* they were in a foreign land spiritually—because they knew they were *en route* for home.

The hymns of Charles Wesley were then, in the first place, an *effect* of the Revival, but they were also a *cause*: they unified in emotion, as well as thought, a people who knew who they were and, all-importantly, where they were going; they taught them the grounds of their belief and hope. In preparing for the *next* world they sang Charles' own Scriptural, and "clear directions for making (their) calling and election sure", as John wrote, through their faith and good deeds in *this* one. Revelation had produced revolution, as with Paul, Augustine and Martin Luther. The experience at Aldersgate had opened other gates—to thousands, and eventually to millions. The full impact of it would not be felt until the next century, but it spread far across the English-speaking world.

CHAPTER 9

Positively Victorian

To entertain the thought of writing merely a single chapter to cover the little matter of the Church in the nineteenth century, even if we limit it to the Church in England, seems like a lethal concoction of hubris, folly, and ignorance taken in equal parts. If, however, we narrow the field a little by concentrating our attention on those aspects of it which most frequently suffer the strongest criticism, the topic at least begins to take on a recognisable shape and might be considered manageable. Against these widespread criticisms we should, in order to be fair, set those aspects of Church history which do the Church greater honour. This of course is hardly the stuff of popular applause today or widespread respect and knowledge. When Ian Hislop, editor of *Private Eye*, presented his series of programmes on BBC 2 during 2011 celebrating the astonishing moral and social achievements of (mostly Christian) selected Victorians, he did so with the benefit and protection of an ironic-sounding title: *The Victorian Do-Gooders.*

What then are the critical commonplaces most frequently met with about Victorian religiosity? The first strand of thinking, or rather cluster of assumptions, tells us that the Victorians were indeed very religious; they built big ugly churches and filled them with uncomfortable pews designed to keep the lower orders awake but in their place. Part of this way of thinking, perhaps the other side of the coin, points to hypocrisy. Humbug, moralising, do-gooding were, we are told, the accepted order of the day, which salved consciences seared by quadruple guilt about wealth, greed, sexual licence (or repression) and doubt.

Another approach is to see the Victorian Church as the beginning of the end, as institutional religion increasingly lost authority. Its doctrines of creation fell before the onslaught of science, its historic foundation was found wanting by Strauss and Renan, its morality was lampooned under the pen of Charles Dickens and satirised by Thomas Hardy. How could it survive such blows?

Yet survive it did. Indeed, the increase of missionary fervour in the period was almost explosive, if numbers sent out are anything to go by, as we shall see—which brings us to the next area in which so many in today's society feel ill at ease: the picture of those imperial missionaries in their pith helmets bringing "commerce and Christianity" to a benighted country as a way of justifying the ravaging of an entire continent for its natural resources, in order to make little England even richer.

As a preliminary, it is important that we dispense with the idea that the entire extent of Victoria's reign (1837–1901) was in any sense monolithic in its beliefs and attitudes. The 1840s and the 1890s in some ways belong to different worlds—economically, morally, spiritually, and intellectually. It is fair to say that the 1840s afford us a picture of life at its worst for the majority when compared with subsequent decades, during which the country got richer and richer, and machinery and new inventions increasingly replaced some of the hardest physical labour with the repetitive drudgery of the factories. It is easy therefore to see how those who did not have to suffer it could envisage such a process as part of the myth of never-ending human progress. Illiteracy was supplanted by universal education, "pocket boroughs" by more democratic suffrage and the stagecoach by the railway. If we look at social attitudes in specific areas, however, few would think now that progress was evenly distributed, or even existed in some respects. Imperialist attitudes, for instance, did not progress (as we would see it now) but probably became more arrogant, more selfish and less liberal in the later part of Victoria's reign. A. N. Wilson senses a coarsening of attitudes from as early as the 1850s in his study, *The Victorians*.[230]

A number of historians see the decades of decisive change as being the 1860s and 1870s. Economically, wealth began to be seen as a matter of "cash flow" rather than capital; it was also in these decades, it has been suggested, when so many of the sons of the thrifty and successful businessmen started to spend their fathers' investments. Morally, abstinence and earnestness were no longer the prime virtues or goals. Oscar Wilde could not have chosen his punning play title on the importance of being earnest before the 1870s had happened. Spiritually, the country had become secularised to a surprising degree. The workshop of the world had become, in part, the playground.

One defining moment was the day in 1868 when the last hanging took place in public. On the one hand it is a recognition of the revulsion felt about the most draconian penal code in Europe; on the other it might be seen as a symbol of the hypocrisy of a society that still expended the lives of the poor quite casually, but now preferred not to be seen to do so.

To my mind, just as there is something discreditable about the late Victorian cynicism found in some writers and artists, and in the attitudes of, say, Cecil Rhodes towards the best ideals of Empire, so there is something magnificent, even awe-inspiring about so many of the earlier Victorians. Instead of delusions of grandeur, there had been some humility; instead of condescension, respect (in many cases) for those whom Kipling, the greatest exponent of Empire, would call the "new-caught, sullen peoples", while rightly applauding the otherwise unsung heroes—ordinary soldiers and minor officials—in both his poetry and stories. In sum, there had been a closer approximation to Christian values, which included duty and service.

The poet Matthew Arnold recognised this as early as 1857. Arnold's father, Thomas, (a product of the Evangelicals) had been the great reforming Headmaster of Rugby School who brought Christian values and some accountability, as well as scholarship, into the bleak world of Victorian education depicted in *Tom Brown's Schooldays*. In his poem "Rugby Chapel", the son eulogises the father. He draws a distinction between those "Who all round me to-day / Bluster or cringe, and make life / Hideous, and arid, and vile", and those who, like his father, "strain on", refusing to "go round / In an eddy of purposeless dust", and who "wouldst not *alone* / Be saved", but who "Gavest the weary thy hand", of which "we saw / Nothing"—surely the best sort of "stiff upper lip" which does not reveal how much it costs to help others.

Marian Evans, better known as the novelist George Eliot, wrote a poem much less well known than her prose, in which she longs to join

the choir invisible
Of those immortal dead . . .
In deeds of daring rectitude, in scorn
Of miserable aims that end with self . . .
Whose music is the gladness of the world.

The unself-centredness, as well as the unself-consciousness of the best early Victorians is what strikes a modern reader about them; the fact that they knew that what is right is right, and what is more, that they were on the side of right. Few of us have such certitude today but, as William Buchan noticed, their astounding energy, unlimited intellectual striving and moral courage were amazing.

Religious Humbug?

We must come to the first of our common assumptions: that the Victorians, early or late, were very religious. Certainly, there was a divide in their thinking which came to a head sometime after 1860, but the very large number of nineteenth-century churches whose building began even before Victoria came to the throne were not there to accommodate a growing number of worshippers. Rather, they were built to draw the unchurched and disaffected poor into churches that otherwise were too distant from the new and densely packed areas of towns and cities that grew so fast in an industrial age. In 1851, on 30 March, a census established that only 40 per cent of the population were in church—and half the population of the country lived in cities: they were not godly places. Ordinary people were alienated from a Church which discriminated against the poor by the attitudes, education, dress, behaviour, wealth and living conditions of its clergy and well-to-do laity. There are accounts of the poor being ashamed to show themselves in Anglican churches where the congregation dressed to be seen. Despite the shortage of clergy for the new cities, there was a reluctance to recruit men from "lower social positions". This of course was not the case so much with the Dissenting Church, where the very plainness of the architecture of the chapels, as well as the far less moneyed lifestyle of its ministers, meant that the poor were not alienated in the same way, and their social cohesion was, therefore, far greater. Moreover, because of the legacy of the Test Act (not repealed until 1828), no one belonging to such churches and chapels had been admitted to public office, so they naturally attracted those who were not ambitious in that regard.

In Chapter 2 of Dickens' *David Copperfield* (1850), there is an etching of "Our Pew at Church" which it is instructive to compare with the Hogarth illustration discussed in my Chapter 8.[231] The illustration by Phiz (Hablot Knight Browne) depicts a church rather fuller than that in *The Sleeping Congregation*, and most of those we see are less obviously bored. The preacher is less repellent, but somehow still looks ineffectual as he stoops myopically over his script. Nowhere to be seen however are the ragged poor. The ladies are neatly bonnetted, the gentlemen have frock coats and cravats. The high backs of the box pews seem to ensure that each of their inmates will not have to suffer invasion by a stranger. Pews were frequently rented out by churches and the better-off would pay for their personal space, even though they were all too often not occupying it. There were even churches in which all the pews were rented so there was literally no room at all for the poor in them. In the novel, the young David drifts off to sleep in the sermon, falls off his seat with a crash and is taken out "more dead than alive" by his nurse, Peggotty.

This environment was made even less attractive by a liturgy marked by responses, canticles and the pointing of psalms which no uneducated person could properly join in with. It seems that Mrs C. F. Alexander's rather easier to sing hymn "All Things Bright and Beautiful", in which we are infamously told:

> The rich man in his castle
> The poor man at his gate
> GOD made them high and lowly
> And ordered their estate

was not just a rhyme but a living reality for the majority of Victorians. They had forgotten Mary's song, the Magnificat, from their own Bible and *Book of Common Prayer*: "He hath put down the mighty from their seats and hath exalted the humble and meek. He hath filled the hungry with good things and the rich he hath sent empty away."[232] They had forgotten the message of the Prophets and the warnings from the Epistle of James. It was a mistake which to this day the Anglican Church suffers fallout from. "The Tory Party at prayer" image lingers on despite everything done to dispel it.

The Victorians liked religious ritual for formal occasions, and to mark the rites of passage because it gave shape to life, and because colour and spectacle were otherwise largely missing from the everyday world. It was altogether a more formal age in which hierarchy and deference were paramount social constructs. But it was not an age in which there was an almost universal awareness of the presence of God in human affairs—as earlier ages had been. W. E. Henley's defiant poem "Invictus" and Matthew Arnold's "Dover Beach" are memorable articulations of alternative views held by many, either saying courageously "*I* am the captain of my soul", or regretfully listening to the "melancholy, long, withdrawing roar" of the sea of faith, and believing these were the only realistic options in a society no longer confident of its Christian origins and values.

When we look later therefore, at the work that the Church did in both the earlier and later part of the century, we need to remember that it was achieved against a current of opinion which far from uniformly supported its endeavours. Carlyle, writing to Thomas Erskine in 1847, reflected that Christianity had become "a paltry, mealy-mouthed 'religion of cowards'", and he included those "on the Howard and Fry side as on every other" in his indictment.[233] Rather later, Chesterton, writing in his autobiography, reminded his readers that he was old enough to remember the Victorian Age and that it had "all the vices that are now called virtues; religious doubt, intellectual unrest, a hungry credulity about new things, a complete lack of equilibrium".[234]

Nevertheless, we may be told, however irreligious a large section of Victorian England was, the Church itself was hypocritical: it preached one thing and practised another. The charge, as we have seen, cannot be avoided. A. N. Wilson speaks of the double standards the Victorian age seemed capable of living with, and of a society changing more rapidly than any other anywhere. But it is hard to think that our own society does not indulge itself like this as well. The charge of hypocrisy is a very easy one to make against Christians for the very reason that when standards are set as high as those that Christ set his followers, it is hard to see how anyone can avoid the charge. We all like to appear better than we are—and are frequently ashamed of the gap between aspiration and actualisation. But it is better to have the aspiration than be without it. Christ himself was subject to the charge of hypocrisy on at least four occasions, according to the Gospel records—a puzzling inclusion for those who consider the documents unreliable or complete fabrications.[235] Richard Dawkins considers that even Mother Theresa was a sanctimonious hypocrite, so it seems there is no escaping the charge even for the innocent, if people as good as she was make others feel uncomfortable. What the critics fail to spot is that we are all in the same boat. No one wants their least moral side brought into the light, save those who are trying to make a name the opposite way—for their very lack of virtue. But even then the desire to outclass others in infamy and wickedness still shows the same basic selfish competitiveness as the rest of us, but with a reversed set of norms. The charge of hypocrisy, then, though true enough and extremely unattractive is not the sole preserve of the Victorian Church. All but the very few are, to some degree, hypocritical. Victorians laboured under conflicting moods of doubt and faith, but their consciences urged them to good deeds, strengthened by force of habit and example. Far from free to speak their minds on religious issues still so fresh and raw, hypocrisy became an inevitable by-product of such rapid change.

The Beginning of the End?

To an objective observer, especially one unfamiliar with Church history, the body blows which the Victorian Church suffered from the advancement of science, from the critiques of historians and theologians, and from the satire of the poets and novelists must have appeared terminal. Yet this was not to be the case, if we are to judge from the fervent activity of nineteenth-century Christians in England, both at home and doing frontier work abroad. Such a "resurrection" was not unprecedented: G.

K. Chesterton describes the *five* deaths of the Church in one of his essays, and Charles Williams reminds his readers that Christendom led the attack on the slave trade and won, just at the point when "Christendom was all but dead", save for the bright light of the Evangelical Revival.[236] C. S. Lewis wrote of the Church: "Each time they put down the earth on the grave, life breaks out somewhere else."[237]

This is not the place to rehearse how Archbishop Ussher's 4004 BC date for the creation of the universe, or how Paley's *Evidences* were demolished by Lyell, Darwin and others. That story has been told often enough. But we do need to remind ourselves of how this impacted on society, and the Church in particular. The answer of course is that there were a broad range of responses—from the biologist Philip Gosse (supposedly accurately drawn by his son Edmund in *Father and Son*), who considered that God must have placed the fossils in the rocks in order to tempt geologists away from the faith, through to Charles Kingsley, who strongly opposed such an idea, gladly welcomed the interface between science and religion, and found that, rightly interpreted, they belonged together. But for many, the impact was anxiety and doubt. If man was nothing but an evolving animal, then the fundamentally motivating belief in the immortality of the soul (with rewards in heaven and pains in hell) was removed wholesale. For many Victorians such a loss of belief was unthinkable or suicidal. All their long-term goals, all their sense of purpose, all their belief in progress towards a better world, were threatened with immediate dissolution.

But there is another story to be told here too, one that Alister McGrath tells in his book *The Twilight of Atheism*.[238] It fits very well with my contention that "the evil that men do" will either live on, or where there is none, will be invented—especially when it comes to Church history in the popular mind.

William Paley's *A View of the Evidences of Christianity* (1794) had contended that, since God is good and omniscient, he made things without the need for their modification or change, and that the early chapters of Genesis could be read as an historical account. However, Darwin's observations of fossils suggested to him that some species had died out, while living species with redundant vestigial structures gave the appearance of having adapted from some previous evolutionary state where those structures had served a purpose. The "special creation", therefore, of each species as they appear to us today, no longer fitted the facts. T. H. Huxley debated the issue with Bishop Wilberforce, as we all know, in 1860. The biased and misleading caricature that we are given today of that debate was, however, drawn in 1890, a whole generation later, and depicts, as McGrath describes, an inadequately informed cleric attempting to score cheap points off the scientist who emerges with dignity, as opposed to the Bishop who is ludicrously outclassed and discredited.

The reality, says McGrath, was very different. Darwin, in the very year of the debate, acknowledged that Wilberforce's critique of *On the Origin of Species* was extremely clever and that he needed to modify his theory in the light of that critique. Moreover, McGrath continues, contemporary accounts of the debate tell us a story markedly different from the 1890 one peddled by journalists in the "naughty nineties", when there was intellectual capital and financial gain to be made from myth-making about an obscurantist Bishop from a bygone era.

The impact of science, after all, on the everyday world of the man in the street in the second half of the century was enormous, as Jacob Bronowski has shown.[239] Gas light, ticker tape, anaesthetics, bridges and ships all attested to the successful, life-enhancing enquiries, experimentation and decision making processes of science. If such a person enquired further he would quickly come across electro-magnetism, pathology, and work on sound, light and electricity. The world of academic theology had no such popular laurels to display. Or rather, what such a rarefied world could and did reveal was shown to those least likely to be able to relate the story of its benefits in the corridors of power: the poor, the disenfranchised, the sick, the disabled, and those very distant from English shores; namely, the people for whom Wilberforce, Shaftesbury and a host of others worked—precisely because the universe they inhabited was *not* a purely Darwinian one where nature *alone* worked to form the human condition, unameliorated by providence and love.

So, when Huxley's view prevailed in the Oxford debate on evolution, it was a victory for scientific method: after that, science would win over theology because it *was* science. In the popular mind, any other approach had been displaced. Today, nobody says in order to reinforce their argument, "It's simply not theological to think that way", but we often hear "It's simply not *scientific* to think that way." Science rightly holds sway because it is such a successful way of achieving results. Unfortunately some beliefs slip under the radar and masquerade as scientific when they are not.

In the second half of the nineteenth century, the impact on faith was such that educated people who were believers had to adapt *how* they believed. God now had to fit into science rather than vice-versa. It was respectable, socially and intellectually, to believe in Christianity in this new sort of way—slightly distanced from too close an adherence to Scripture; from too literal a belief in miracles. Unbelief, in turn, became something that could be talked about and was no longer a shocking departure from the way one ought to behave. Indeed, Huxley and Mill and Eliot and their like were acutely conscious of themselves as highly moral beings, but nervously exhausted, as Bronowski says, by the strain of shunning evil without the same rationale for doing so that their forbears had enjoyed.[240] Whether we have yet found a sufficient substitute for Christian belief that will act as "salt and light" (in Christian terms) or, for the secular mindset, a source of values that will underpin human social behaviour strongly enough to make humanity do good and avoid evil is a matter for urgent debate if Britain and the rest of Europe are set to become increasingly secular. The New Atheists think we have those values, of course, but the evidence from the newspapers would suggest otherwise. Richard Dawkins' books may have been extremely popular, but his attempts to discredit theology as an intellectually respectable discipline, and to acclaim science as sole arbiter of whether something is knowable or not, or even worth knowing, have been dismal failures and recognised as such by a wide range of academic voices, some of the most scathing being atheists and agnostics. The majority in the Christian Church has no awkwardness at all in accepting that God's method of producing his crown of creation, humanity, was evolutionary and was a process which took billions of years rather than thousands. Indeed, such insights have enriched both our understanding of Scripture and theology.

So far, our secular scientific age has come up variously with enlightened self-interest, the Utilitarian "greatest happiness" theory, the survival of the fittest, and the wishful thinking that the awesome nature of our world and cosmos is enough to make us behave well. That's not an impressive list when judged by its results. Despite the number of signatories to human rights documents (based on values derived from Christianity), there seems to be little adherence to them when states and individuals decide they are inconvenient, as Amnesty International has shown. It is not only the Church that has failed to love its neighbour.

The advancement of science does not seem to have rung the death knell of the Church, or even, so far, to have been the beginning of the end. Indeed, anecdotal evidence suggests that there are more Christians working today in the sciences in British universities than there are in other faculties.

Science, of course, was not the only point at which the Victorian Church came under attack. The foundations of faith were also rocked by the fact that theologians and historians were using the same methods of examining the Biblical texts as they applied to other documents.

Ludwig Feuerbach (1804–1872), the German philosopher and anthropologist, had already argued that human need had produced the idea of God, rather than the reverse—the traditional idea that God had created human need to remind us of our dependence on him.[241] According to Feuerbach, Christianity as a living reality had long vanished. George Eliot translated both Feuerbach, and David Friedrich Strauss's *Life of Jesus* (1836), ten years after its publication.[242] Strauss had argued that were no historical grounds for supernatural religion, thus reducing Christianity to a mere example of how humanity generates myths which it comes to believe as true. C. S. Lewis would later reverse this by saying that the myth of the dying and rising god had existed from the beginning, a myth which God proceeded to write into history in the crucifixion and resurrection of Christ—the earlier mythical versions being good dreams of a prophetic nature which were preparatory in purpose.

A greater impact was made by Ernest Renan (1823–1892), who felt the historical Jesus to have been a purely human figure without supernatural powers but with an enormous ego whom the early Church elevated to divine status.[243] This is a view which still obtains today of course but is frequently used as an excuse for not having to think about the whole picture of Jesus in the Gospels—the records as we have them. Many prefer to leave out the supernatural on a priori grounds, attributing not only the miraculous element, but also many of the most profound words of Christ, to a later generation of acolytes, thereby ignoring the undeniable historical impact of this enigmatic figure on the mid-first-century Roman world.

Ordinary readers have been encouraged all too easily, by a number of scholars, to miss the integrity and cohesion of the words with the deeds of the portrait (surely a uniquely startling conjunction) in each Gospel. Lewis's remark that such people are looking for fern seed but missing an elephant in broad daylight is well made. If the records are fabrication, or if much of their core is a later accretion, then surely those who created the fiction were themselves making a work of supreme genius—but what we know, or can deduce, about the authors does not allow for this. The "demythologisers" do not seem to have taken away from the compelling power of the portraits of Christ for those who will read the accounts. Chesterton's *bon mot* could be applied here: it is not that Christianity has been tried and found wanting, but that it has been found hard, and not tried. The very reluctance of many moderns to engage with the evidence is a pointer to that. One previous Director of Studies in Mathematics at the University of Cambridge, on asking his colleagues at high table why they dismissed the evidence for the resurrection, was told simply that they did not like to contemplate such possibilities. Huxley had to admit that the only final case against miracles was the dogma that they did not happen. Science, as well as scholarship, sometimes has to discover, or recognise, its own limitations.

Even more widespread than the impact of either the scientists or the textual critics was, inevitably, the reading matter of the wider literate public. Dickens, Tennyson, Arnold and Hardy, each approached in different ways the conduct of the institutional Church, and its more unattractive (to them) or least easily believed dogmas. Each had a large readership of different social groupings. George Eliot, perhaps the greatest writer of all of the Victorians, had a different approach again, deeply influenced by scientific discovery.

Dickens, having experienced poverty, felt that Christians preaching morality to the poor before such people had the means of enjoying such a luxury was useless (the Evangelical Charles Kingsley thought the same). Decent housing, sanitation and light should be the object of reform, rather than godliness in the first instance. In *Bleak House* (1853), he presents us with two ludicrously funny but highly unattractive ladies, Mrs Jellyby and Mrs Pardiggle (wonderful names!). Mrs Jellyby spends so much time on missionary work "educating the natives of Borrioboola-Gha on the left bank of the Niger" that her neglected daughter, Caddy, wishes she and all of the family were dead. Mrs Pardiggle, by contrast, conducts her philanthropy at home. Her children too are "weazened and shrivelled . . . absolutely ferocious with discontent", even more so than the brickmaker and his family, living in degradation, who are the recipients of the "rapacious benevolence" of this lady of prominent nose and loud voice, "who had the effect of wanting a great deal of room".

When she visits his broken-windowed hovel surrounded by pigsties and stagnant pools, he tells her:

> No I an't read the little book wot you left. There an't nobody
> here as knows how to read it . . . No, I don't never mean
> for to go to church. I shouldn't be expected there, if I did;
> the beadle's too gen-teel for me. And how did my wife get
> that black eye? Why, I giv' it her.

Dickens is merciless in this scene, making every sentence count against the unwelcome Pardiggles of the world. He also allows his narrator, who accompanies Mrs Pardiggle, to feel "very uncomfortable", intrusive and out of place, with an "irremovable iron barrier" existing between the parties thrust together. The "little book" referred to in the passage above is described as being unreadable even by Robinson Crusoe on his desert island. Dickens knew his audience would recognise the type, for without that his satire would have no edge, no purpose.

Another character in *Bleak House*, Mr Chadband, is a lay preacher, "a large yellow man, with a fat smile", whose oily and self-regarding rhetoric whilst preaching both to and about the boy Jo, the penniless, destitute crossing sweeper, is such that he can say of the lad:

> this brother, present here among us, is devoid of parents,
> devoid of relations, devoid of flocks and herds, devoid of
> gold, of silver, and of precious stones, because he is devoid
> of the light . . . the light of Terewth.

Such a short extract cannot give the proper flavour of Dickens' prose here, and of his astonishing power to render such cant and hypocrisy,

the worst aspects of Victorian religiosity, a laughing-stock. It is needless
to add that Chadband does nothing whatever to alleviate Jo's poverty.
Indeed, the sermon ends with a complete debacle during which young
Jo, having understood nothing whatever of what was going on, slips out,
but is given a supper (without any sermonising) by the maid, Guster, as
he goes. Satirical characterisation in Dickens' novels worked the same way
as TV satires on the clergy do today: they draw on a stereotype but they
also reinforce it, thereby deepening the chasm between clergy and public.

Recent biographers of Dickens have ignored the importance of religious
feeling in his novels, but Humphry House, in *The Dickens World* spent
a chapter on the topic and quotes Dickens' paper "Sunday under Three
Heads", in which an idyllic country scene is pictured.[244] House suggests
that Dickens, when young, would have liked to have seen a pattern of
behaviour all over the country where minister and congregation shared
a "devotion as far removed from affectation or display as from coldness
or indifference", as the novelist wrote. His compassion for the poor and
loathing of evil, as well as this imagined idyll, derived from his inherited
liberal Protestantism as well as from Romanticism.

Tennyson's doubts, his struggle with geological timescales, his reference
to nature "red in tooth and claw", and his emergence to a watery faith also
played their part in the dilution of faith. He was Poet Laureate, author
of "The Charge of the Light Brigade", a figure who spoke for the literate
part of the nation. For him, as for many of them, doubt was as much a
part of his psyche as faith. "In Memoriam" comforted people with the
idea that "There is more faith in honest doubt, / Believe me, than in half
the creeds." Poets as well as novelists express what others feel but might
not so easily articulate, thereby making it more real, more present as a
theme in society, a topic for discussion.

Thomas Hardy shocked the later Victorian public more deeply than
any other popular writer. He not only questioned the existence of God, but
also his goodness (if he did exist), and the behaviour of clergy who acted
as if he was not good, or as if they were unaware of the consequences of
their often crass behaviour. There was little gentle satire in Hardy when
it came to the writing of mature novels like *The Mayor of Casterbridge*,
Tess of the d'Urbervilles, and *Jude the Obscure*. In these great novels Hardy
presents us with a universe variously blind, indifferent, and hostile to

human goodness and endeavour. Providence is replaced by a Fate which turns even the best into playthings of the "President of the Immortals". Hardy's clergy are not only inadequate to their high calling but lack the human decency and awareness of others (especially their suffering) that he blesses his rustic characters with. The evangelical Mr Clare in *Tess* seems to have bred sons (Angel in particular) who are so steeped in Victorian "respectability" that the parable of the mote and the beam in the subject's eye is one they simply seem unable to apply in the real world. Angel Clare throws out his bride, the gorgeous Tess, on their wedding night for confessing the same sin to him that he has just confessed to her. The hypocrisy and double standards are deeply alienating. Jude (containing a lot of Hardy himself) is a figure spurned by the university authorities (dominated by clerics) because he is poor, insufficiently educated, and of the wrong class. Hardy's criticism of the Christian status quo is unmistakeable, as rejection of one kind or another at the hands of the Church and society reduces Jude and his family to poverty, despair and death. The death of Tess's unbaptised baby, and her own death by hanging as punishment for the passionate murder of her seducer and one-time preacher Alec, concludes one of the greatest Victorian novels, in which the status of women, of the uneducated, and the poor are all championed against a society which Hardy depicts as riven with double standards, and a Church divorced from compassion and any desire for change. Sadly, Hardy himself seems to have been unable to command a much better attitude to women in his own life, or at least to his first wife Emma, according to three modern biographers, Robert Gittings, Patricia Ingham and Claire Tomalin. Ingham in particular does not gloss over Hardy's inconsistency and illogicality in his attitude to Christianity, and while she is fair to Hardy it is hard, on reading the book, not to see him as making sense in his novels of his own life, his failures and disappointments, at the Church's and society's expense.

George Eliot, who at the height of her fame was the greatest literary figure of her day, worked a different way, though she also put much of her own passion into her characters. Nowhere is this clearer than in Maggie Tulliver, the heroine of *The Mill on the Floss* (1860), her most autobiographical novel, but one which is without Hardy's desire to vent his discontent on the Establishment. She knew deep inside her the power of a motivating evangelical faith and wrote admiringly about religion, though she could not, in all conscience, share in it. Maggie is adrift on the tide of passion but looks to the past for permanence, "where duty lies".

For Maggie, "thirsty for all knowledge", this conflict can end only in death. She has "a blind, unconscious yearning for something that would link together the wonderful impressions of this mysterious life". Through Maggie and other characters, Eliot brings to the fore, in a new way, the idea that (as D. H. Lawrence implied in the psychological drama of his novels) the most real action of our lives is internal—something that Freud would explore further in more scientific terms. She shows us that people's mental evolution is linked to their environment, just as Darwin showed their physical evolution was. She also encouraged a soul-searching honesty about motives and inner truth which empowered readers to face their own doubts and discuss them. Eliot's characters are in revolt against compromise; Hardy's often need to *learn* compromise. Her ideas strive towards horizons and her sympathies are wider than anyone's. All this worked against the narrow rigidity of powerful sections of the Victorian Church, which, where it was not enlivened by motives of love and service of Christ and neighbour, was all too likely to be compromised in the ways we have already seen.

Matthew Arnold wrote in *Literature and Dogma* (1873) that the object of the book was "to reassure those who feel attachment to Christianity, to the Bible, but who recognise the growing discredit befalling the miracles and the supernatural".[245] This discredit, he goes on to say, is just and necessary. Nevertheless, he writes, the *message* of the Bible with regard to conduct is essential to civilisation, and his alarm is precisely about this. In particular, he sees "what everyone sees to constitute the special moral feature of our time: *the masses* are losing the Bible and its religion".[246] J. A. Froude, friend and biographer of Thomas Carlyle, wrote of his friend's views in the 1860s that he believed "the power of the established religion was growing less; but it was not yet entirely gone, and it was the only hold that was left on the most vital of all truths".[247] Interestingly, Emerson had said similar things to Harvard Divinity students a generation earlier in 1838: "What hold the public worship had on man is gone."[248] But it seems every age says the same about itself. D. C. Somervell wrote in 1929: "Faith has lost its hold upon the majority of modern men and women."[249] *Literature and Dogma* is therefore a highly eloquent and beautiful example of the Victorian's dilemma: she or he loves the Bible, the figure of Jesus, the supreme selflessness of New Testament injunctions, but disbelieves the supernatural elements and cannot accept that the New Testament writers did not make mistakes; ones which compounded the misunderstanding about Jesus already visited upon the disciples by virtue of the fact that they were so greatly inferior to their Master in every form of understanding and morality. Cogent replies were published to Arnold, but his gentleness, morality and standing as a poet were as influential to his readers as his arguments. His insistence that the purpose and object of religion is "conduct" and that conduct is "three-fourths of life" which "men and nations fall by" is also so characteristic of Eliot, Huxley and the other agnostics.[250] They have the highest ethical code but it is coupled with an inability to see that it is not behaviour in the first place that religion seeks to establish, but contact with the divine. His definition of religion as ethics heightened by feeling further drives home the Victorian emphasis on morality—as if, after the death of serious theology, this must be elevated in its place.[251]

Commercial Travellers?

David Livingstone died in 1873, the year that Arnold published his remark about the masses losing the Bible and its religion. There is something paradoxical about the coincidence of date. Livingstone died, bereft of all European company, deep in Africa. If churches in England were so empty or moribund or corrupt, why were they exporting so many products to the ends of the earth? What Livingtone was doing, and what other missionaries from Britain and other parts of Europe were doing in Africa and all over the globe, was not remotely like the work of Mrs Pardiggle or as Mrs Jellyby imagined it to be. The view that the missionaries were simply imperialists in disguise is mistaken.

We need to start with a backward glance at the formation of earlier missions.

In the post-medieval period the history of mission has been far more than mere proselytism, the search for converts. In the great age of discovery there had been a strong sense, in the reigns of Edward VI and Elizabeth I, that any journeyings to the ends of the earth should have "the sowing of Christianity"[252] as their chief intent—if they were to prosper. The founder of their faith had instructed that it should be preached to every tribe and nation, so when Cabot planned his voyage to Cathay it was unthinkable that the participants should do less than take the gospel to share with those so benighted by its absence. Sir Walter Raleigh presented the Virginian Company with a present of £100 "for the propagation of the Christian religion"[253] when he parted from them.[254] In the seventeenth century, Richard Baxter, the Puritan divine, along with others, enlarged a charter (first created by Cromwell) designed "to seek the outward welfare" of the colonies as well as the "salvation of their immortal souls".[255] These were to be the twin intentions of thousands of missionaries for the next three hundred years or more.

It was, however, the Moravians in the 1730s who, as a church, were among the earliest Protestants to form the idea of reaching out in an organised, deliberate way to the "savage and perishing tribes" in places as far apart as Greenland, the West Indies, and Ceylon.[256] This extraordinary group of believers had a far-reaching effect on John Wesley, who in turn must be seen as a primary source for the inception of the modern missionary period which is marked out by the *absence* of connection with the state. The Evangelical Revival brought into new focus the worth of the individual before God and the necessity of a personal relationship with him. William Carey, often seen as the father of modern missions, considered the conversion of the heathen an obligation for all Christians. Under his influence the Baptist Missionary Society was founded in 1792, and by June 1793 Carey was on his way to India, a sum of £13 2s 6d having been subscribed. From that point on there was never a decade until 1900 which was without the formation of a new society, funded by donation. In most decades there were two, three, or four new societies added to the list so that by the end of the nineteenth century nearly forty major societies were in existence in Britain alone, along with three or four hundred smaller agencies. There were some twenty-five large societies in the United States founded with similar intentions.

During this high period of the formation of such societies the Church in England was clearly not moribund but rather highly active—at least among those who read the Scriptures and acted on them. Nor was the Church unable to pursue its mission at home, though this took a form different from that which had preceded it. Missionaries, clergy, philanthropists of every kind (the "do-gooders") were busy on a huge number of home fronts socially and politically. But what were the missionaries doing in foreign fields? Oscar Wilde, in a demeaning jest, called them "commercial travellers".[257] Witty as ever, Wilde combined a subtle truth with a deadly and unjust calumny.

We shall start our answer with David Livingstone, medic, explorer and missionary, even now a household name, because he was a supremely heroic figure to most literate Victorians, and because when he told his audience at the Senate House in Cambridge in 1857, "I go back to Africa to try to make an open path for commerce and Christianity" they loved it, and the picture it created for them.[258] For some, however, his meaning was ambiguous: a useful ambiguity which would allow Christianity to be used as a means of commercial enterprise and gain, as opposed to using commerce as a means of bringing Christianity to the peoples of Africa. The latter was unquestionably Livingstone's intention, and his unique achievement. In his 1857 book, *Missionary Travels*, he is explicit at the start that he had early resolved to devote his life to the betterment of humanity's lot. He was not the first to catch the vision that the way to end the slave trade in Africa was not the force of the Royal Navy but something more subtle; more integral to the lives of the Africans. Thomas Fowell Buxton, successor to William Wilberforce as leader of the crusade against slavery, had spoken at the first anniversary meeting (at Exeter Hall) of the Society for the Extinction of the Slave trade in 1840. Like Wilberforce, Buxton was deeply involved in the work of overseas missions and he knew that despite legislation and the work of the Royal Navy, something more enduring was needed. "The true ransom for Africa will be found in her fertile soil", he argued. "It is the Bible and the plough that must regenerate Africa."[259] He strongly opined that explorations should be made into the potential Africa held for agricultural and commercial development with a view to denying the profiteers in human flesh their markets by the creation of better ones based on Christian practices. The

Union Jack would protect such settlements. Among the audience at that Exeter Hall meeting in 1840 was a rather quiet twenty-seven-year-old medical student from Charing Cross Hospital: David Livingstone. By 1841 that extraordinary young man was in Cape Town and destined to spend the next twenty years making journeys such as the world had never seen. Geoffrey Moorhouse says of him in *The Missionaries*: "Alone he would do more to kill the slave trade and exalt the Christian missionary profession than all the glittering meetings . . . held in Exeter Hall or anywhere else on the face of the earth."[260]

Paradoxically, Livingstone is often described as a failure in missionary terms—converting only one person in his entire travels, one who would lapse in his faith quite spectacularly. This seems to be a misunderstanding of mission in general and of Livingstone in particular. It is also a hallmark of the first generation of missionaries: in one Society, twenty missionaries died to achieve twenty converts. Carey had baptised only one convert after seven years' labour. *Missionary Travels* is explicit about the motivation for such unrewarding work; Livingstone goes to some length to explain his "affectionate love to Him who bought us with His blood" and his "sense of deep obligation to Him". But he also says that he will not be recounting his evangelistic labours in the past so much as what still remains to be done. Most importantly, he says: "In the glow of love which Christianity inspires, I soon resolved to devote my life to the alleviation of human misery." After more than 500 pages detailing his journeys up to that point he remarks: "I view the end of the geographical feat as the beginning of the missionary enterprise. I take the latter term in its most extended signification, and include every effort made for the amelioration of our race." He then goes on to list scientists, soldiers, sailors (rescuing the victims of "heartless men-stealers") and merchants as well as missionaries. But Livingstone does not neglect the Bible, which he calls "the Magna Charta of all the rights and privileges of modern civilisation"—a view similar to Matthew Arnold's seen earlier. Speaking of his friend Sebituane's journey, he says: "he opened up the way for me—let us hope also for the Bible." Livingstone describes the slave trade, as engaged in by the "American race", as "the gigantic evil", and makes a detailed analysis of how through commerce "an effectual blow will be struck at the slave-trade".[261]

Many years later, in 1871, he witnessed a terrible massacre by slavers at Nyangwe in the Congo. His account of that day (now available in the original manuscript through spectral imaging) was published by *The Times* and provoked outrage when Stanley brought it back. Livingstone's heart for Africans is revealed in his conclusion that "If my disclosures regarding the terrible Ujijian slavery should lead to the suppression of the East Coast slave trade, I shall regard that as a greater matter than the discovery of all the Nile sources." An unambiguous statement if ever there was one. He consistently puts commerce second to Christianity in importance as a means of bringing hope to Africa: "We ought to encourage the Africans to cultivate for our markets, as the most effectual means, *next to the Gospel,* of *their* elevation." No "commercial traveller" there, but a man of unique energies, gifts, dedication and love for Africa and its people. But Livingstone was no sentimentalist. He speaks of impenetrable areas full of "hordes of bloody savages" where "no white man could have gone without leaving his skull to ornament some village". Equally he learned that "there are vast numbers of good people in the world."[262] If there was a tendency amongst those at home to romanticise the work of missionaries in general, it was because the actuality of the situation—the disease, indifference and obstinacy of the indigenous peoples—was often too depressing to recount.[263] Half a century after Livingstone's travels, General Smuts, one of the toughest South Africans, wrote of his 1916 campaign in equatorial Africa: "The malarial mosquito everywhere . . . the deadly tsetse fly . . . a wild luxuriance of parasitic life, breeding tropical diseases . . . the pitiless African sun . . . much-reduced rations."[264] Africa was no place for a holiday.

We have now forgotten, or find it politically incorrect to remember, what Africa, and those parts of the Empire untouched by the gospel, were like in the nineteenth century. J. C. Lambert's book, *The Romance of Missionary Heroism,*[265] may focus solely on the good that missionaries did, but it is a welcome antidote to the rather cynical misrepresentation often painted of them today: their life of privilege, their employment of servants expected to fetch and carry for them, and their imposition of ludicrously inappropriate Western standards of behaviour, dress and belief—while all the time belittling or even destroying African culture. Certainly this happened, but equally there was considerable identification with the indigenous peoples, self-imposed poverty, continual hardship and discomfort, and an inevitable social isolation from all the familiar things we take for granted. Whether working in Africa, Asia, America or Oceania, the missionaries were as likely to come across cruelty, injustice, infanticide, cannibalism and human sacrifice as they were to find peace-loving communities exemplifying "the noble savage", untainted by the greed and other vices of the white man. In fact, tribal life was frequently extremely brutal and violent; Laurence Keeley, an anthropologist at the University of Illinois, has calculated that one in three members of a variety of tribal societies died in war. Stephen Pinker, in his book on the decline of violence through history, *The Better Angels of our Nature*, shows hunter-gatherer societies lost a minimum of 15 per cent of their peoples to warfare, while the Wars of Religion in seventeenth-century Europe accounted for only 2 per cent of deaths.[266] Villagers and missionaries were in many places in constant fear of attack, and religious practices were often a matter of appeasing savage gods. Life spans were often short for those the missionaries served—cut off by disease, violence, tribal customs and beliefs. For instance, in Nigeria, and elsewhere, slaves were sacrificed on the death of their masters; slaves were also accepted as substitutes for the misdemeanours of their masters; and twins were killed at birth. The lives of the missionaries were sometimes even shorter. Livingstone remarks at one point, near the end of his book, that all the Africans he had so far met "eagerly caught up the idea of living in peace as the probable effect of the Gospel".[267] It was not something they had had the privilege of enjoying. Medicine and healing, agriculture, clean water, literacy and peace were large gifts to exchange for the absurdities of inappropriately clothing the native peoples in ways designed not to offend the whites, and for failing to recognise the value of their cultures.

Some missionary enterprises were of course disastrous. The first expedition up the Niger in 1841, backed by the government, and led by a Royal Navy captain, lost fifty-one of its 145 members to tropical diseases within the year.[268] Further expeditions had more success, though the connection of mission work with politics was a dangerous precedent. It would mean that the imperialists could more easily use the missions as scouts for their own purposes. One good outcome, however, for those who lived "on the left bank of the Niger", as Mrs Jellyby must have been delighted to think, was that they could see which side their bread was buttered. Tribes who were "perpetually at war with each other", as Moorhouse says,[269] saw the advantages of desisting and enjoyed peace.

One famous disaster in particular illustrates both the high-mindedness and selfless endeavour, as well as the folly and naivety of the Victorian missionary. Tierra del Fuego, even today, is surely one of the most forbidding and remotely inhospitable places outside Antarctica, which it faces. Darwin, on board the *Beagle* in 1826, thought its people possibly sub-human, so primitive were their lives and appearances. Despite this, or perhaps because of it, a young British naval officer, Allen Gardiner, hired an unseaworthy schooner and an incompetent crew (there was no money) and amazingly reached his goal. Finding himself entirely unprovided for on his arrival, he made the dangerous journey home, and then tried four more times, unsuccessfully, to reach the Fuegians. The last attempt, in 1850, was catastrophic. He and his crew had left behind their ammunition for shooting game, they spoke not a word of the native languages, and on arrival they had to hide when the natives threatened them. Their bodies were eventually found in their refuge where they had died slowly from starvation and the extreme cold. What this little vignette shows perfectly is that Gardiner, in one sense, knew exactly what lay ahead of him in terms of an alien people, an absolute remoteness, and unsurvivable conditions without sufficient precautionary measures. And despite all this he made four expeditions beyond his first—which must have shown him what he was in for. Pettifer and Bradley, in their 1990 book, trace the legacy of these futile attempts which were ultimately to lead to the extinction of a people.[270] But can we blame Gardiner and his successors for this? It was not the missionaries who extinguished the Fuegians but the Argentine navy and government. The navy arrived as they would have done anyway, irrespective of missionary presence in "Fireland", and they brought with them a secret killer: measles. It was followed by scrofula and influenza against which the natives had no resistance. To add to this, in the 1890s Argentina sold off their traditional hunting-grounds to sheep farmers, and in the conflicts that developed over land use, a bounty of £1 was offered for each dead native.[271]

The whole Tierra del Fuego episode illustrates not just the extraordinary compulsion of Victorian missionaries, their godly folly and immense strength of purpose, but also the dilemma of all primary mission work. The Victorians had to ask themselves: should the gospel precede or follow the incursion of Western civilisations into others, in an age when such incursions are part of accepted expansionist behaviour? If it were to precede, it becomes a harbinger and opens up a territory to the less scrupulous who would follow—with firearms, alcohol and perhaps servitude if not slavery. But if the gospel has to follow, the damage is done already, and it is heart-breakingly difficult to share the gospel with a vitiated people who associate the intruder's skin colour with the anguish of slavery, the labour of the mine, the dissolution of the tribe and the dereliction of their hunting-grounds. What is astonishing is that in Africa, despite the long history of enslavement to Europeans, those early missionaries did make an impact of quite staggering proportions, though, as was often the case, patience and faith were needed. In Uganda, for example, baptisms rose from 200 in the year 1890 to roughly 100,000 in 1914. Had their ministrations been characteristically like Mrs Pardiggle's they would surely have had less success. It is interesting that in 1965 S. G. Evans predicted that it would be extremely difficult for colonies in Africa to throw off imperialism without throwing off Christianity. The last half-century has proved him entirely wrong. Today, Africa is, by some reckonings, the most Christian of continents.

Matthew Parris writes regularly for *The Times* and is a very highly respected journalist and broadcaster. He is also an avowed atheist. In 2008 he wrote an article which three years later he was to call the one that "provoked a greater response" than any other *Times* column he had written, in which he admitted reaching a conclusion which "embarrassed [his] growing belief that there is no God".[272] His expressed view was that though he applauded the practical work of the mission churches there, it is actually the gospel which is essential to Africa. He wrote: "In Africa, Christianity changes people's hearts. It brings spiritual transformation. The rebirth is real. The change is good." It is convenient to allow that the medicine and the literacy, are what count in Africa, but Parris's point is the reverse. What really counts are not these things but the faith in Christ—which liberates the people, not into deference or subservience, but into openness, confidence, diligence, optimism and honesty. Tribal belief which suppresses individuality is replaced by the new conception of a place in the universe made by a loving God. Anxiety, stemming from fear of evil spirits, ancestors and the natural world, wrote Parris, "strikes deep" into the African psyche, with the result that curiosity is stunted, initiative avoided.

Christianity, he says, "smashes straight through" such a framework of thought with its "direct, personal, two-way link between the individual and God". It is a view supported by his travels across the continent from Algiers to Nairobi through nine different countries. If we want Africa to "walk tall", he concluded, it needs a belief system. Removing Christian evangelism "may leave the continent at the mercy of a malign fusion of Nike, the witch doctor, the mobile phone and the machete". Brave and generous words. He might have added, as he did in a later article, that Africa needs more honesty, dependability and incorruptibility—not swagger and pride. Currently, Africa is reckoned to have 32 per cent of the planet's natural resources, but contributes only 2 per cent of the world's production—an appalling statistic, but not an inevitable one. The Church in Zimbabwe, for instance, by linking Christian farmers together and training them in agriculture, is starting to reverse the grim decline imposed on them by decades of tyranny and mismanagement. Similar schemes are operating in other African states. Dr Alison Morgan, in her book *The Wild Gospel* shows how Uganda has been transformed by nationwide prayer initiatives and a new emphasis by the government on integrity and sexual morality: AIDS has decreased, as has inflation, while these issues were being addressed with concerted prayer.[273] Economic and social problems were accepted as having underlying spiritual causes.

The number and geographical extent of Africa's Christian churches today suggests that missionary work has not only been a success but that the work of the Church has been quite distinct from that of the Empire, the last vestiges of which were discarded at least fifty years ago. To conflate the two is a dangerous mistake: in accepting the value of the one, we would have in that case to accept the value of the other. And nothing divides historians and the interested public like the history of the Empire: it is often seen as either a very good or a very bad thing, as Ben Macintyre has pointed out.[274] In reality, it cannot have been like that; there was much to admire and much to deplore. We can be both proud and humbled depending on which facets of it we look at. John Darwin's 2012 book,

Unfinished Empire: The Global Expansion of Britain, demonstrates that
the assumption of post-colonial historians that imperial rule was evil and
selfish, without room for altruism, is simply wrong and far too simplistic.[275]
Science and technology, the work ethic, medicine and education we can
be proud of; racism, patronisation and exploitation we deplore. Kwasi
Kwarteng argues that we still need the values of the British Empire, and
that one reason why the experience of those under imperial rule was
so various was the huge discretion local officials were allowed in their
administration—which derived from a policy of fostering individualism,
initiative and competition (especially in the public schools) in a time
without modern means of communication.[276] When messages between
continents take weeks to be exchanged, decisions have to be taken without
reference to higher authority. Kwarteng goes on to cite Rhodes, Kitchener
and T. E. Lawrence as men who got on through merit, enterprise, courage
and ability rather than just class. Figures such as Frederick Lugard,
Governor of Nigeria, looked for honesty, self-control, truthfulness and
an absence of vanity. Milner in South Africa chose for his "kindergarten"
men like John Buchan—of exceptional promise rather than distinguished
background. Kwarteng's view is that most engineers, missionaries, civil
servants, doctors and lawyers wanted to improve the lives of those they
had chosen to work among. As for the Raj, even mainstream Indian
historians today widely acknowledge that the Empire was in many ways
a blessing in disguise, exposing India to democracy, the rule of law and
a socio-economic system not based on caste.

What, then, did the missionaries achieve that the Empire's best
administrators would not have? Matthew Parris has given one answer,
but there are more.

H. M. Stanley's *In Darkest Africa* (1890) was a Victorian best-seller.
J. Scott Keltie, Librarian to the Royal Geographical Society at the time,
wrote a long introduction to it, where he describes how Stanley had to
fight the tribesmen of the Victoria Nyanza area "to secure a free passage
over a continent that is *virtually no man's land*".[277] The phrase today strikes
us as both arrogant and ignorant, but in 1890 few would have recognised
it as such, and it was the view of a spokesman for a "scientific" body. A
generation earlier, in 1866, even after Livingstone's visit to England and the
publication of *Missionary Travels,* the *Anthropological Review* described

his kind as "Nigger Worshippers" because of his sympathy with Africa's plight.[278] Richard Burton, and other high profile explorers, also took for granted the permanent racial inferiority of black people, and the futility of trying to change their culture by religion or by any other means.[279]

The weakness of many missionaries may have been to harbour views of cultural or even racial superiority, but their efforts (variously amusing or more culpable) to make the African adopt the language of Shakespeare or the dress code of middle England indicate precisely the reverse attitude of the *Anthropological Review*: the Church believed in the African's capacity for change and the missionaries knew it to be worthwhile expending their lives trying to achieve it—sometimes against all odds.

Treating a person in this way as someone who can learn and improve may be somewhat patronising, but is at the heart of education. To be told you cannot learn, or to be treated with that assumption, is utterly damning. Missionaries gave hope and self-belief which a good part of the scientific community failed to do. Yes, missionaries often led lives of privilege (though there were also outstanding examples of the opposite) but in some cases these can be seen as an attempt to model what the Europeans, products of their time as we all are, envisaged to be what the Africans might eventually aspire to. The failure of so many Englishmen to learn the native language was also a mistake but this was a function of education as much as anything. Early Protestant missionaries were often artisan recruits who had neither the intellectual ability, nor training, nor imagination to see its importance. By contrast, Dr Livingstone, who was highly educated, albeit much self-taught, wrote that he found the voyage home awkward because he had hardly spoken a word of English since his arrival in Africa. Linguistic adequacy was later to be recognised as important, and by the mid twentieth century the Gospels were available in 400 African languages, and the acquisition of tribal languages and the translation of Scripture continues today.

One further contribution of the missionaries, which arises from their counter-cultural stance about the capacity for change and development within the African peoples, came to fruition as the colonies sought their independence. That independence was gained more as a result of the activity of the Church than any other single body or pressure group.

Education had always been a primary function of the missions. They may have taught European values and concepts, but many of those truths were universal tools for understanding the world. The village mission school under the acacia tree, or in a hut built of wattle and daub, where the missionary taught Bible stories and the alphabet, was the only road out of poverty, ignorance and superstition for most Africans. From these schools at least fifteen African presidents emerged—amongst them such figures as Jomo Kenyatta, Kenneth Kaunda and Joshua Nkomo. Pettifer and Bradley show that it was the compounds of mission schools which gave rise to most of those who led their countries through colonialism towards independence.[280]

Nor can it be said that the administrators of the missionary societies were tardy in their support of the independence movements. The 1908 Lambeth Conference encouraged the formation of native episcopates and the adaptation of liturgy and organisation according to local needs. Moorhouse has shown that when, after the First World War, local labour was desperately needed on farms owned by Europeans, the Church opposed government moves which would exploit African labourers. By the 1920s missions were recognising that giving Africans responsibility for their own affairs was the best policy,[281] and that Britain had to see them not as instruments of its own economic advantage but as fellow beings, to be assisted to the highest possible development. Moorhouse's final chapter on "The Achievement", though sobering, is heart-warming in equal measure, especially in the way he shows that the architects of missionary policy, from both Protestant and Catholic wings of the Church, soon became the most pressing force on colonial governments in the preparation of their subjects for political independence.[282]

Missionaries have suffered from bad press in recent years. The evil that some undoubtedly did lives after them, but as a class their achievements in the betterment of millions of lives were unrivalled by anyone else working in the developing world. They were frail, flawed, occasionally downright stupid, but what they gave Africa was the opportunity to enter the modern world as equals. Without the Church, and with only the state to guide or nurture them, Africa would not have been offered that in the same way, if at all. As the then Bishop of Stepney wrote in 1905 in *Empire and the Century*, a 900-page collection of essays "on Imperial Problems and Possibilities by Various Writers": "We look to the Church to help in counteracting the dissolving and disintegrating influence with which our Western civilisation inevitably affects the races whom it touches."[283] Though he sees Empire and the Church as needing to work together he has no doubt as to whom we should look for the antidote to the destructive powers of imperial rule, saying that "native Churches (must) develop on their own lines, untrammelled by the limitations of merely British religious history."[284] His essay is flanked by one on commerce and another on defence, by different authors; perhaps that is indication enough as to why he is able to predict the equal partnership of churches in the Empire being achieved before an equal partnership of any other kind. A later archbishop, William Temple, at his enthronement in 1942, spoke of God building up a Christian fellowship of the world-wide Church which was the major development of his time. Today, the Churches in countries that once were colonial are some of the strongest in the world.

Wilberforce and Abolition

It may seem odd to return to slavery and its abolition after quoting a text dating from one hundred years later, but no book dealing with the failures and successes of the Church could neglect to consider such a world-changing event and the Christians who achieved it. The Slave Trade Act of March 1807 was not just the first great reform of the nineteenth century in England, but the greatest of those reforms. Its explosive power provided the impetus for so many reforms that followed—a process of reformation based on Christian principles which continued for the next century and a half. Despite the magnitude of the task and the impact of its successful conclusion, there are those who ask why it took so long, and why it is that the Bible does not condemn slavery.

1807 was a culminating moment in Wilberforce's long campaign which was itself the result of his conversion to evangelical Christianity. It was a campaign based on hard work, evidence and principle rather than sentiment, one which demanded years of poring over documents and studying the allegations of cruelty, atrocity, rape and murder. It cost Wilberforce and his allies their peace, their social and political reputations, and their health. The fact that they achieved this greatest of reforms against the whole weight of history, when every economic argument from America, Spain, France and Portugal was ranged against them, is rightly celebrated today. The British government too can be applauded for pursuing the policy on the high seas straight after the Act. Royal Navy squadrons intercepted slavers who plied the Atlantic each year with their chained cargo of 60,000 slaves. Over the next fifty years the navy would free some 150,000 slaves in this way. For many years two hundred ships were engaged in the task.

Initially, much of the reaction to the legislation was uncomprehending. Not only those employing slaves, and those whose unresting factories (through the use of cheap child labour) depended on the raw materials the slaves produced, but much of polite society from French statesmen to Oxford dons failed to see quite what the fuss was about. Most otherwise humane people had taken slavery for granted. If we go back to 1720, the date of Daniel Defoe's *Robinson Crusoe*, the hero shows no misgivings about it: the humane treatment and ownership of slaves is deemed to be perfectly godly. At the end of that century Nelson and Napoleon were both supporting slavery. Two accounts from 1840s America included in Carey's *Faber Book of Reportage*, one of the sale of a boy in front of his despairing mother and the other of the torture of a black slave girl, show the absolute indifference of most of those watching the events to the suffering that slavery imposed.[285] A. W. Kinglake, in *Eothen*, seems himself to be indifferent to the plight of the slaves in the Cairo slave-market at about the same date.[286] The essayist R. W. Emerson, in his essay "Race", writing about America in the 1850s, reckoned its population to be about twenty million, "exclusive of slaves"—who presumably didn't count.[287] A. N. Wilson quotes the "kindly minded" Thackeray's view: "Sambo is not my man and my brother."[288] As late as 1911, the *Encyclopaedia Britannica*, in its entry on South Africa, included the following: "The black man is not simply a morally and intellectually undeveloped European, and education, except in rare instances, does not put him on an equality with the European."[289] Three years later, in 1914, Indian troops shipped over to France to fight a remote European war were to find that white nurses were not allowed to treat them medically. Nearly 10,000 men died in two

months.[290] A combination, therefore, of a more pronounced indifference
to human suffering, the belief that black races were self-evidently inferior,
and "compelling" economic reasons, was sufficient to underpin early
nineteenth-century society's view that slavery was a permanent and
natural fact of human existence.

Nevertheless, we must ask why the Church took so long to achieve
abolition when slaves were being notoriously abused. The Book of Exodus
(ch. 21) had made clear that slaves should not be abused and should be
treated justly. Moreover, provision was made for the dignity of slaves in,
for instance, their being allowed to have a family. Negatively, however,
the answer to the question must be that throughout history Christians
have compromised. The Sermon on the Mount is so radical that achieving
its standards, remaining in the world but not of it, defeats us. Even so,
Christianity from the earliest times has been opposed to slavery in its
fundamental teachings. Slipped in among the pages of the New Testament
is the "Book" of Philemon, described once as a "cover-note" Paul wrote to
ensure the friendly reception (by his master) of the runaway slave Onesimus.
Philemon was asked to accept him back—not merely as a slave but as a
"beloved brother". This was revolutionary. Although it was possible in the
ancient world for slaves to become free, the "freedman" usually remained
dependent on his master, and any idea of a former slave becoming your
brother must have sounded bizarre and unnerving. J. B. Lightfoot, writing
from Trinity College Cambridge, in his scholarly 1875 commentary on
the letter, describes it as "the earliest prelude to these magnificent social
victories" as he looks back at the abolition of slavery in his century.[291]

It is curious therefore that MacCulloch believes this letter to be
foundational in the justifying of slavery on the grounds that there is no
suggestion that Onesimus was to gain his freedom from Philemon. It is
surely more likely and convincing that Paul is here not asking Philemon
point blank merely to liberate his slave but to go much further: to treat
him as a brother and therefore a free man from birth. Paul had led both
of them to Christ, the Saviour and Liberator; he now reminds Philemon
of his Christian obligation to treat the other man as a fellow believer: as
"one in Christ Jesus". Paul was not known for making light demands of
his fellow converts and this is no exception. Why was such a slight letter
preserved and revered if the recipient had not acted on it but had gone

against Paul's wishes? Such a view accords with Paul's reminder to the Galatians that there is neither "slave nor free", but that there is equality of status in the new kingdom which Jesus has inaugurated.

Why then does Paul not urge all Christians to rise up against slavery? Is this not more evidence of the opium of the people influencing them to accept their lot, miserable though it may be? The answer to that is very positively "no", because even for a figure as radical and counter-cultural as Paul, the eradication of slavery would have been not only unthinkable, but unworkable in New Testament times: it was the economic basis of the whole Roman world in which, unlike Hebrew slaves, Roman slaves had no protection under the law and no conjugal rights or rights at all. Wealthy Roman landowners often had thousands of slaves. To remove slavery would not only bring about the ruin of the Roman world and the immediate invasion of barbarism, but it would also leave millions of slaves without employment or security or any means of making a living. The British government compensated slave owners; no such help would be forthcoming from Roman emperors. No, the way forward was to convert the world to Christ; to change entirely the way men saw each other and so destroy slavery by mutual reappraisal of our origins and purpose. All people would realise "in Christ" that no one owns anyone; all people everywhere are not their own for "you have been bought with a price". We do not own others; just the reverse—we are owned by God.

What Paul and the first generation of Christians achieved was to inculcate just that attitude. Many Christians were slaves themselves, but in being Christians too, they enjoyed "brotherhood" with those who were not. Many Christians also freed their slaves. In the post-apostolic age, St Patrick, a one-time slave, was fiercely opposed to slavery. Jonathan Hill, in *What has Christianity Ever Done for Us?*, states that slavery had virtually died out by the Middle Ages in Europe—as a result of continued faithful teaching.[292] When Spain re-introduced slavery in the fifteenth century, three popes successively condemned it—but to little effect. Despite further papal declarations, settlers in the New World justified the enslavement of blacks by claiming them to be less than human, or at least deeply inferior (a claim which, as we have seen, continued in some form right into the twentieth century). In the eighteenth century, John Wesley was deeply affected enough, on reading a Quaker account of the evils of slavery, to write his own *Thoughts Upon Slavery* two years later in 1774, in which he is absolute in his loathing of the practice, to the point of saying that Britain should be "sunk in the depths of the sea" rather than pay so high a price as slavery for its prosperity. He reminds everyone that "slaves are procured by means nothing near so innocent as picking of pockets, house-breaking or robbery upon the highway." Three years later in another book he calls slavery the worst reproach to Britain in its history—an "execrable traffic".[293] Men-buyers, he says, are on a level with men-stealers. Later, in his final days, he urged Wilberforce to continue his fight against it. By 1789, Wilberforce had already presented his first Abolition Bill to the House of Commons.

Wilberforce fought for the right to be heard in spite of the denunciations of him by Paine, Cobbett, Hazlitt and others. To such people, he was "an ugly epitome of the devil", expending his time upon "fat, lazy niggers" while Englishmen starved at home without his help.[294] The allegation was entirely unjust. Indeed, he rarely gave less than a quarter of his annual income to the poor, and in one year found that he had given away substantially more than his income. One can only wonder whether Paine and Cobbett did the same.

Despite the recent revival of interest in Wilberforce through biography, documentary and film, those who like to find fault with the Church have continued to do so with him for saying that he considered the conversion of India to Christ a priority above the abolition of slavery. A modern mindset understandably finds this idea difficult. How could the nature of another person's religion possibly be more important than the fate of millions of slaves, who, as Wilberforce himself put it, suffered under a system of "the most unprecedented degradation, and unrelenting cruelty"?[295] One way of answering that is to be theological and say that there were more "slaves" in India than there were in the plantations, but we must do better than that.

The first thing to realise about Wilberforce's remark is that it was made *after* the 1807 Bill had been passed. Making a rhetorical point to highlight a currently neglected need by comparing it with some great thing which has already been achieved is a very different matter from making such a point before the great deed is accomplished. Having abolished the legal basis of the slave trade, it seems entirely acceptable to call something else more important in order to focus attention upon it.

It is also worth thinking about the nature of liberty and the cost to the Abolitionists of struggling to procure this for others. There is danger of a terrible hypocrisy in those who still want to criticise Wilberforce for placing theology before humanity. This was no armchair philosopher fatly pontificating about the heathen while sitting on his hands. He had been given, despite early bereavement, most of the social and intellectual advantages one could ask for, and sacrificed them in a forty-year struggle which cost him dear as he exposed as lies the claims that slave ships were "a comfortable conveyance", rather than places of "pestilence, disease and despair".[296] Like Augustine, Wilberforce saw the world as a place where liberty came through grace and not vice-versa. To be properly free, a man must be saved first in a world where all are enslaved one way or another to sin: behaviour we are responsible for but would rather not have held to our account. Before this is dismissed as twaddle, humbug, or the opium of the people preventing them from claiming their rights, Wilberforce's opponents in this would need to explain that paradoxical clause from the *Book of Common Prayer* about service being perfect freedom. Serving God, according to Jesus and the New Testament writers, is finally evidenced only by the way we treat our neighbour. It is the root of real and ultimate freedom as we escape the tyranny of ourselves and learn what it is to be who we are intended to be. To achieve this freedom there has to be service, and service means action in the here and now. Thus, to make people free to do this by means of accepting the gospel not only confers an infinite benefit upon them, but also necessitates right action from us towards them in their material needs. In giving them the gospel, or freedom from spiritual enslavement, as well as freedom from physical chains, their attitudes towards others and their circumstances are transformed. The freeing of slaves still goes on today in a number of countries, but where a spiritual slavery is ended as well as a physical one (as in Nepal), the experience of the doubly redeemed is notably more profound.

Wilberforce's actions throughout his long political career exemplify his concern for both the material well-being and the spiritual liberty of humanity. It was his own conversion into "the glorious liberty of the children of God" which motivated him.[297] He wrote in his famous *Practical*

View that to the real Christian, "the doctrines of the Gospel constitute the centre to which he gravitates."[298] He wrote to his mother that being thrown into public life as he was, it would be no less than desertion if he were not to use his position for the betterment of others.[299]

Having begun adult life as a member of the fast set who was more interested in the races, balls, gambling and parties than he was in philanthropy, Wilberforce was converted to evangelical Christianity largely through the influence of John Newton and Joseph and Isaac Milner, the latter of whom (a Cambridge professor of maths and President of Queens' College) worked with Charles Simeon. But his new experience of spiritual liberty did not let him luxuriate in it. The popular view that he was obsessed by the need merely to convert others and free foreign slaves does not match the facts, which are that Wilberforce was actively involved in prison reform, elementary education, factory legislation, the prevention of cruelty to children and animals, the reform of the penal code and the organisation of relief for the poor.

Ian Hislop, in his introduction to *The Victorian Do-Gooders*, was unequivocal that Wilberforce had been the driving force behind what he called a moral revolution in Victorian England and that its impact was as great as the French Revolution, or even the Industrial Revolution. But unlike those events, he reminded us, it had been by and large forgotten.[300] Yes, "the good is oft interred with their bones." Shame on us all.

Social and Political Reform

Tucked into a passage of *Literature and Dogma* where Arnold is at pains to tell us that orthodox theology has thwarted our perceptions of what is truly right and wrong, he writes: "The world has accepted . . . the pre-eminence of Righteousness", by which he means the social and individual ideals of Jesus' teaching.[301] This is an extremely interesting insight, the implications of which are seldom considered today. The impact of Christian teaching throughout the Western world makes us accept that people world-wide acknowledge that certain humanitarian norms are to be upheld and that our view of civilisation derives from these principles which are in origin Christian. He goes on to say that "the immense experimental proof of the necessity of it . . . has steadily accumulated."[302] More specifically he says that living according to conscience, renouncing the idea that our own desires are of paramount importance and a mildness of temper are the key elements of righteousness. At the time when Arnold was writing (1873) he had good reason to think that—but only because Christians had started a transformation which is still with us today. This legacy, however, is so pervasive in the West that we can no longer see it without an intent gaze. Where watercolours blend in to each other it is hard to pick out the single hue which was laid down first. Acts of welfare provided today by governments, programmes of social service, are the "parricidal children" (as they have cleverly been called) of the Christian reformers and take their hue from their forebears. If we had lived in Soviet Russia, or any society without Christian norms, having previously experienced them, we would acutely and immediately feel their absence—as Peter Hitchens did living in Moscow as a journalist in the 1990s.[303]

Whether we consider prison reform, the penal code, care for children, relief for the poor, housing for the homeless, medical attention, universal education, action in slum areas, the prohibition of cruelty, the lot of women, or the extension of the franchise, we soon find that the Evangelicals, the Nonconformists, the Christian Socialists, the Puseyites and other Church groupings were deeply involved, not just in financing but in serving at every level of these great causes. What we now take for granted as standard decent behaviour in humanitarian issues, the benchmark that public figures, at least in Britain, like to be seen to aspire to, and which they assume others will support, was by no means always the unspoken norm of social consciousness. Tolerance may now be a hallmark of the values we espouse but it derives from the faith of Christians both famous and anonymous.

It is not the purpose of this book to explore or list the achievements of the very large number of outstanding men and women who changed our view of the suffering of others, but to remind us that the attitudes they encouraged, and supremely exhibited, were Christian ones, and that they did what they did because they were Christians—and not out of some general sense that we all owe each other greater kindness. Wilberforce, by his own admission, was irritable by disposition but "took particular pains to be cheerful and pleasant" for the sake of the gospel.[304] Changes in society have causes, and the cause of this change in all the areas we've discussed was Christian compassion. From this predominantly Christian influence "the world has accepted . . . the pre-eminence of Righteousness" and the evidence of its impact is all around us. Shaftesbury spoke for all Christian reformers when he declared to the Commons on 4 August 1840 that the "white slaves" in the collieries and mines of England were "created, like ourselves, by the same Master, redeemed by the same Saviour, and destined for the same immortality".[305] Like Wilberforce, Shaftesbury paid a huge price for his dedication. Fifty-seven of his sixty years in office were spent without pay, and his father, deploring his son's evangelical zeal, excluded him from the family home for years, and refused him financial help so that he had to borrow in order to educate his children. Despite his First in classics from Oxford, a seat in Parliament at twenty-five and a role in government at twenty-seven, he declined repeated offers of advancement in order to keep himself free of corrupting influence. Yet his "Ten Hours Victory" in the Factory Act of 1847 is no more than the most famous of many victories. His career includes three previous Factory Acts, the Mines and Collieries Act (saving women and children from near slavery underground), the Chimney Sweep Acts (saving boys' crippled health and early deaths), the Lunacy Acts (preserving the dignity and care of the insane), Lodging House Statutes, and Agricultural Gangs Bills protecting children in the countryside. His exploration of the London slums gave new impetus to the drive to establish "ragged schools" for the poorest, and he was President of the Ragged Union, the YMCA, and the Religious Tract Society, among many other responsibilities. He limited the worst excesses of laissez-faire capitalism in an age when, as A. N. Wilson says, its only opposition came from Communism and Christianity. Wilson also remarks that Lord Atlee and Sir Stafford Cripps were more indebted to Shaftesbury than they were to Marx.[306] In the same breath he might have mentioned Keir Hardie, first leader of the Labour Party, who converted to Christianity when he was twenty-two, or Ramsay MacDonald, first Labour Prime Minister, who saw real democracy as being dependent on vital Christianity, in particular, the Free Churches.

What happened in the middle and later parts of Victoria's reign was that through this dissent from prevailing and powerful opinion, whether it was via Nonconformism (a product of the Evangelical revival), High Anglicanism, Christian Socialism, Catholicism, the Quakers or the Evangelicals, a transformation took place at the hands of Christians which changed the face of England. Some mock the moral earnestness that characterised those bringing about this change, but that mockery is a mark of how much we are in their debt. The battles they had to fight do not threaten or appal us in Britain now so the laughter is facile, unthinking. *Oliver* may now be a musical, but they would be fools who thought that Dickens' novel was written so that we could see the inside of a workhouse only to sing along to a jaunty tune—merely to *enjoy* it. In times when your coal may have been fetched underground by a child of six, or your chimney climbed and swept by a boy of eight; when orphans died of starvation or cold in the street; when men were transported for petty crimes born of social injustice; when unguarded factory machines were operated by children for inhuman hours in appalling conditions; when London's poorest lived in unsanitary hovels if they were lucky; when married women were without property rights; and while those in power saw no reason for change, indeed saw strong reasons *against* change, then times were serious, "the worst of times". Even in 1873, about 4,000 people owned half the country. In effect, therefore, a long war against injustice had to be fought, and to be anything other than earnest about such things would be a betrayal. But as a result, decade by decade, things improved.

This earnestness, this sense of mission and the unstinting dedication of our Christian forebears produced a network of charitable institutions— schools, hospitals, orphanages, and rescue houses—which attempted to heal the wounds of a broken society. One measure of how central these concerns were to Christians is that they united with Utilitarians and those with whom they had little in common in order to achieve their humanitarian goals. As A. C. Dawson has said, they were "flint and steel" to each other and from their coming together sprang the spark of moral idealism and a passion for reform which swayed the less concerned.[307] Alone, however, among the Christians engaged in the work, it was the Evangelicals who were successful in pressurising Parliament to pass legislation. A. N. Wilson concludes his chapter on the politics of the 1880s with the view that "the real agents of change were extra-parliamentary" and cites the churches alongside the Trades Union and women's colleges.[308] But looked at over a longer period, it was the Church in one form or another that was pre-eminent in forcing the issues on the public consciousness. As Elie Halevy says in *A History of the English People in the Nineteenth Century*, speaking of the Evangelical Revival: "We shall explain by this movement the extraordinary stability which English Society was destined to enjoy throughout a period of revolutions and crises."[309] Later he speaks of Evangelical religion as the moral cement of English society, which restrained the plutocrats and placed over the working classes a group of leaders in love with virtue.[310]

Secular historians are very ready to say that it would be a mistake to suppose that religion alone produced the new philanthropy and humanitarianism; that Voltaire and Rousseau, Bentham and Mill, were also philanthropists. Of course there is some truth in this but it is impossible to envisage the age developing as it did in terms of concern for our suffering neighbour, both at home and abroad, without the compelling influence of the gospel motivating its greatest figures and impacting through them others who would help because of their example. It would also be difficult to find any of the non-Christian philanthropists who sacrificed so much as did Wilberforce and Shaftesbury, Howard and Fry, Nightingale and Booth, as well as thousands of others in England and across the Empire.

In addition to these, the very greatest demonstrations of compassion and service, there are hundreds of other examples of Christian love acted out through the formation of charities that date from this period. The London City Mission, the Glasgow City Mission, the RSPCA, the YMCA, The Mothers' Union, The National Children's Home, the NSPCC, Dr Barnardo's Homes, the Salvation Army, the George Muller Children's Homes in Bristol, are but a few of the best known of these—all founded by Christians. The number of meals, beds, homes, blankets, jobs, and the less calculable amount of advice, direction and hope afforded freely by these charities and others will never be known in total, but the millions who have benefited over the last 150 years or more have often told their story. Of the roughly 500 charitable organisations founded in the nineteenth century, three-quarters were Evangelical in their establishment.[311]

In this respect the Victorian Church in England was a beacon which the rest of the world has often followed without due recognition or even acknowledgement.

CHAPTER 10

Global War and the Abridgement of Hope

The Sorrow Of God: A Sermon In A Billet

Yes, I used to believe i' Jesus Christ,
And I used to go to Church,
But sin' I left 'ome and came to France,
I've been clean knocked off my perch.[312]

G. A. Studdert Kennedy

In 1919, Hodder and Stoughton published a 241-page book called *Up Against It, or Questions Asked by the Soldiers.*[313] The book was a compilation of lectures given to serving soldiers in France in the YMCA huts where, according to one review of the day, stuck on the flyleaf of my 1919 copy, "a considerable number were University men or highly educated . . . and a very considerable percentage had definitely rejected the dogmas and definitions of the Christian churches". The men "gathered in large numbers to hear" the talks. There were two speakers or authors, one of whom was my grandfather, the Reverend Professor F. J. Paul, who had become a temporary chaplain to the Forces in France. The aim of the book was to address the intellectual and moral objections of the soldiers to Christianity—men who by the time the talks were given had the Somme and Passchendaele behind them; men who were part of an army that was experiencing on average the loss of 5,000 men every day.

The talks are instructive, but for our purposes, and for history, their titles are almost more so. "Is the World an Iceberg or a Ship?", "Can God be Good When There is so Much Suffering in the World?", "Has Christianity Broken Down?", "Is the Bible a Back Number?" and "What is Wrong With the Churches?". Such questions as these, posed by the troops, while in one sense being perennial, afford an immediate insight into what thinking men were asking themselves in moments of reflection among the onslaughts and horrors they both endured and perpetrated, actions described by the poet Wilfred Owen as "superhuman inhumanities, immemorial shames".[314]

The fascination which the First World War exercises over our generation is manifest—in the stream of novels, films, documentaries and revisionist history books which it gives rise to. That is understandable enough when 2010 and 2011 saw the very last combatants of that war slip beyond our reach as they were finally laid to rest. The first-hand experience of any of its battles is now beyond any living memory and we are curiously reluctant to let it go. Of course it is a matter of scale: the statistics in terms of casualties are unimaginable (Wade Davis says 10,000 new junior officers were needed every month to fill the boots of the dead), but so is the scale of armaments and expenditure (three million shells fell in five hours on the British Fifth Army in the 1918 Spring Offensive).[315] The futility of so much of the action still makes one's gorge rise in anger, and the incompetence of many generals leaves one open mouthed in dismay. As Vera Brittain wrote in her elegiac autobiography, *Testament of Youth* (1933): "There is so much . . . to cry for here that one might weep for ever and yet not shed enough tears to wash away the pitiableness of it all."[316] "My subject is war, and the pity of war", wrote Wilfred Owen—and the horror and the pity continue to compel and have filled innumerable books.[317] What needs to be considered in this book is the impact of the war on the Church and people's perception of it. Those "Questions Asked by the Soldiers" were asked with good reason, and they were not alone in their doubts. What happened spiritually to "the lost generation" and why? How did this evil done by men change just about everything?

There is an interesting passage in one of Owen's letters in which the poet reveals that it is behaviour and action that create and destroy faith (his at least) rather than ideas. Speaking of a "Northumberland lad" he saw in

Keswick, he wrote: "The watching of his conduct, conversation, expression of countenance during meetings, bids fair to speak louder to my soul than the thunderings of twenty latter-day Prophets from their rostra upon these everlasting hills."[318] It is a concept that we shall bump into again in time of war with regard to the Jews, and again when we consider the impact of secularism. Owen found that the collapse of his adolescent faith was not the result of the sort of evidence the Victorians struggled with, but of the actions and attitudes of the people he had to live with after leaving home. The absence of love, the predominance of self-will, the imposition of violence, and the prolongation of these things into daily norms create a mindset which often, though not ineluctably, leads to disbelief irrespective of intellectually held convictions. The two World Wars subjected millions to conditions which mirrored bestial life and promoted bestial attitudes through the imposition of violence on an unprecedented scale in a world which had learned to live without it. Those few who survived a long period in the trenches and then returned home frequently found the world they returned to so uncomprehending of the horrors endured, and so utterly divorced from the reality they had experienced, that to speak about it was an absolute impossibility. Remarks to Siegfried Sassoon such as "death is nothing", made by manicured well-meaning religious ladies curious that the recuperating soldier had a certain dislike of discussing the topic, were hard to stomach and impossible to reply to. The same was true when, trying to avoid difficult topics of conversation after dinner, his hosts would speak about the "the ineffectiveness of ecclesiastical administrative bodies", a topic that must have seemed of utter inconsequence to a participant on the Western Front.[319] But as Sassoon noted in his memoirs, there was little else that elderly people could do when the reality was that, as Owen wrote from the Front in a letter of 29 October 1918, "Shells made by women in Birmingham are at this moment burying little children alive not very far from here."[320] Robert Graves, in his autobiography, simply remarked that at home "civilians talked a foreign language".[321]

Despite this, writers of genius—Graves, Sassoon, Owen—and hundreds of lesser poets forged lines of blood and steel in a white heat of rage and pity. The rest kept silent, aware that every word was utterly inadequate for the weight they needed it to bear. Occasionally, one broke ranks after decades of repressed horror or guilt in the way that Harry Patch did with his account *The Last Fighting Tommy*, written two years before his death, aged 111.[322] Patch was the only surviving veteran of the trenches when he published the book; the only remaining person able to recall the mud of Passchendaele and the sound of the whistle that thrust hapless thousands over the top, who "breasted the surf of bullets" as Owen described it, while "the whole sky burned / With fury against them."[323]

For many, "hell's upsurge" into life made faith impossible. Patch was one such. At the start of Chapter 8 he describes being demobbed at the end of the war. He writes:

> I left the army with my faith in the Church of England shattered. When I came home, I joined Combe Down church choir to try to get the faith back, but in the end I went because I enjoyed the music and had friends there, but the belief? It didn't come. Armistice Day parade—no. Cassock and surplice—no. I felt shattered, absolutely, and I didn't discuss the war with anyone from then on, and nobody brought it up if they could help it.[324]

A testimony heart-rending in its simplicity and sadness. Like Owen, Patch had not been convinced in his disbelief by ideas, but by actions; by the endless brutalisation that war inflicts. Vera Brittain, the most famous of the Voluntary Aid Detachment nurses in the First World War, wrote that she had "a touching faith in the efficacy of prayer, which superstitiously survived until the Great War proved to me, once for all, that there was nothing in it". The cause of her loss was not far to seek. While nursing, she reckoned: "Some of the things in our ward are so horrible that it seems as if no merciful dispensation of the Universe could allow them and one's consciousness to exist at the same time." She found herself wishing she had never been born. At the end of the book, after her years of relentless grief, horror, revulsion and hardening to the everyday sights of a battlefield hospital, she describes life as "a brief interval between darkness and darkness in which to fulfil obligations".[325]

Robert Graves, in his autobiography, *Goodbye To All That* (1929), says that Good Friday 1916 was the last occasion on which he ever attended a church service, apart from weddings and so on. But he also says of the regimental chaplains: "if they had shown one-tenth the courage, endurance, and other human qualities that the regimental doctors showed, we agreed the British Expeditionary Force might well have started a religious revival."[326] Actions, therefore, and not ideas or words, would have been the key to men's belief in Graves' view. He is however fair to them in telling us that Anglican chaplains were under orders not to get mixed up in the fighting, but of course those who did (Catholic chaplains wanted to administer last rites where they could) were hugely respected by the troops. Abstract ideas therefore had little to do with loss of faith: it was personal experience of faith flourishing in the midst of brutality which convicted men of faith's reality and relevance. Despite Graves' strictures, others found the presence of a chaplain in rest billets or in a hospital ward a huge comfort. Private Norman Demuth, of the 1/5th Battalion, London Regiment, found himself thinking deeply about God while sitting on the firing-step of the front line, and understood why the chaplains never stayed long in one place—they got in the way of all the frenetic activity. He recollected: "when I was wounded and got to the hospital I thanked heaven for the padres, they were wonderful." Sergeant Daniels, Royal Artillery, spoke of a chaplain "risking his life to come into the front-line trenches", and of how pleased he was to see him. In praying with the padre, the brave sixteen-year-old was given hope. Many found the Salvation Army as good as its name. Trooper George Jameson, 1st Battalion, Northumberland Hussars, speaking of them placed on the side of Vimy Ridge under constant shellfire, reflected: "How they survived there I don't know. Wonderful people. In the middle of nowhere to suddenly walk into a place and get a piping hot pot of tea, it was a great reviver." Church Unit canteens were nearer to the front-line than the Expeditionary Force ones, according to Lieutenant Burke, 2nd Battalion, Devonshire Regiment. "They were marvellous, those people, especially the Salvation Army." Another "forgotten voice" found a padre by his side during an attack in no man's land and under "very heavy machine-gun fire".[327] The padre had brought him a tin of "woodbines"—a popular brand of cigarettes. The most famous of the padres to do this was "Woodbine Willie", the poet-padre G. A. Studdert Kennedy, who published *The Unutterable Beauty*, his collected poems, in 1927. The poem bearing his nickname as its title he placed significantly first:

Woodbine Willie

They gave me this name like their nature,
Compacted of laughter and tears,
A sweet that was born of the bitter
A joke that was torn from the years

Of their travail and torture, Christ's fools,
Atoning my sins with their blood,
Who grinned in their agony sharing
The glorious madness of God.

Their name! Let me hear it—the symbol
Of unpaid—unpayable debt,
For the men to whom I owed God's Peace,
I put off with a cigarette.[328]

The poem has something of Sassoon's bitter irony in the hammer blow of
its final line. It is worth quoting in full because it speaks so frankly of the
dilemma of the best chaplains, the necessary impossibility of their task. To
be chaplains, they could not fight, but in not fighting some suffered regret,
guilt and shame comparable to that of conscientious objectors who were
widely derided. In fact, 185 chaplains died in action and a large number
were wounded. Three were awarded the Victoria Cross and many others
the DSO and MC. In Rose Macaulay's 1916 pacifist novel, *Non-Combatants
and Others*, the Christian character West says "to have one's friends in
danger and not be in danger oneself—it fills one with futile rage."[329] This
was equally true of ordinary soldiers who were invalided out yet wanted
to return to active service in order to support their friends. Wilfred Owen
especially felt this. Sassoon, recuperating at "Nutwood Manor" from a
bullet wound in the neck, found, despite the kindness of his hosts, that
Arras and the Somme "beckoned me with their bombardments and the
reality of the men who endured them . . . Seen from a distance, the war
had a sombre and unforgettable fascination for its bondsmen."[330]

The unique bonding which sharing in battle confers on combatants
is one thing, but vision is another. Vision, or intensity of insight as to the

nature of the world, of reality, was perhaps inevitable, as R. C. Sherriff suggested in the play based on his own experiences in the trenches, *Journey's End*, given the heightened nervous state of those involved.[331] Ultimately it was a state that might end in madness, where in Owen's line in "Mental Cases", "Sunlight seems a blood-smear; night comes blood-black."[332] But another vision was possible, at least for those who survived without the curse of madness, a vision given shape by Studdert Kennedy in his book *The Word and the Work*. Kennedy was awarded the MC and knew the reality of battle. He describes in the book running through a wood in no man's land on 7 June 1917 while it was being heavily shelled, and while he was mad with fright. As he ran he tripped over the corpse of an undersized, underfed German boy with a hole in his head. He goes on:

> It seemed to me that the boy disappeared and in his place there lay the Christ upon His Cross, and cried, "Inasmuch as ye have done it unto the least of these my little ones ye have done it unto me." From that moment on I never saw a battlefield as anything but a Crucifix. I see the Cross set up in every slum, in every filthy overcrowded quarter, in every vulgar flaring street that speaks of luxury and waste of life. I see Him staring up at me from the pages of the newspaper that tells of a tortured, lost, bewildered world.[333]

Such a vision is of course completely life-changing, and something of Kennedy's vision was shared by other Christians working to the same end. If the contribution of those who acted out of Christian compassion in following Christ's searching and mysterious statement, "Whatever you did for one of the least of these brothers of mine, you did for me" (Matthew 25:40) were tallied up, it would have to include, in addition to the chaplains and padres, thousands of doctors, nurses, Red Cross and YMCA workers, and in addition, countless volunteers at home providing for the 185,000 cold and hungry prisoners of war suffering in German prison camps. As always, the unsung smaller deeds of the unrecorded many made a huge difference to untold numbers.

Loss of faith then, though entirely understandable, was not inevitable. The long Studdert Kennedy poem quoted briefly as an epigraph to this chapter imagines God's heart breaking as he looks down on the carnage, powerless to stop it without denying us our freedom. The soldier narrating the poem pities a grieving God:

> I'd rather be dead, wiv a 'ole through my 'ead,
> I would, by a damn long sight,
> Than be livin' wi' you on your 'eavenly throne,
> Lookin' down on yon bloody 'eap
> That were once a boy full o' life and joy,
> And 'earing his mother weep.[334]

Bold lines at any time, especially then. Lines which speak not of God's indifference, but his suffering and grief, and even his shame—which the soldier wants no part of. Nevertheless, though men's views were occasioned by a brutality and horror which corrupted and distorted how they saw the world, their intellectual questions still needed an answer. Many felt that Christianity was discredited by being invoked on both sides of the military divide, the Church a spent force, and the Bible "a back number".

The Professor Paul answered these questions of nearly a century ago in terms which to my mind seem curiously modern. In the first place, he accepts that "we find the Christian subjects of the belligerent Powers approving whole-heartedly of the aims and methods of their respective countries", and he clearly distances himself from that view.[335] But he goes on to consider a cause of the war which historians today also accept, namely the ambition of Germany. This, he says, was virtually a repudiation of Christianity, tracing influences back to Nietzsche's glorification of the super-man with his corruption of the Sermon on the Mount into the aggressive creed: "Ye have heard . . . how in old times it was said, blessed are the meek, for they shall inherit the earth; but I say unto you, Blessed are the valiant, for they shall make the earth their throne." The Kaiser followed this lead in the sense that his was "the ideal of Napoleon, not of Christ; of Corsica, not of Calvary". The temptation was that of old in the desert when all the kingdoms of the world were on display; for Germany "the lure was too strong to be resisted; they yielded, surrendering themselves to an ideal that was the direct opposite of the Christian". Professor Paul then contrasts this with Christ's injunction, "whosoever desires to be first

among you must be the servant of all." Moreover, he says, Christianity
proclaims "the sacredness of human personality, the supreme value of every
individual before God". This is a doctrine which German tyranny would
banish—as proven by its treatment of not only its colonies, but its own
people. The Kaiser's confidence in God therefore was blind presumption,
indeed blasphemy; his fervent piety mere delusion. It is surely hard to
argue with this view, one held despite the fact that both the professor and
his wife trained in Germany and had strong ties with it. When war broke
out, "it was almost civil war to me", he wrote.[336]

Refreshingly he does not exculpate Britain entirely, citing "the flagrant
injustice of our social system and of our industrial life" as indictments of
our way of life. (Studdert Kennedy was emphatic about this six years later
in 1925.) He concludes the lecture however by making the powerful point
that what has failed is not Christianity, but "the attempt to do without
Christianity".[337]

"Is then the Church a spent force in Britain and Europe?" comes as a
question needing an answer. *Up Against It* treats this too with refreshing
frankness. Paul begins with the view that probably less than 10 per cent
of the population have any real connection with the Christian Church
and that even for those involved it is "utterly impossible to say that all is
well". He acknowledges, in fact forcibly emphasises, that the weaknesses
of the Church are at least six-fold: too much attention to creed and too
little to conduct; the prominence of class-distinctions when there should
be none; hostility between denominations; over-emphasis on original sin
which results in a kill-joy attitude; the pursuit of vested interests; and a
negative attitude towards science. Finally he adds, and most importantly,
"the unchristian life of many professing Christians". That is an astonishing
list to read from the pen of an evangelical clergyman in 1917 or 1918. My
grandfather knew very well that for most people, as Wilfred Owen said
in the letter referred to earlier, "the construction they put on Christianity
depends almost entirely upon the lives of the Christians they know."[338]

One further important answer had to be given to the troops if they
were to believe in a God who loved them despite every appearance to
the contrary: they should be able to trust the Bible's picture of him. The
nature of this lecture is perhaps the most surprising of all, given its time,
for here is not a cleric asking his flock to believe in the literal inspiration

of every Biblical word in the way some fundamentalist groups would today, but rather showing an understanding of a Revelation which grows over time and culminates in the incarnation of Jesus; a group of writings which record the gradual revelation of God—neither a hand book of history, nor of science, the Book is nevertheless, the lecturer says, the unique way for mankind to find its Saviour.[339]

If we have diverted from our central concern of the impact of the war on the religious attitudes of the age, the diversion has served to illuminate the doubts of those profoundly scarred by their experience of battle or their loss at home as a result of it. The lectures in the YMCA huts and the publication of *Up Against It* may have answered some of those doubts, but for others unable or less inclined to listen, their experience of the Church was too frequently negative.

Three strands of dissatisfaction seem to dominate the experience of those disaffected: the clergy were either irrelevant, or worse, they were warmongering, or they were simply incomprehensible and incompetent. As an example of the first, Sassoon, on sick leave and reading the newspaper on top of a bus, came across the Archbishop of Canterbury's "Message to the Nation About the War and the Gospel". Smiling sardonically he read a passage in which the great cleric kindly reflected that in the exceptional circumstances of the war people might "make a temporary departure from our rule. I have no hesitation", he wrote, "in saying that in the need which these weeks present, men and women may with a clear conscience *do field-work on Sundays.*"[340] Bitter satire must have been a tempting response—"How generous of him not even to hesitate"—but Sassoon merely remembered the intense bombardment in front of Arras on Easter Sunday that year and wondered if the Archbishop had given sanction for that.

Warmongering clergy evoked stronger responses than those elicited by the merely irrelevant from people who endured the realities of warfare first-hand. In 1917, Owen wrote to his mother that passivity, "one of Christ's essential commands", would never filter into the dogma of any national church. He went on: "I think pulpit professionals are ignoring it very skilfully and successfully indeed."[341] The double alliteration in the line deliberately emphasises the scorn which Owen poured into that sentence. Sassoon, contemplating whether to go to church, reckoned that he would find more religion in the *Golden Treasury* than in a church which only gave approval to men of military age when they were in khaki. He decided it wouldn't help and he wouldn't go. Vera Brittain was irritated by the tranquil way elderly Oxford viewed the prospect of death for its young men, and doubted the message from the pulpits there that the call of her country was the call of God.

The third strand of dissatisfaction was that the clergy simply were not up to explaining how the war and Christianity fitted together. Sassoon captures this perfectly in his poem "They" (1916), in which the Bishop is confronted by soldiers who have variously been blinded, suffered amputation, other wounds or syphilis, and want some answers. The poem's last line is: "And the Bishop said: 'The ways of God are strange!'"[342] An insultingly inadequate response, but not one, we must hope, that was ever uttered in quite those circumstances.

So the problem for the Church was a double one: first, that the brutalities of mass and mechanised warfare had produced a large youthful section of society disinclined to believe in the goodness of God; and second, that its clergy were seen to be irrelevant, belligerent, or unequal to the task of dealing with the war's consequences.

Two things, however, need to be remembered in coming to terms with this. The first is that the very scarring and degradation that so many suffered in terms of their personality also meant that they saw the Church through pained eyes and distorted vision. When life has gone badly wrong it is natural to want to find an object of blame. The Church, the clergy and God, were all conveniently vulnerable to attack. For many, the only actions that could carry weight with men "who rushed in the body to enter hell" and who were "crawling slowly back", as Owen puts it,[343] were military ones which were mostly denied to officials of the Church—chaplains or padres. For lay Christians who served as troops, even if they preserved both their lives and their faith, trying to make sense to others of what was happening, in a reasoned argument, must have been impossibly difficult. Such men went "to hell and back", as the cliché would have it, and the phrase hides a truth which needs bringing out—for those who did survive such experiences *had* in a sense died and come back again as different people. "I don't take the cigarette out of my mouth when I write

Deceased over their letters", Owen confided to Sassoon on 10 October 1918, three weeks before he was killed.[344]

Desensitisation to sudden death was one thing; sexual degradation another. Graves claimed that at the Red Lamp, the army brothel in Bethune, each woman served nearly a battalion of men every week "for as long as she lasted".[345] Other sorts of degeneration took place too. Vera Brittain recounts how at school she told her headmistress that she felt about thirty, and was told in reply that the war had that effect on anyone who realised it at all.[346] In fact, the war aged most people—through physical and mental exhaustion, anxiety, grief and fear; and because of the promises, lies, and disappointed hopes it bred cynicism, so destructive of belief and aspiration and goodness. Brittain, working as a nurse in Camberwell at the time, wrote to her fiancé Roland:

> I sometimes feel that little by little the Individuality of You
> is being as surely buried as the bodies are of those who lie
> beneath the trenches of Flanders and France.[347]

Graves found that the flashbacks he suffered for ten years after the war were nearly always of his first four months in France: "the emotion-recording apparatus seemed to have failed after Loos."[348] This sort of ruination of personality, the attrition of certain sorts of feeling, seems to me to be as significant as the more obvious disabilities troops suffered by way of nightmares, nausea and the fear of spaces and places, in being a cause of their inability to respond to the good news of the gospel, whichever way they encountered it. Something irreplaceable had died in many of those who suffered most, and to revive it, resuscitate it, was a nearly impossible task for those who had not shared in the experience.

This has been illuminated recently in a place no one has looked for it before: in the life of George Mallory and his fellow climbers on Everest in the expeditions of the 1920s. Wade Davis' *Into the Silence* shows that with the exception of Sandy Irvine (who was too young), all the main Everest mountaineers of that time had been through the war and had suffered profoundly. Their attitude to the mountain was formed by it: their probable deaths upon it of little consequence in comparison with what they had all been through. The individuals in those teams illustrate what this chapter has been indicating: a profound personality change took place in so many participants which often involved a catastrophic loss of faith, but might result in the opposite. Mallory wrote on arrival at the Front: "Life seems to have no meaning if war has a place in it."[349] Arthur Wakefield, nicknamed the Archdeacon, would, like Graves, never enter a church again after his war experiences, despite his piety beforehand. Oliver Wheeler suffered no opprobrium from fellow expedition members when he missed the funeral of a fellow mountaineer who died on the approach walk to the mountain. He recorded the death in his diary next to a comment on the weather. Men who had watched others die in their thousands had lost some capacity for pity, perhaps; it would have been at least one of the understandable outcomes of such horror. I know, as a climber, that today on a mountain expedition such an attitude would be unthinkable. Davis discerns a different attitude to death among civilians too in the post-1919 period: cremation suddenly became a far more popular choice (it was hardly heard of in the nineteenth century). But in a world reeling from an *absence* of so many bodies—200,000 simply obliterated by high explosives or lost in the swamps of Passchendaele, 55,000 of whom are remembered on the Menin Gate Memorial—the idea of the necessity of a marked grave had been severely challenged.

But just as Studdert Kennedy had found an alternative way of dealing with the trauma, so also did at least one of the mountaineers. Davis shows that the careers of two of the men on the mountain had been uncannily similar. Both Howard Somervell and Arthur Wakefield were medical doctors; both were outstanding climbers; both had enlisted as army medics; both had been present at the carnage on the first day of the Battle of the Somme; both had been accepted by the Everest Committee to take part in the 1922 expedition. Wakefield renounced his faith and refused to enter a church building of any kind after his experiences of battle. Somervell never returned to Europe after Everest: he spent the next forty years in India, a pioneer in the treatment of leprosy who was moved by Christian compassion to the unceasing work of seeing 150 patients a day for the rest of his working life. Sympathetic though we should be to Wakefield, we should not be deceived into seeing these responses as merely equal and opposite reactions—in the way loose thinking often characterises such things. They are not morally equivalent. Wakefield simply refrained from something he no longer liked doing and turned it into a matter of principle. Somervell re-directed the entire course of his life into the service of others. Nothing could be more different.

As we know, for those who did return home from the Front, whether whole or maimed and scarred, the post-war world offered little: two million unemployed; half a million ex-soldiers on the streets begging for food; unrest, isolation, exhaustion in coping with a combination of past and present, capped off by a peace treaty which thinking people like Sassoon, Graves and Brittain knew would cause another war. The Depression was not only economic. Wade Davis quotes Churchill, speaking to his constituents on Armistice Day 1922:

> What a disappointment the twentieth century has been . . . How terrible and melancholy . . . we have seen in every country a dissolution, a weakening of bonds . . . a decay of faith, an abridgement of hope, on which the structure and ultimate existence of civilised society depends.[350]

George Santayana, the Harvard philosopher and essayist, by 1922 saw the war as not the end of conflicts but the expression of the natural human condition. The same year saw the publication of perhaps T. S. Eliot's most famous poem; he called it "The Waste Land". Sassoon wrote in *The Weald of Youth* that in 1914 he could not have known that the next twenty-five years would be "a cemetery for the civilised delusions of the nineteenth century".[351]

The Church had a monumental task ahead of it if any ground was to be regained and in twenty more years it would be plunged again into atrocities that would engulf even more of the globe. It would need outstanding leaders and thinkers to survive not only the brutalising and bestial influence of another war, but the attacks of the secularisation which flourished in its aftermath. Those leaders were raised up but at times it must have seemed increasingly that they were faced with no less than Goliath.

CHAPTER 11

Tyranny, Secularism and Dystopia

No single event could be more symbolically apt for dashed hopes than the sinking of RMS *Titanic* in 1912. The sudden and utterly unexpected demise of a ship so opulent, so much the embodiment of the first great age of expanding wealth, of travel and of globalisation, fits exactly with the scale of the economic collapse during and after the First World War. The 300-foot gash in its 882-foot side is a powerful metaphor for the extent to which the modern world was wounded—and the inadequate provision and selfish usage of the twenty lifeboats show how careless and hubristic Western society had become. The ship embodied both the pride and capabilities of the Victorians, and yet their unconscious vulnerability as well. As Thomas Hardy put it in his menacing poem of 1915, subtitled "Lines on the loss of the *Titanic*":

> In a solitude of the sea
> Deep from human vanity,
> And the Pride of Life that planned
>   her, stilly couches she.[352]

Something in the late Victorians' psyche had told them that of course their good fortune could not last. Kipling's "Recessional" (1897) has as its refrain "Lest we forget", a warning against the perils of hubris, and the disastrous Boer War two years later, with its concentration camps in which more than 20,000 women and children died of disease, starvation and exposure, foreshadowed the shape of things to come.[353] The fashionable *fin de siècle* cynicism of the aesthetes too had been a warning. But no one could know quite how far and how fast things would change by the end of the new century, and what that change would do to man's sense of his place in the universe.

My intention in this final historical chapter is to offer five brief points of focus: to consider the impact of the Second World War and to gauge how far German Christians were infected by Nazism; to look at the social impact of the steady rise of overt secularism; to consider the Church's impact on society in countering that; to examine some of the charges against the Church in this period; and finally to catch a glimpse of the state of the world-wide Church.

World War II

It would be facile to suggest that the Second World War was the sole or predominant cause of Europe's desire to live in a post-Christian world, but it is fair to say that it played a very large part in the process of secularisation. On average, 27,000 people died every day from 1939–1945: 3 per cent of Europe's population. In that time, as Michael Burleigh noted in the opening chapter of his magisterial 2010 volume, *Moral Combat* (Harper Press), Hitler's intention was to replace Judaeo-Christian ideas of conscience with something far more atavistic. What, however, is more significant than the statistics is the fact that that information about the war's destructiveness of life, property, goodness and hope was, and is, so widely disseminated—as well as the fact that people in Europe had forgotten, or enjoyed living without, violence of this order. Peter Hitchens, reflecting on the decline of Christianity in the twentieth century in his book, *The Rage against God* (2010), does go as far as saying that the two wars did more to damage Christianity than any other single force: the wars simply trampled underfoot virtues such as gentleness, honesty and charity.[354] There is also the fact that in England, at the post-war 1948 Lambeth Conference, the bishops ceded the Church's welfare role to governments by concluding that the state is an agent in providing this under God. The pre-war organisation of 60,000 Anglican district visitors was simply abandoned, and parish institutions fell apart, leaving thousands unconnected to the Church by their earlier pre-war link. Moreover, a nation which had in previous generations enjoyed the social benefits of the Evangelical Revival and then the Victorian philanthropists had either by 1939 become unused to the actuality of war or had blanked out the twenty-year-old memory of the last one. Revealingly, the art historian Ernest Gombrich, writing *A Little History of the World* in 1936, confidently declared that the Enlightenment had been a "truly new age", when torture, ethnic cleansing, and religious persecution were finally eradicated from civilisation. But in an addendum to later editions of the book he confessed that his view had been abruptly changed by the Second World War and subsequent events.[355]

One of those events was of course the Holocaust, an event of such magnitude and significance that it altered the meaning of the word and of all subsequent Jewish and European history. It is a piece of the past that has worried Christian commentators as much as anyone because "baptised Christians" helped perpetrate it. To others of course it can be yet a further indication of God's indifference or absence. How are we to respond to these two very different perspectives? The second is a specific example of the argument from suffering against God's existence—expressed very neatly by Daniel Finkelstein when he wrote that "the idea that there is an all-seeing God who can find your missing dog if you pray to him, but somehow overlooked the Holocaust, does seem improbable."[356] In this rather loaded and loose thinking, however, like is not being compared with like. The two events cannot be meaningfully compared when the factors causing them have no similarities. In the case of the lost dog, there is no intentional human evil which caused it to wander off and inadvertently cause distress. In the case of the Holocaust there emphatically was—of the most determined and resolute kind. The actions of the dog and the will of God were not here consciously opposed. The actions of Hitler, Himmler and the SS most certainly were opposed to his will in the most deliberate way. God may not ultimately be thwarted ("God can raise up children for Abraham from these stones")[357], but in allowing us our freedom, and the goodness that we derive directly from it, he also allows us terrible destructive powers. God was no more absent from the death camps than he was from any other places of horror in history. Indeed, one of the questions that has to be asked by historians is why and how did the Jews in the camps keep their faith through such terrible darkness? Ultimately their faith was stronger than everything that was designed to kill it.

The dismay we feel, from the other perspective, that the Holocaust was perpetrated in part by those calling themselves Christians also needs comment in such a book as this. First, we need to ask ourselves whether we really believe that the vile people involved were sincere practising Christians at the time when they carried out their infamous actions. Some authentically felt that they were, but we need to remember what they had signed up to by simply being members of the Nazi Party and how far that indicates that they had become estranged from their Christian calling and profession.

In the 1939 census of the Greater German Reich, the population declared themselves, in round numbers, to be 42 million Protestants, 2 million Catholics, 2.7 million Neo-Pagans, 1.2 million without belief, and 300,000 Jews. The majority of the 3 million Nazi Party members registered themselves as Christians. Surely these figures tell a story. Had the country been so overwhelmingly Christian as these statistics suggest, how could it, for the six years since Hitler had become chancellor, have tolerated what had happened? The Weimar Republic had turned into a one-party state, a dictatorship, a police state in fact. Opponents of it were not only intimidated but executed. Even as early as 1934, on the infamous Night of the Long Knives, 200 SA leaders (originally Hitler's private army) were executed by the Nazis. Every soldier in this militarised state had, by the same date, to swear an oath stating his "unconditional obedience to the Fuhrer", and from the earliest days Hitler had advanced extreme racialism amongst his policies—which included meeting violence with violence and removing Jews from all positions of leadership. In 1924 Hitler had described the swastika on the Nazi flag as representing the struggle for the victory of the Aryan man. In 1925 he published *Mein Kampf*, in which he describes Jews as symbols of evil and personifications of the devil.[358]

There was therefore no room for doubt that National Socialism policy and practice were utterly un-Christian. Indeed by 1935 the Gestapo had arrested 700 Protestant ministers who opposed these policies. The later removal, torture and murder of many further priests and ministers would never have been possible, nor would the Holocaust, if 44 million

"Christians" had been alert and obedient to God. Those who were
(Niemoller, Schneider, Galen, Fath, Bonhoeffer and hundreds of others)
often paid with their lives—and who can say how any of us might have
reacted to such a deadly mix of seduction and intimidation? The blend
of propaganda, mendacity, ruthlessness, and shameless devilish ambition
is a terrifying combination when linked to irresponsible power. The
Church as a whole failed in this overwhelming challenge, as it confusedly
misunderstood, then connived at, then gave way to Nazi intentions,
delivered as they were from time to time in reassurances for the public
couched in hypocritically cynical religious phrasing. Even so, we should
also reflect that the historic Church's doctrines and practices were not
those that Nazism adopted but rather ones they opposed, not least by the
creation of their own pagan cults and by closing down Christian schools
and Sunday schools. If members of the SS and other criminals had once
upon a time been baptised in infancy, that merely serves to show that,
whether sacrament or not, the action is not efficacious in producing a
Christian life without the willing cooperation and faithfulness of the
person concerned. If a church is to stand and do any good in the world
it has to be more than a club whose membership criterion is subjection
to a ritual imposed by parents on their unwitting infants.

Christians still have to face the fact that Christendom has a long
history of anti-Semitism, and that this must have contributed to the
German collaboration with Nazism. MacCulloch has a brilliant and
characteristically fair analysis of the degree to which this took place, citing
among its causes hatred of the Weimar Republic (producing pro-Nazi
sympathies), the Lutheran contrast between law and Gospel (and thus
between Judaism and Christianity), and a natural conservatism among
Christians even in the Confessing Church (opposing extreme nationalism),
which led ordinary people to feel they had to support a lawfully elected
government, albeit a Nazi one.[359] It has been widely thought that Pope
Pius XII did not help matters, for though he said nothing to the German
government on learning of a plan to assassinate Hitler in 1939, no more
did he speak out by openly naming the Jews as an oppressed and tortured
minority. However, J. G. Lawler, in a trend-reversing book, *Were the
Popes Against the Jews? Tracking the Myths, Confronting the Ideologues,*
makes clear that much of what has been said about papal anti-Semitism

is ideological rather than historical.[360] In particular, despite allegations to the contrary, Pius XII *did* mention the word "Jew" and condemned racism in his very first encyclical of 1939 thereby repudiating Hitler and his policies. Other Christian thinkers also spoke out, men such as Helmuth von Moltke, an officer in German military intelligence, who used his powerful legal intellect to oppose Nazism on grounds of its illegality and smuggled out a letter telling the British that increasing numbers of Germans were realising that not only had they been led astray but that their actions were sinful. Ben Macintyre, the historian and journalist, has told his story and quoted von Moltke's words shortly before he was hanged after capture by the Gestapo to the effect that what the Third Reich was terrified of was the discussion by anyone of "the practical, ethical demands of Christianity".[361] Von Moltke gathered a circle of resistance around him, as did other Christian intelligence officers, as well as soldiers like the Catholic von Stauffenberg, who thought it a sin not to act against Hitler in his assassination attempt. Despite these brave men and some heroes of faith and martyrs, there were far too many who became corrupted bystanders or active participants in racism and atrocity.

The "Long Peace" from 1945, as Steven Pinker has called it, may have constituted the least war-torn years in the history of our species but they have surely not been as creditable as the rational optimists (enjoying the picture of a successful and growing secularity) would sometimes like to make out, given the extraordinary privilege and security that most of the Western nations have benefited from during the last hundred years. The post-war generation expected the world to come together, but in recent years the UN, EU, WHO, IMF and other international organisations have lost authority and failed to produce the peace and global cooperation that we hoped for. To enumerate their failings would simply be to quote the frequent headlines of the last two decades, but most notably the UN signally failed to stop genocide in Rwanda or ethnic cleansing in former Yugoslavia, and year after year failed to confront Saddam Hussein effectively. Nevertheless, democratisation, the nation state, international trade and the work of the UN have managed to pre-empt some conflicts. In addition, travel, medicine, education, housing and welfare, the media, technology, a transformation in the role of women, the collapse of Communism and the growth of human rights have all improved the lot of most people in the West. Given this considerable improvement in the life experience (and life expectancy) of the majority, it is worth asking why we have not done better; why personal happiness seems as distant as ever for so many; and why the sinking of the *Titanic* remains such a potent symbol. How much is secularism, and the *decline* of the Church rather than its existence, actually part of the problem? It is not an issue the media devote much time to.

Secularism and its Consequences

The zeitgeist tells us that the Church is certainly to blame for many aspects of society's ills. Public intellectuals such as Matt Ridley confidently assert in the press that a destructive intolerance has been the hallmark of Christian behaviour for a thousand years—a one-sided and mistaken view which this book has sought to redress (ironically, it was the National Secular Society, not the Church, which Michael White in *The Guardian* characterised as having an intolerant impulse to inflict their views on others).[362] But even if it were more true than not, there is something suspect when intolerance is seen as the ultimate evil, more serious than criminality, drug abuse, fraud, war, trafficking and terrorism, for example. Not only has the Church *not* been at the forefront of these developments, but its work has directly countered them in recent decades, while a secularist outlook leaves the world without any final authority to confront and condemn them.

It is surely not fanciful to realise that a secular worldview which diminishes or negates an overarching meaningfulness to individual existence, which denies our being made in the image of God, which rejects the sacredness of a God-given life, absolute moral standards and life after death, is one that promotes selfishness—if only because altruism is not a demand or requirement that can be made of us within such a view. In fact, one could argue that the New Atheists have sought to hide this through their aggressive stance on the history of religions. But a more reasonable atheist writer like Alain de Botton, though perhaps patronising to believers, sees the weakness of a secular age and acknowledges that religion helps to provide order and meaning, to ameliorate our lives and make sense of what appears to be the tragic and universal condemnation of us all: death.[363] Religion also gives us a code of etiquette about how to behave, soothing rituals to enact, wonderful art and architecture and a sense of mystery. Myths such as that set in the Garden of Eden prompt us to examine ourselves in a healthy and social way, and they contain profound truths. In that particular story the guilt and shifting of blame, the breakdown of relationships, and the resultant fear should speak volumes to a world which spent £8,000 billion on arms in the last decade, a world in which six times as much public money is spent on research for weapons as research for health protection, and a world where on average in less economically developed countries there is one soldier per 240 people but only one doctor per 1,950. If the world were an imaginary village of 100 people, it has been calculated, 48 would live on less than $2 a day, 23 would have no adequate shelter, 17 would be illiterate, 16 would be undernourished, and 13 wouldn't have safe drinking water.[364] In the hugely wealthy West, the abuse of drugs and alcohol, family breakdown, the neglect of children and the old, and bulging prison populations are the commonplaces of our largely religionless lives. Moreover, the disparity between rich and poor is increasing—one of the greatest causes of social unrest. Joseph Stiglitz, one-time chief economist of the World Bank and a Nobel Laureate, in his book *The Price of Inequality*, shows that in America between 2002 and 2007 the richest 1 per cent appropriated 65 per cent of the increase in the national income.[365] He condemns this as morally offensive and economically damaging. Unrestrained human want seems insatiable. As faith has declined in our century so has social cohesion. It is reasonable therefore to remind ourselves and others that the only thing that has not been a steadily increasing social factor in the twentieth century, out of those listed above, has been convinced Christian belief. What has been substituted is the belief that life is only sacred if we choose to call it so; that our genes are selfish and our drives evolutionary; that moral standards fly in the face in the face of biology; that death is the end of all and divine justice meted out in an afterlife mere wishful thinking at best.

Such assumptions underlie Joanna Bourke's book, *What it Means to be Human*, which has no theological reference or even undertones to maintain the distinction between humans and non-humans; it settles for the view that since the distinction is not unequivocal in the natural world we simply have to agree that our humanity and value are to be found in our earthbound selves, the product of biological evolution.[366] This loss of conviction about the uniqueness of humanity brings into question the whole moral framework of a previous age. Instead, convenience and choice become the predominating factors in such issues as euthanasia, abortion, human rights (the UN Declaration being "outdated"), cloning, torture, natural disasters, humanitarian aid, justice and imprisonment. Evil becomes that which I personally don't like or which society is threatened by. It certainly cannot be, in such a view, an external force bent on human destruction. Instead, people express views such as that famine and disaster are "nature's way" (what does that mean?) of dealing with population growth (and are therefore somehow legitimised, or rather our complacency in regarding them is legitimised), and even that the unique scale of violence in human warfare is nature's way of providing food for scavenger species. As abstract ideas these strike me as repellent but they are worse than that if they ever influence even a single individual to be only a shade more indifferent to human suffering. In my view the reality is that they do however provide an evasion strategy which is an unacknowledged excuse for many people's desire to remain irresponsible.

Fortunately, Christians and those of other faiths are not alone in seeing that militant atheism is not only unattractive in its current presentation by its proponents, but socially negative in its effect. As Janice Turner, columnist for *The Times* (who calls herself "a lifelong unbeliever") asked of Dawkins and company: "How are their crass insults . . . adding to a sane and necessary discussion about religion's place in our public life?". Dawkins' infamous remark that Catholicism is the "world's second most evil religion" is a good case in point.[367] How is he qualified to make such a statement with any degree of authority? His books and articles suggest that he knows next to nothing about it. David Aaronovitch, another writer for *The Times*, suggested rather that atheists should want religion around. Although it can be oppressive or abusive, he allows that this is not unique to religion, and that churches, mosques or synagogues can support individuals' consciences and help ensure that when a dictator transgresses moral boundaries the voices of the oppressed are heard.[368] Moreover, where there is no absolute moral code, and where we can change it to suit ourselves, who is to say that the outrages enforced upon a society by a Pol Pot or a Mao or Stalin are any less right than the promulgations of any previous or subsequent regime? As we have seen, it was true even in the terrors of Nazi Germany that it was the Church, or at least part of it, which found a voice to speak out with.

Being part of a gathering who celebrate, remember, hope and pray together is transformative, as Jonathan Sacks, one-time Chief Rabbi, has said. Grief and joy can find their just proportions in such communities, as can forgiveness. Remarkable examples of reconciliation as a result of Christian forgiveness have arisen in countries as diverse as South Africa and Northern Ireland in recent times. It is doubtful whether any secular view of the world could be the fount of such profoundly moving scenes as arose from the shattered lives of bereaved Christians who literally or metaphorically embraced those who murdered their loved ones in both war zones. But Sacks also mentions that self-righteousness is "the most toxic of all emotions".[369] Such an attitude, I would add, is something Christian theology also forbids us, "miserable offenders" that we are.[370]

We should also remember that some of the worst excesses of religious enthusiasm looked at earlier in this book, such as the Inquisition, have their secular counterparts today, even in an age where toleration is often supposed to be the supreme virtue.

In reality, as an age, we are not tolerant at all in a number of areas. At first sight it may seem that it is the murky processes of "rendition" or waterboarding which remind us most of the Inquisition's methods of getting suspects to give us the answers we want to hear, but on reflection, the more subtle intolerance is political correctness, which restricts our freedom of speech and seeks to change hearts and minds. It is curious that in such a secular society, if you tweet some drunken racial abuse about a footballer, you are liable to be locked up (it happened). Exercise your conscience by wearing a cross at work (as Nadia Eweida did) and British Airways may suspend you from work and an employment tribunal find against you. Offer to pray with a patient and your job may be on the line (it happened). Continue with the age-old tradition of opening a council meeting with prayer, as happened in Devon, and someone will take offence, claiming you are infringing their human rights. Call someone "love" or "dearie", or hang a cross in the windscreen of a vehicle you drive for a living, and you may be disciplined. Section 5 of the 1986 Public Order Act made it a criminal offence to use words in such a way that they were deemed insulting and therefore caused distress. The frightening result of this has been that cases as different as the use of a placard to denounce Scientology and the case of Dale McAlpine saying in a public place that homosexual activity is sinful have been brought to court. Truly speech is no longer free when such restrictions obtain. It is ironically the one issue which brings Christians and the National Secular Society into alliance, as Peter Tatchell has said.[371] The law should be reformed when dissent is disallowed. Cullen Murphy's book, *God's Jury*, looks at such inquisitorial techniques in the modern world, and suggests that Silicon Valley, or perhaps the courts, are more likely sources of this sort of outrage than the Church.[372]

Another area of intolerance and restriction of the freedom of speech is in the scientific world, where the medieval requirement that you must assent to religious propositions if you wish to pursue your research has now, in certain quarters, been worryingly reversed. Witness the furore over the 2010 award of the Templeton Prize to Lord Rees, variously President of the Royal Society, Astronomer Royal, Nobel Prize winner, Master of Trinity College, Cambridge, and member of the Order of Merit. In brief, Britain's "top scientist". Yet because he advocates "peaceful co-existence" between science and religion because they are concerned with "different domains", as he calls them, he is attacked by other scientists who deplore his being given the Prize—including Dawkins, who has called him a "compliant quisling" for his tolerant attitudes. He also of course may have been singled out because although he is optimistic about our *technological* ability to provide solutions for the world's growing population, he is pessimistic about whether the science will be appropriately applied.[373]

In February 2012, an official report called "Clearing the Ground" for Christians in Parliament, an All-Party Parliamentary Group, found that there were "significant problems" with both the law itself and its current interpretation in terms of freedom of speech and action by Christians.[374] Following the report, the headline in the *Daily Telegraph* ran: "We Need Reforms To Protect The Rights Of Christians".[375] One final example of this completely inequitable situation is to be found currently in the very place where Britons should be proud to uphold the tradition of liberality:

the university, surely the home of free speech if ever there was one. Yet in 2006, two university student unions, Birmingham and Exeter, denied their university's Christian Unions (CUs) the same rights of holding meetings as other affiliated societies, on the grounds that their leadership and membership, based on adherence to the doctrines of the historic faith, was not open to all, namely to members of other faiths or none! There is an inherent and obvious absurdity in this, namely, that such people by definition would not in any sense want or be able to hold such a position. Yet six years later this situation was still not resolved, nor the CUs admitted as student union societies. It is hard to believe that such a situation can be legal in this country. It smacks of the intolerance of a Middle Eastern theocracy. The "Recommendations" section of the Parliamentary report rightly stated therefore that the government should "provide a simple way for strengthening the protection for freedom of belief and help to foster a culture that more authentically respects a diversity of views and identities".[376] The "Executive Summary" of the report also recommended: "There are specific and necessary steps which the government should take . . . to enable Christians and other faiths to have greater confidence in their freedom to express their beliefs."[377] Such conclusions are not lightly reached by those in public office such as these MPs. The cause of this restricted freedom may be religious illiteracy, but the effect on ordinary people is a lack of tolerance by a tyrannically overbearing majority.

However, it is of course easier to point to the inadequacies of contemporary society than it is to be convincing (or convinced) that these are directly linked to the decline of religious practice or Christian belief. In two areas however the link can be made relatively easily: alcohol abuse and (separately) the decline of the family.

Alcohol Abuse

There are clear indications in Scripture that alcohol, while not forbidden, is to be taken only in moderation and that drunkenness is to be avoided on all occasions. Both Old Testament and New Testament are clear about this. Drunkenness is shameful, and certain periods of Christian history have been notable for the strength of social opinion or of legislation militating against it. In the first half of the eighteenth century, alcohol abuse was so widespread as to be a national scandal. It was the Evangelical Revival which played the single greatest role in bringing it under control. Through the nineteenth and twentieth centuries there was a clear preconception that if you were religious, drunkenness was incompatible with your profession of faith. Today drunkenness is endemic among young people (and older) who feel no moral compunction about what they do to themselves and others by such behaviour. Indeed, the sole aim of the weekend (starting on Thursday if the queues outside nightclubs are any indication) for many under the age of twenty-five is precisely to get drunk—frequently as an end in itself. The current (if passing) slang of "getting wasted" to describe the process is significant. Waste is precisely what happens—waste of time, of money, of health, of work, of life. Yet are the physical conditions of this generation so painful that the oblivion of alcohol is preferable to them? Clearly not if we are to compare their lot with the hours and conditions of work, and the standard of living, of previous generations. So the pain they suffer to make such a state preferable to daily normality must be psychological. Young Christians, by contrast, know they are blessed by God, recipients of a precious gift, on a meaningful journey, and going to a destination that will outshine all earthly cities. Alcohol abuse is a refuge only for those living outside such realities. The statistics are astounding and alarming.

The Office for National Statistics states that over 5,000 deaths in England and Wales year-on-year are caused by alcohol (figures released in 2015 show 8,416 alcohol-related deaths in the UK in 2013). The cost to the NHS is in the region of £3 billion a year, and £55 billion when you take into account crime, public disorder, damage to families, criminal justice, social services and costs to employers. Mortality from liver disease has shown a fivefold increase in people under sixty-five in the past thirty years—when other major causes of death (suicide remains a notable exception) have dropped over the same period. The human misery which ensues from the loss of a job, or driving licence, or relationship, or anxiety about health, an unwanted pregnancy and venereal disease, are other huge areas of concern. Any society suffering this sort of disintegration can hardly be called happy or successful. Any Christian community would not suffer, and has not undergone, this sort of pandemic, for where the Kingdom of God is, alcohol abuse will not be much in evidence.

That sounds, of course, unpalatably smug to a non-believer (and possibly to some believers as well), but it is hard to refute. Indeed, the only reason to want to refute it is prejudice—the prejudice of a secular society that has impoverished itself by being ill at ease in discussing morality and which is wary of art or literature that has an ethical intention. There is of course no doubt that the monotheistic religions have their intentions too and that an element of the Church is insensitive in its handling of them. But a prejudice that clouds judgement exists on both sides. When a journalist as able as Oliver Kamm, for example, can write insultingly that C. S. Lewis was "a minor literary scholar and Christian apologist of rare crudity", we know we are no longer dealing with a rational viewpoint but one that has taken exception to the fact that a figure of some importance has declared his colours (T. S. Eliot suffered comparably).[378]

Leaving aside the quite unsustainable insult not only of the "crudity" of Lewis's apologetics, but the gratuitous addition of the superlative "rare" (both of which words give away the real motive of the attack), if we are to keep our perspective we need to remember that rather more weighty figures than Kamm, such as Helen Gardner, Donald Davie, A. L. Rowse, and John Wain, professor of poetry at Oxford, all applauded his work.[379] Nevill Coghill, professor of English at Oxford, mentioning no less than four of Lewis's critical works, described them as magistral books, saying he did not know of any critic of our times who could equal such an achievement.[380] William Empson respected Lewis, saying he had "read everything, and remembered everything he had read".[381] More recently, Rowan, Lord Williams (one-time Lady Margaret Professor of divinity at Oxford) has described *The Chronicles of Narnia* as a "remarkable achievement" showing "great prescience" about issues of human uniqueness much in focus today, sixty years on.[382] My point is that highly intelligent people such as Kamm will make judgements wide of the mark on finding their world is threatened when someone they admire is found to take a Christian writer seriously. Someone with a higher degree of objectivity would be able to share de Botton's view that religions deserve attention at least for the scope and ambition of their concepts, recognising that their achievements outrank with ease even the greatest secular movements in history.

We have diverted from the case of pointing up that a decline in faith has brought with it certain social evils in order to illustrate for a moment that such a case will not readily be accepted by opponents of the Church, and to alert the unsuspecting that blind prejudice may masquerade as cool objectivity on both sides of the divide.

Let us turn our attention now to a second social evil of enormous consequence: increasing dysfunctionality in the family.

The Decline of the Family Unit

In September 2009, Sir Paul Coleridge, then one of our most senior judges in the Family Division of the High Court, gave the Explore Lecture to the House of Commons. In it he spoke of the family as being in need of protection as a species which is now endangered.[383] He spoke with the authority of one with four decades of experience in the profession. His thesis, which was reported at length in the press, was that family life has been integral to and coterminous with a healthy and stable society, but that in some urban areas in Britain family life is no longer recognisable, for it no longer exists. Family breakdown dominates the courts, which every day see thousands of families seeking their help. The effect on both parents and children is well documented, not least that children from broken homes are less likely to achieve their potential than others. Over the next twenty years, Coleridge said, the impact on people in Britain will be as destructive as global warming and more so than economic decline. Almost every child who we find in trouble with the courts or police is the product of a dysfunctional family life. Such was Coleridge's considered public view delivered to the Commons.

At any one time there are an estimated 3.8 million children caught up in the family justice system. The breakdown in relationships costs £46 billion a year—though this is a trivial statistic when measured against the human costs of misery, aggression, mental health, depression, demotivation at school and at work and so on. Currently at least 40 per cent of marriages in the UK end in divorce, and there is no significant change in the curve of the annual increases. In November 2011, the NSPCC published a report claiming that in Britain 200,000 babies were at risk from parents either addicted to drugs or alcohol, or with inappropriately treated mental health problems, or in a violent relationship.[384] These three problems are more likely than anything else to result in a young child being abused or neglected. Significantly, in the 2007 research findings of the UN Children's Fund, children in the UK were judged to be unhappier than those in any other developed country, and this included measurements of family and peer relationships, educational well-being and behaviours, as well as subjective and material well-being.

Getting married, of course, is much less popular than it used to be: there were only 241,000 marriages in 2010, the lowest number in nearly a hundred years. Divorce figures, however, for 2013–2014 show 230,000 people going through this trauma annually in England and Wales. Cohabitation, meanwhile, tripled between 2001 and 2014 and is expected to continue to rise. A baby born to parents who cohabit is ten times more likely to suffer its parents separating than one born to parents who are married. Data released in 2014 by the Institute of Education and taken from the Millennium Cohort Study of 19,000 children born in 2000 and 2001 shows that now only 61 per cent of eleven-year-olds share a home with both parents. In 1969 it was 90 per cent. Of these eleven-year-olds in lone and step-parent families, more than a quarter have behavioural difficulties, which contrasts sharply with merely one in ten of such children in homes with both natural parents.[385]

The question naturally arises then as to how this situation came about, and Sir Paul points in his lecture to three factors: the arrival of the contraceptive pill, women's liberation, and a change in expectations with regard to how exciting married life should be.[386] He also mentions in passing that we no longer have any underpinning cultural acceptance of Christian values as expressed in the Bible. But this surely is more fundamental than the other points which are symptomatic of that underlying cause. This is not to be entirely negative about these social changes, which brought about good as well as doing harm, but it is to say that getting married in a church, making public vows before God and man about the permanence of marriage and the centrally and mutually unselfish nature of the contract, is a better grounding for family life (and therefore social cohesion) than cohabitation or marriage in a beach restaurant with lots of self-centred pre-nuptial legal provisos. Two-thirds of civil weddings are now celebrated in approved premises including golf clubhouses and football grounds. This association of marriage with recreation rather than religion can hardly be missed. It betokens a lack of seriousness.

It must also be true that the traditional Christian practice, still widely adopted prior to the arrival of the pill in the sixties, of not sleeping with your partner prior to the wedding ceremony, made each person more special and unique to the other than the now commonplace practice of having multiple sexual partners before ever committing to some sort of circumscribed vows in a register office. The sexual act being reserved entirely to a sharing with only one other is a more emotive and powerful seal of the uniqueness of a relationship than any other in the physical material world. The efficacy of marriage in terms of its ability to keep families together was statistically demonstrated in the report from the Centre for Social Justice in 2009, which revealed that only 8 per cent of married parents, compared with 43 per cent of unmarried parents, had separated before their child's fifth birthday. This was even after taking into account data such as income, age, and education. The report, which Sir Paul quoted, went on to say that "The empirical evidence . . . shows that intact marriages tend to provide more beneficial outcomes for adults and children than cohabitation or single parenthood."[387] Those outcomes for children cover health, education, and financial security—familial and relational outcomes too.

Yet successive governments and parliaments have failed to give marriage sufficient active support. Put another way, children living with both birth parents are less likely to have poor cognitive development, education and employment outcomes. Twenty-eight per cent of children in lone parent households live in relative poverty, so marriage is an economic issue, as the USA's Federal Reserve Bank has noted, saying that family structure accounts for some key trends in employment and income. In our own country, one in three children live without their father. In March 2013, 68,000 children were "cared for" by the state,[388] and about a quarter of those in our prisons today began life in this way.[389] Children in Britain's poorest households are three time more likely to suffer from father-absence than those in the most affluent homes. Research by the Centre for Social Justice also shows that it is marriage rates which divide the bottom from the top of society, not just income.

Professor Sir Denis Pereira Gray, one of the nation's most distinguished doctors, has drawn attention to the fact that marriage is also a public health issue. Death rates of children in their first year are significantly lower for married parents in every social class—as analysed in the Child Health Statistical Review.[390]

Marriage is also an educational issue. In November 2014, a survey by Resolution, the 6,500-strong association of family lawyers, found that almost two thirds of children whose parents went through a divorce said that the break-up had adversely affected their GCSE performance.[391] The survey results also suggested that parents' divorces triggered eating disorders and substance abuse in children, symptoms of stress which schools are only too aware of and to which teachers often have to make the first response—a matter for which they are not usually trained. All the evidence from other countries tells the same story. The report made the main front page headline of *The Times*, but successive governments fail to act adequately on these findings. Canada and the USA have invested in the family far more heavily than Britain; Canada's tax benefit for married couples is five times more generous than this country currently sees fit to provide as a marriage incentive.

Dull as they may appear on paper, what these facts together indicate is that Christian faith and commitment are central pillars of the longevity of marriage; that marriage is the bedrock of family life; that family life is central to children achieving their potential, and to society therefore remaining stable and in turn achieving a high degree of happiness and well-being. In fact, Christian marriage has been a gift of inestimable value to Western society. The corollary is that where this Christian commitment is lacking there will be a tendency for this logical sequence to cease to operate with its resultant impact of social instability and individual suffering: exactly the process we see at work today.

Of course, the ancient non-Christian world had marriage ceremonies, but they were not binding or mutually committing in the way that the Christian ceremony has been in Christendom. Nor were they based on the understanding of Scripture (however badly carried out in reality) that there should be obedience and mutual service, as Paul makes clear the Christian pattern is (in Ephesians and elsewhere). But Christian marriage is not only a matter of love, respect and service, it is also permanent, even indissoluble, depending on how Christ's statements are to be taken. On top of this, Christian marriage is sacramental, a profound symbol in the material world of how things are in the spiritual world. The relationship of a man and his wife should be one that mirrors for us day by day the relationship of Christ and his Church. The one lays down his life for the other—as also taught in Ephesians. This sacramental permanent monogamy is in distinct contrast not only to secular marriage, but also to that provided for by the Qur'an, which allows for sexual relations with up to four wives and any number of concubines. There are today only two Islamic countries that have laws against polygamy. But both Muslims and Christians are appalled at a society like ours which allows internet service providers to provide access to dating sites which encourage extra-marital affairs. How can a responsible society countenance such a toxic business as the encouragement of infidelity? In truth, we bring so much suffering upon ourselves. As J. A. Froude wrote of Carlyle's view one hundred and fifty years ago, "Modern society . . . breeds in its own heart the instruments of its punishment."[392] Sir Paul Coleridge's launch of the Marriage Foundation in April 2012, which made the front pages and is backed by senior Church figures, was an unusual and bold step for a judge but hugely welcome.

Further Consequences of Secularity

It is all too easy to point to one's own age as being in a state of moral degeneration so I don't want to spend too long on what Prime Minister David Cameron called, after the city riots of 2011, "the slow motion moral collapse" of society in Britain.[393] Those riots were attributed in major part—by the official enquiry—to the effects of materialism in our culture, but some further points need to be made to indicate that, while there are positives about current secularity, society's failure to preserve Christian thinking and traditions of behaviour has been an unequivocal loss.

Three consequences of this in particular are worth noting. The first is that an absence of absolutes in regard to behaviour means that no boundaries remain unchallenged, and that when an idea which was perceived as unethical throughout the Christian era is seriously proposed, there is no bedrock in a godless society on which to mount a solid opposing argument. Take for example the issue not just of abortion but the killing of newborns proposed by two doctors in the *Journal of Medical Ethics* in 2012. Newborns, they claim, are not really persons at all yet and do not have any moral rights to existence. The article, entitled "After-birth Abortion: Why Should the Baby Live?", written by Doctors Giubilini and Minerva, argues that killing the baby should be permissible in all cases where abortion is, and in addition when a baby turns out disabled unexpectedly.[394]

Perhaps the expression of this idea is almost inevitable, given that in 2012 figures were released for 2010 which reveal that of the 189,000 abortions in England and Wales in that year, 64,000 terminations were performed on women who had already aborted a foetus. 50,000 of these were performed on unmarried women. Repeat abortions alone cost the NHS in the region of £1 million per week and it is becoming clear that the procedure in many instances is becoming just another form of birth control. The thinking here reflects that in other ethical areas where the emphasis has shifted from the sanctity of life as a given, a starting-point from which it is presumed we agree, to a matter, as seen earlier, of choice and of convenience. The psychological damage as well as the financial cost has to be faced. But if the distinction between human and non-human is considered hard to establish, if God is not part of the equation but is replaced by evolutionary drives, then it is much harder to oppose this sort of thinking and conduct. After all, the main secular argument for accountable behaviour which is offered as an antidote to moral decline is that it is necessary for a stable society. But this is an abstract concept which makes very little impact on an individual in the heat of the moment: such a person is not governed by a worldview in which they are morally accountable to a being infinitely greater, wiser and better than themselves, nor will such an idea restrain an action which can be to a degree justified by "situational ethics" and hardly be ranked as important in the greater scheme of abstractly "promoting a stable society".

Where the underlying assumptions are that we have only one life, and getting what we can out of it is the first responsibility for a human being, there will inevitably be a self-serving nature to the tone of society, and a vacation from responsibility towards others. Attempts will be made to preserve an ethical framework by the setting up of government bodies to deal with those who are less fortunate, but these are subtly undercut by the feeling that personal morality is something I work out for myself, that cannot be imposed from outside, and that I don't have to listen to sermons or lectures about. Nevertheless we like to keep our consciences clear in an overwhelmingly consumerist society, and we do this, as John Humphrys points out in *Beyond Words*, by subtle shifts of language.[395] We buy something with American Express, and suddenly "Desire can be Virtuous", as their advertisement put it, since some of the money for the goods was promised to the Global Fund for Africa. Morality thus becomes cost free to the individual, and more significantly, a matter of feeling good about yourself. We can now spoil ourselves rotten and yet reckon this is good for our souls. Very clever. George Orwell would have been proud of such an excellent example of "doublethink". Humphrys also points out that the insidious intrusion of "your" into the names of both products and producers changes the world from being Copernican to being an endless extension of oneself. Marks and Spencer became "Your Marks and Spencer", which it obviously is not unless you are a shareholder.[396] The world increasingly now exists to make us comfortable, rather than being a testing-ground with demands made on our behaviour by its Creator. Such a change is hardly a formula for contentment.

As society becomes more selfish it also becomes more enraged, since every inconvenience turns into an infringement of "my time" or "my rights" or "my space". A study by the Mental Health Foundation found that a quarter of Britons worry about the intensity of their anger. Yet the world most of us live in is more comfortable, more safe, more pampered than ever before. Despite this, whether shopping in the high street or driving the roads, people sense an underlying rage, at least in many of our cities. The journalist Peter Hitchens noticed how civility had sharply declined in Britain during his five years away and attributed it in large part to the way Christianity has so rapidly vanished from public consciousness in the UK[397] Of course we might add that there are causes, one main one being the way in which the internet, TV, cars and pressures of work have all contributed to an increasing ability (or necessity) for isolation from each other, which means we become decreasingly able to cope with intrusion, delay or inconvenience.

Making self-fulfilment the conscious target in place of the virtue of the self-sacrifice of a previous generation has made our society a more violent, more fragmented and less predictable place for our children to live in, and the breakdown of family life is one of the most catastrophic results, as we have seen. We have a greater number of vulnerable children now than ever before in the modern era.

I do not believe that to say society is *not* in decline, because we have the welfare state, free education, tolerance and medical and technological advances, is any sort of answer to the picture I have drawn thus far. Economic prosperity has enabled us to deliver these advances but they have produced their own evils or been abused or have failed to create the solutions to social problems that were expected—not least in the area of education.[398] Our world is a very long way from what it should be, given the resources we pour into attempting solutions to its problems.

A second consequence of our failure to preserve a Christian worldview and traditions is a certain absurdity and lack of sense of proportion which has entered aspects of daily living. Nowhere is this more patent than in the area of "human rights", which I place in inverted commas because some of the grounds for legal cases dealing with them are invisible to the naked eye. Take for instance the gentleman who alleged in court that, along with the content of the lectures on his MA course, the design of the seats he had to sit on to hear the lectures infringed his rights as a male because they did not suit the shape of the male bottom. Or the woman who took legal action against the government in January 2012 under the Human Rights Act because she was forced to do two weeks' work experience in Poundland, which she considered was of no value to her (she lost her case that August, but then won in the Court of Appeal in February 2013).[399] The expression is so revealing because it shows not only an absolute failure to recognise that the job might have been useful in the relief of someone else, but also a complete failure to see that giving our labour in such a place teaches us what millions go through every day: that work is often a grind, that we are no better than the next person, and that even in repetitive labour there can be kindness and joy. Hundreds of cases of this kind could be adduced.

The third consequence worth noting (and it is one that increasingly features in the intelligent press) is that if the atheists were to have their way and manage to erase religion not only from public life but from private consciousness there would be a vacuum. The question has to be asked as to what we would replace it with. Beauty? Art? Morality? Science? Admittedly these are huge issues, and it is only too evident that on a personal level we do not have to believe in God to be moral creatures. Mainstream Christian theology does not say that either. We all know many good people who are non-believers (Christian theology in this respect talks about how God has dealt with those parts of us that are *not* good and how pervasive those parts can become). But, nevertheless, aesthetic views and moral beliefs seem ineffective in making a radical change to individual people's lives. The SS were famous for their love of art and music, and had their own warped morality. The culture of Ancient Greece was a marvel, but it didn't last, nor did it impact on how you treated your own slaves, your women and your children. Christendom has lasted twenty times as long as the Athenian miracle and although there have been all the vicissitudes we have looked at, its achievements in terms of human respect and relationships have utterly outshone Athens.

Professor James Quinn Wilson, once dubbed the cleverest man in America, in his lifelong career working on the moral sense, criminality and the state, came to the conclusion that it is *private* virtue that is critical in establishing public order. Moral relativism is simply wrong, he found, and he marshalled the scientific evidence for his view.[400]

Militant atheists love to tell the world that they are at least as good as religious people, and even better, because they don't need a God to make them be like that; but there is an insincerity and irrationality in their use of language which the first week of an undergraduate philosophy course would expose. They claim the moral high ground against a creed which, according to Richard Dawkins in *The Times*, should win a prize for its futile pointlessness as well as its moral depravity.[401] Strange that so many outstandingly good people have believed and acted on such a creed, then. The irrationality of this was pointed out by Professor Edgar Andrews (author of *Who Made God?*) in reply to the article: you cannot have moral indignation without first having morality, and since Dawkins admits in *The Selfish Gene* that society based on the gene's ruthless selfishness would be very nasty, his moral stance is at complete variance with his beliefs which, strictly speaking, are surely more "futile" on any analysis than the Christian creed.[402] Morality and fairness are, in an atheist's worldview, ultimately about convenience and niceness. Crimes are wrong because they are inconvenient to individuals and society. Furthermore, if genes and environment determine our behaviour, why do we lock someone up when they do "wrong"? In what sense can it have been "their fault"? We already show our hesitance and moral uncertainty in this area by frequently using the word "inappropriate" in place of "wrong" in public notices of dismissal or disciplinary action. A society properly coming to terms with the logical implications of this would be a society in chaos which is why no one wants to. It would also be a society without religious communities—a seeming utopia for those who believe religion poisons everything, but in reality dystopian, since those communities offer charity, promote a sense of responsibility to others, provide a place to belong, and create ceremonies to mark important rites of passage. A society without these would be bereft indeed. There may be inconsistencies in religious belief, but no more so than in the belief systems of the non-religious.

What we see in Britain today, and perhaps further afield, is a society at a crossroads where no one is sure who has right of way. There is hesitance, confusion, anger, lack of understanding and insistence on one's own rights, as our belief in what is acceptable and what is not changes so rapidly. If you silence God, starve and frighten his people, deny any knowledge of him to the children (because it is "child abuse"), and then excise him from history, there will not only be a gap but a desert where merciless winds will blow. Already families are in collapse, alcohol abuse is endemic, education is failing to reach even its reduced goals, politicians struggle to keep their finger in the dyke, and each and every day people are deafened and desensitised by relentless "breaking" news packaged to keep us watching, while banner headlines in the press are more interested in sales figures than the truth.

Today's opiate of the people is not religion but entertainment—albeit in the guise of information. The sole refuge which teaches love based on absolutes could become the one place those in need feel unable to go: the Church. Perhaps it has already for many. Philip Larkin, considered by many Britain's greatest post-war writer, wrote most perceptively (if depressingly) about this in his great poem with its punning title "Church Going".[403] Having entered an empty church he reflects on what will happen when churches fall out of use altogether. Interestingly, in the final stanza, he thinks people will continue to visit the buildings, even if only because they have the reputation that they were places of wisdom in which a hunger to be serious, not merely entertained, might be fed.

If enough has been said to suggest that a post-Christian world which has marginalized the Church, at least in the UK, is far from what it ought to be and that it is the *decline* of Christianity rather than its presence which is the problem, what more can be said in the Church's defence? Fortunately there is further evidence we can bring forward to show the Church to be central to the cure rather than contributing to the disease.

Cure or Disease?

At this point both Christians and non-Christians have to keep a sense of perspective, because matters have to be weighed objectively without recourse to the sort of emotive statements so prevalent in the tabloids. It is undeniable that in some respects, especially in aspects of human sexuality for instance, sections of the Church have badly failed in their witness to Christ and in love of their neighbour. Very strong views about homosexuality dominate press reportage about Church matters from time to time and it is an issue that divides Christians deeply. There has been cruel and unfair discrimination by some Christians, as well as love and understanding by others. Nevertheless, the injustice which some homosexuals have suffered, if it is to be weighed against either the good the Church has done, say, this last fifty years, or the violent persecution it has suffered in that time, is in global terms not highly significant. No cruelty or injustice is ever to be condoned and must be condemned, but such actions and attitudes in this area also abound in the secular world far beyond the bounds of the Church. Recrimination should not be allowed to distract the Church from its task, or society from the rightful recognition of the positive social impact of the modern Church.

Sadly, we have also to come to terms with the repeated revelations, beloved of the press, that priests have sexually abused boys in their charge. This revolts any civilised person and the result has been damaged lives and massive damage to the Roman Catholic Church in particular—especially for failing to deal with the abuses and for covering them up. Yet it can hardly be claimed that other secular institutions (schools of all sorts, and the BBC it seems, included) were not engaged in the same practice of turning a blind eye to the sexual abuse of both young boys and girls by those in authority or enjoying celebrity. Nor can it be said that the Church approved or that it in any way allowed such horrors as part of its doctrine. Indeed, the perpetrators have almost universally hung their heads in shame and knew their misdeeds from the start. Their actions were selfish and damaging and utterly wrong, without excuse, but these failings were wider than just the Church. They were widespread in predominantly or exclusively male institutions where boys and men lived and worked together or where the economics of celebrity was more important than the blighting of a young life. The Church in the instances of this abuse simply failed to be better than the rest of society, much of which turned a blind eye.

Something should also be said about Roman Catholic pronouncements on birth control, in response to which Pope Benedict and his predecessors incurred the wrath of many within and outside the Church. Unlike the previous issue this, precisely, *is* a matter of doctrine and there is no escaping responsibility here when condoms are seen to be evil though they are a means of preventing the spread of AIDS. But surely the weakness of the doctrine is not that it is of itself wicked but that it is too idealistic. The proper way to prevent this suffering, says Catholicism, is abstinence and fidelity, rather than gratification and irresponsibility, which is not the Christian way. There would be no AIDS crisis if sexual relations were confined to man and wife and if single people were celibate. Such a view will never be popular, but we have seen already the impact of the outcome of neglecting this teaching on the family even where AIDS is not rife. Fidelity in marriage and abstinence outside it has been the teaching of the Church from the earliest times. What has been wrong in the current situation has been to try to apply it too rigidly to those without sufficient Christian commitment or indeed any at all. There are signs now that the Vatican might shift its ground a little but it is unlikely to be a rushed process.

Again, perspective has to be sought here, and while many may be critical of the Church's stance on this issue, it is pertinent to remember work done by Catholic priests the world over in supporting and living alongside the poor and dispossessed—not least in South America, where, in the last fifty years, there have been regular clashes between Church and repressive governments, and where clergy pay with their lives for standing up for justice for the poor. Since the Second Vatican Council there has been a focus on the responsibilities of the laity too to work for a just social order. Actions as far apart as help for immigrants in Mexico, asylum seekers in Australia, and North African refugees in Europe have all been taken and originated at high levels in the Catholic Church while being supported by the rank and file members.

We all remember the death of Archbishop Oscar Romero of San Salvador, assassinated as he celebrated the eucharist in a hospital chapel in 1980. He is one of ten twentieth-century martyrs whose image is carved above the Great West Door of Westminster Abbey. He gave his life in the fight against poverty, social injustice and the use of torture.

What further may be said in defence of the Church's concern for those outside its immediate flock, as well as those within? Statistics may be used to support all sorts of things, but in terms of health and well-being the Church would seem to be a winner in saving the coffers of the state by encouraging healthy, trouble-free citizenship. In *The Twilight of Atheism*, McGrath cites a 1998 Harvard Medical School conference report which found that almost all family doctors in America considered prayer, meditation and other religious practices to be beneficial to the healing process.[404] Similarly, the creation of community and the sense of belonging has been shown to be beneficial, and even a country as secular as France has had to take into account the helpful social outcomes of the religion of its immigrant communities.

Large-scale academic or government studies provide one sort of evidence but at the other end of the scale is the evidence of small-scale projects which are so ubiquitous and constant as to be literally uncountable world-wide. Nevertheless, the evidence for these would be forthcoming if anyone were to do the research. A glance through the pages of recent numbers of even a single Christian periodical give a flavour of what the Church is doing in any part of any year we choose to examine. In the magazine of merely one Christian organisation, I counted twenty-eight separate areas of concern and social action for the betterment of the world.[405] They included: Christian volunteers working for an aid and development project in Afghanistan; literacy in Burkina Faso; raising funds to combat leprosy; orphanages and schools for "Untouchables" in India; help for the victims of terrorism; working towards an end to violence; help for those in prison; conflict resolution in the home; affordable housing; how to cope with redundancy; debt counselling; food distribution; parenting courses; teenage relationships; the promotion of family life; strengthening local communities; encouraging political engagement; befriending internationals in Northern Ireland; work in education; working alongside drug addicts, gypsy communities and alcoholics; street pastors in city centres; helping those with physical and learning disabilities; welcoming Olympic athletes; how to make films which promote charities; and a ministry to journalists!

A glance at a later issue added many more topics, such as the continuing struggle against racism, help in hospitals and nursing homes, support for persecuted minorities, reconciliation processes in Northern Ireland, further humanitarian work abroad, combating human trafficking, the work of Christian Aid, care for migrant workers, ethical banking and business practice, and honest electioneering. That particular magazine also happened to be an edition which marked the death of John Stott, who in an issue of *Time* in 2005 was accounted to be among the one hundred most influential people in the world.[406] He was a humble evangelical vicar of a London church who transformed the lives of millions by his faithful "double listening", as he called it, to both the voice of God and the needs of society.

We should also not forget the financial contribution made through the Christian practice of tithing incomes and other giving. In his 2010 Toronto debate with Christopher Hitchens, Tony Blair referred to the fact that, in 2007, religious organizations in the United States gave one and a half times the amount of aid that the US government did.[407] That's a pretty impressive amount.

If we need further evidence of the Church's concern and action in the world it is worth stating that more than 200 million hours a year are given by evangelical Christians alone to voluntary work in the UK every year.[408] That's worth more than a billion pounds, in the crudest monetary terms, and worth so much more in terms of changed communities. Other sections of the Church may do as well or better. In Trafford, best known as the home of Manchester United, the churches of the borough employ more youth workers, have more buildings, and reach more young people than the local authority. Half the voluntary projects in that local community are run by faith groups. Naturally, next to none of this extraordinary panoply of service is reported in the mass media because of the reasons we have explored in earlier chapters. Contrarily, the failings of the Church continue to make headlines—because the evil that men do continues to live after them, or live on with them.

Nevertheless, given all that has been said, can *any* other voluntary organisation even hold a candle to the depth and extent of the community work and social commitment of the churches in this country and many others?

Education Again

This overview, which has briefly given some idea of the breadth of the social action of the Church in communities world-wide, has made little specific mention of a provision made for education which is perhaps unique to the UK. From the beginning we have seen that education and the Church have been natural allies and the continuing link has been strong throughout the twentieth and twenty-first centuries. The fact that there have been attempts to weaken that link is shown every time the Church is attacked precisely for its guardianship of that association.

It was only in 1870 that School Boards enabled even the poorest to attend elementary school by paying their fees, and in 1880 that education became compulsory in England and Wales up to the age of ten; before that the Church had founded school after school, especially the National Schools established throughout the nineteenth century. In 1944, the Butler Act recognised that the purpose of education in Britain was "the spiritual, moral, mental and physical development of pupils"; William Temple, Archbishop of Canterbury and one of the most able men of his time, helped create that wording.[409] In 1988, the Reform Act added the wording "and of society" to that phrase, which widens the intentionality of the Act considerably. Since the Church of England has about 5,000 schools in the maintained sector, this was a way of acknowledging their origin and continuing purpose. Indeed, the founding purpose of many of these nineteenth-century schools was to educate pupils (frequently the poor) in the principles of the established Church throughout England and Wales. They offered an education founded on the Gospel and Christian values. This continuing tradition, along with the high numbers of such schools (and their success), has annoyed the more militant atheists, who speak of "indoctrination", a useful catchword but ludicrously misapplied term. Their ire is increased by the fact that the vast majority of independent schools also have a church foundation of some sort. Of these schools, again, the vast majority are highly successful in providing what parents seek for their children.

There is however a further benefit of these schools with a Christian character or foundation, which refutes one line of attack from the secularists, the one which claims that faith schools are divisive. In November 2009,

Professor David Jesson published a paper which examined the inspection reports of 400 secondary and 700 primary schools inspected between March and June 2009. His findings established the reverse of the "divisive" claim. The Ofsted information was emphatic. The data for primary schools showed both community schools and faith schools achieved exactly the same gradings in terms of promoting community cohesion (2.2 on a scale of 1 to 4). The data for secondary schools however, even more counter-intuitively, indicated clear evidence that faith schools were awarded substantially higher inspection gradings for promoting community cohesion than community schools, according to Professor Jesson.[410]

What Ofsted inspectors were looking for was, among other things, evidence that the schools had strategies for dealing with discriminating behaviour directed against both groups inside the school and under-represented groups outside the school. Schools with a religious foundation and purpose therefore showed that taking faith seriously meant valuing dialogue, as well as respecting differences between groups in the community. Being clear about your own values is a natural and easy standpoint from which to teach children that other people's values are important too; respect therefore comes more easily. Dilution of faith is not the way to community cohesion. For instance, when young Muslims have not been taught the core beliefs and values of mainstream Islam is when they are more easy to radicalise.

Nevertheless, despite this (or perhaps because of it), the charge is levelled that such schools "indoctrinate" their pupils. The first thing to say here is that whoever makes such a charge has clearly never taught in a school of any kind. After a lifetime in teaching (across three continents and eight schools, and having visited more than I care to remember), I know that children of every age are immensely canny and simply do not accept any sort of faith unquestioningly just because "the teacher says so". In 2011 a child of six wrote to God asking how he "got invented". Her journalist (and atheist) father sent the letter on to Rowan (later Lord) Williams (then Archbishop of Canterbury) whose reply was a classic of wisdom, humility and clear thinking.[411] A moment's reflection will show why such questioning takes place. Indoctrination, save where the victim is a willing one, is largely impossible when it is overt and conscious in an open society such as ours. It is the *unconscious* infiltration of ideas which is by far the more effective. Any school which takes its foundational faith seriously will be working counter-culturally, against the grain of society, by presenting an alternative way of looking at the post-Christian world, the assumptions of which pervade every space and waking moment of our lives. From our earliest infancy we imbibe the assumptions and views of our parents and whatever society is around us. Naturally therefore, if that society is largely irreligious, the majority have that bias from the start. Those growing up in the minority of religious or Christian homes will admittedly, to start with, imbibe the opposite view. But the moment they set foot outside the door, go shopping, turn on the TV, listen to contemporary music or mix with friends at school they will find every shade of contrary opinion as young people struggle to make sense of a society in constant flux. What a faith school does then is not to stifle debate, but promote it by presenting a self-consistent intellectually intelligible view of the world which is defensible in a debate about what is really true.

The means of doing this in schools, however, are constrained by every other consideration and demand on time. For perhaps ten minutes in a day, in a school that begins with a religious assembly, pupils are asked to consider an alternative worldview to the one that bombards them the moment they leave the school premises and one which has not been inactive inside the gates. That's ten minutes of conscious (and frequently unpopular) "indoctrination" (really?) out of 1,440 minutes of unconscious and unopposed infiltration of "normality" on every day of every week of every month—a normality which urges us by every possible means through the media to conform to it in our beliefs and lifestyles. Just ask a teenage group when they last saw a film, listened to music or read a magazine which promoted a Christian worldview!

Faith *indoctrination*? I don't think so! How could it be? It's not unconscious, it's not continuous and it's not the sole option. On the contrary, the way we grow to be independent is by the consideration of alternatives to those we grow up with. The indoctrination comes from a world which does not want the Christian alternative to have any voice in the public square, a world we have seen much more of in recent years. The most militant atheists would like all such voices stifled by denying children the right to hear something different from that which every influence *other* than the Church provides, something which is consciously presented as a different way of living. Such people have called this presentation child abuse. Funny thing, that. I would have thought the abuse was in the denial of the minority alternative, not in its provision.

One further point remains to be made. How are atheists to respond to the fact that, should they send their offspring to a faith (primary) school, the child may be taught to say their prayers and then believe that one way or another those prayers will be answered? The first obvious reply to this objection is that when a child is entered for a school it is not the same thing as entering a restaurant where you may choose from a menu. Schools make public statements about their educational provision and if parents wish for their children to attend, in sending them, they accept the whole package. If on reflection they dislike the package the child may be withdrawn. Second, it is hard to see that such a view is anything greatly to worry about, since any child, as we have seen, will immediately be told in the "real world" that God is not there to answer prayers anyway. Moreover, most atheist parents will have forewarned their children of this "nonsense" beforehand. In addition, Church of England schools (the majority of faith foundations) are known for their exam results, as Alice Thomson (an unbeliever) remarked, rather than as training academies for the Church.[412] Whatever their opponents may say, the Christian schools in this country seem remarkably good at sending out better-than-average students—whichever way you judge them. This is not good news for those who hope the Church will either wither away or immolate itself in flames of controversy of its own making. Nor is the state of the Church world-wide, good news for our opponents.

Growth of the Church World-Wide

In 2009 the editor of *The Economist* and its Washington bureau chief co-wrote *God is Back*, a wide-ranging analysis of the resurgence of religious belief across the globe.[413] Their thesis is that democracy, market forces, technology, and the quest for community are combining to produce this result. Secular fury about this arises from exasperation that modernity has not killed off religion, as was expected both in the 1960s and at the turn of the century. The authors' prediction is rather that religion will continue to move back towards the centre of intellectual life—even though Europe will remain predominantly secular.

During the season of Lent in 2011, *The Times* ran a six-part series of pull-out pages on "Christians".[414] In concluding the series, Michael Burleigh, a writer and journalist of international distinction, as well as a professor of history, wrote an article under the headline "The Long Withdrawing Roar of Secularism"—an ironic take on Matthew Arnold's famous poem "Dover Beach", where the roar of the metaphorical tide going out over the pebbled beach was applied to faith, rather than its opposite. In the article, Burleigh talks about the explosive global growth of a faith to which one-third of the world's population adhere, and which outnumbers Islam by about half a billion. In common with other periods of history when the Church has seemed at its weakest, it now shows, he says, a remarkable capacity for regenerating itself.[415] Church attendance in the UK may be at an all-time low, but only at a time when in the developing world its growth is astonishing.

As the world's economic focus has turned away from Europe to Asia and the Pacific Rim countries, so Christian churches have grown in numbers and dynamism in just those areas—China being the most remarkable. It has perhaps 100 million or more attending churches, even though many of these contravene state regulations and face repression and persecution. Maoism and capitalism as a mix has not filled Chinese hearts. The gospel has—to the point at which it is worth serious risk (life and liberty) to worship Christ or even lay hands on a Bible. In fact, as has often been said, there have been more Christian martyrs in the last hundred years than in any previous century, and we should not imagine that Stalin's purges or Nazism make up the extent of that persecution. "Open Doors", a charity which serves persecuted Christians world-wide, publishes a list of fifty countries where there is persecution. In 2011, the three countries which the charity considered most difficult for Christians to survive in were North Korea (arrests, murders and labour camps), Iran and Afghanistan.[416] A Catholic report of the same year named thirty-four countries where Christians were "Persecuted and Forgotten", as the report was entitled.[417] Michael Binyon, writing for *The Times*, drew attention to the fact that Hindus and Muslims are leading the attacks on Christians, but that China and North Korea are also responsible for violent government opposition to Christians and that churches are under attack across half the globe.[418] The columnist Melanie Phillips has recently drawn attention to the plight of Christians in Iraq, Syria and Pakistan, saying that the global onslaught on the Christian Church goes almost totally unremarked in the press.[419] The 1981 UN declaration on religious freedoms does not seem to be securing protection for as many as 100 million Christians in the places where they need it. Many in the West do not realise that where there is autocracy, it is impossible for the autocrat to tolerate any higher power, any absolute beyond space and time, since it would constitute a rival regime and the possibility of opposition.

Despite this persecution, the figures supplied by *The Times* are far from discouraging in global terms. Catholicism alone has well over a billion adherents, at least nominally, and the *Atlas of Global Christianity* for 2010 puts the number of believers in Russia alone, who belong to the Eastern Orthodox Church, at over 100 million.[420] World-wide, Anglicanism incorporates 85 million believers in thirty-four countries, and the growth of the evangelical Church throughout the world has been marked for many years and is expected to continue. Currently it is estimated that there are 600 million Evangelicals, the fastest-growing section of that grouping being Pentecostalism. In particular, this wing of the Church is changing the face of some South American countries (Venezuela, for example, has quadrupled its Christian population in the last twelve years.) In North America, the Church is more pervasive than at any time in the last 300 years, and twenty-five per cent of Americans claim to be Evangelicals. Astonishingly, in Iran and Afghanistan, albeit from a tiny and persecuted base, the annual growth of Evangelicals is between 15 and 20 per cent. Countries as various as Kuwait, Mongolia, Greenland and the Gambia are seeing evangelical growth rates of 7 or 8 per cent. By contrast, according to Christian Research, the Church in the UK will have lost a worrying 1.1 million children between 1990 and 2020—unless the unexpected happens, which, given the history of the Church, we should be expecting and praying for. But it is curious to think that this last statistic will give our most militant opponents pleasure, when on the evidence provided here it will actually damage society and be a significant personal loss to each child so affected.

CHAPTER 12

Epilogue?

Well, of course, there is no epilogue to the story of the Church. Nothing can supersede or come after it when so many of its members are already busy in heaven. There is no conclusion to eternity. If we are Christians we should make no mistake: God has a destination and a destiny for his Church which just keeps getting better. Heaven and earth will both be full of his glory, which is inexhaustible, and his kingdom will hold sway in both realms. Of the *increase* of his government and peace there shall be no end. But such talk can be inflammatory and needs careful qualification, because it is just such beliefs that have led the Church into dreadful errors of different kinds in the past. Four points will serve us well in avoiding the repetition of those mistakes.

The first is about power. The Church should never hark back to some past imaginary golden age when standards, or behaviour, or law were somehow more Christian than now because the Church had more influence or power. The human race has been uniformly disinclined to renounce its natural selfish rebelliousness towards a God who asks so much at the same time as giving so much. In times when the Church had power to enforce certain codes of behaviour, the apparently good conduct of those who were oppressed was, as a result, frequently no more than skin deep and the veneer of faith in the oppressors was probably even thinner. In earlier days this new and radical faith had been dismissed as "the religion of slaves", which it was, in that it appealed to those who could identify with its persecuted and crucified Saviour. It is unimaginable now that Christianity might again become the tool of emperors to use against their subject peoples, but petty tyrants can still sometimes try that in their churches—though the outcome is always a disaster for all. We must not, therefore, in the first place, long for position, worldly authority or political power. Philip Pullman's figure of Jesus in his "story" *The Good Man Jesus and the Scoundrel Christ* depicts Jesus towards the end of the book praying that the Church should stay poor, without power and of course modest.[421] Pullman seems not to be without a view of what the Church should be; he has simply missed so much of what it was and is.

Second, the Church must insist to the world that however hard they press us to say otherwise, our final authority to speak is not grounded in any charity or goodness we may bring to the world (though the Church has provided that without rival, as we have seen). It is rather grounded in the fact that our faith is rational and historical, based on evidence and subject to scrutiny. Secularists like to characterise our concern for historicity and truth as naive and boring. They like to say that since, at best, no one can know for sure about the foundations of Christian belief, we should leave that concept behind, catch up with the last hundred years of thinking and accept that the best we can hope for is that religion should not get in the way of progress and be a useful optional extra for those who need it. None of this should be accepted for one minute. Reasonableness is not applicable only to science or other measurable matters. It is entirely reasonable to believe that God exists and that he may choose to reveal himself to his creatures, as some of our most able philosophers and scientists have attested to. The New Testament documents provide very good and reasonable grounds on which to base our belief in the divinity of Christ. If we allow the supernatural to leach out of Christianity we lose what is distinct, what is true and what is simply essential about the faith. We would be, as St Paul said, "of all men the most to be pitied".

Third, we must re-kindle our vision of heaven and our preaching about it. Having our eyes set on the reality of heaven is, paradoxically, the most effective way of bringing it closer to earth for others. Believing that the mind of God held something in store for them was the prime motivator of our forebears and the great heroes of faith in improving the world for their fellow men. Worldly suffering was to them a slight matter in relation to the endless joy that was set before them. From Polycarp to Bonhoeffer, from Blandina to Gladys Aylward, men and women have proved by their lives and in their deaths that heaven was a reality to them and the source of their altruism on earth. By contrast, there is today something of a reluctance to talk about heaven, an embarrassment perhaps; a feeling that such talk is smug, or may be seen as delusional, or a compensation well suited to those who are losers on earth. At worst it is seen by unbelievers as a bribe to get people to be good. All these can be true in circles where heaven is misunderstood, but previous ages were less circumspect about their celebration of the afterlife, as so much music and art shows. We too should celebrate it. The New Testament is itself redolent of heaven on page after page. Jesus, Paul, Peter and John all speak of it as something to be desired above all things, and, naturally, as a blissful release from the agonies of the world. That of course is why we in the West speak of it so little—because our lives are not agonised, for the most part, as theirs were. We are not only mostly comfortable, but pampered.

Yet the conquest of death still eludes us, and that is why our proclamation of heaven should be unashamed: it stands as a marvellous foil to the failure of the world to come to terms with what it imagines as extinction. Death is still, for those without faith, "an absolute bummer", as Robert Crampton calls it.[422] Doctors dislike discussing its imminence with patients, family members with elderly parents, even clergy with parishioners. Our language is full of euphemisms which help us to avoid using the word. Death is inevitable and universal and yet it is incomprehensible in so many ways— the contemplation of one's own non-existence is seemingly impossible. It is seen by the world as a pure negative, the most final of all full stops at the end of the last sentence of the last paragraph of the last chapter of the last book. After it, there is nothing. It is the negation of everything. There is hardly much to recommend it on such a view, save as the cessation of suffering for those to whom life has become intolerable. The historian Edward Gibbon confessed in his autobiography that the failure of hope would always tinge the evening of life. From the eighteenth century onwards, non-Christian writers have variously expressed disappointment, resentment and bewilderment in contemplating their own death. Some, like Yeats, have turned to the comparative permanence of great art to escape the fact of mortality, but the final words of his collected poems, used as his epitaph, are chilling in their detachment: "Cast a cold eye / On life, on death. / Horseman, pass by".[423]

Yet for the Christian, death is the exciting gateway to *heaven*. What a reversal of attitude that belief entails! Death, the gateway, means that at last we can see face to face the One who has loved us and desired us to be with him since before the beginning of time, the only One who is more excited about our arrival even than we are! The One who wanted it to happen so much that he gave absolutely everything to achieve it. We all long to be thought well of, to be appreciated, to be commended, to be praised for what we have striven to do well, and here at last is the One who knows exactly what we did—and did not do—and gives the Christian unqualified assurance of his acceptance of us, warts and all, in Christ: "Well done, good and faithful servant." The metaphors of Scripture and of writers down the ages serve only as a stumbling attempt to do justice to the utter awe of the occasion, one unlike anything we could possibly have experienced before

Why then is it difficult for many of us to want heaven in the way we want other things? One reason is that we are not taught to think about it properly, if at all. On the contrary, all our training is to focus on the rewards of this world and the completion of our aims and ambitions *before* we die. Books abound on places to visit, things to do, and which books to read before you die. Christians, however, should be conscious of all the things they may be asked to do, expected to be capable of, *after* they die. We are told in the parable that some will be in charge of many cities. Figurative it may be, but it does not suggest a life of sitting around on our hands—or on a cloud. One of the most memorable things in Dawkins' *The God Delusion* is the anecdote in which Cardinal Basil Hume, when dying, is visited by the Abbot of Ampleforth, who *congratulates* him, wishing he could join him.[424] If we believe in heaven, that is the right attitude to have. Mr Valiant-For-Truth, at the end of *The Pilgrim's Progress*, quietly said, "Death, where is thy sting?", as he entered the river of Death, and then "Grave, where is thy victory?", as he passed over to the other side. C. S. Lewis speaks of heaven as the story which goes on and on—the opposite of the final full stop—and of chapters which are always better than the one before; of term-time giving way to holidays.[425] In the final three chapters of *Perelandra*, Ransom is in the presence of the King and Queen of that world, who paint a picture of Maleldil's intentions for the universe and the place of his creatures within it.[426] Lewis conveys, as few others can, a sense of the unspeakable majesty of God, the boundless size and glory of his plans and the destined greatness of man when he is redeemed. We need to re-capture this vision. John Bunyan wrote of the Celestial City seen on the horizon from the Delectable Mountains as being the culmination of Christian and Hopeful's journey. He does not get beyond the City, not just because that is his goal, but more profoundly because there *is* nowhere beyond the City. Its glory goes on forever. *Civitas Dei* is also *Civitas Aeternitatis*. The story and the journey may go on but not through space or time. The map has been rolled up, for the view is clear and the earthly traveller has arrived to be re-clothed for all that lies ahead. The clock has been discarded, for time is no longer of the essence. Indeed, time simply is no longer, for living in the joy of the moment becomes a continuous unbroken experience: all previous plans and hopes have been transcended and so forgotten. It is my belief that we are closest to eternity when we are utterly taken out of ourselves, because we are entirely caught up in awe at the life or presence of something or someone even more wonderful than we are. The "I" of this world is taken over in its entirety by the "Thou" of heaven. We are allowed glimpses of it here, but in heaven it will be constant and perfect reality. Our imaginations, grounded in Scripture, need to be renewed so that in a world so mercilessly forcing its purposes upon us we keep the picture of heaven always and only just beneath the surface of all that we do.

Last, we must do good to all. Our charity must be unlimited in its extent and generous in its depth. The world will not thank us or be impressed if we give solely to Church causes—though we may choose to channel that aid through Christian hands. History shows that for the most part the Church has provided a shelter from the storm for the needy in every age—but at other times we have been slow or unduly selective in our responses. The world continues to be full of suffering, and we always have the poor with us, so the humbling reality of that will not be completely eradicated. The marvel is that the world is also full, as has been said, of those *overcoming* suffering, and the Church must be the principal agent in the world for enabling that to happen. Where it fails to do so, it fails in its mission.

In 2008, Barack Obama used a powerful metaphor in his victory speech in Chicago, one he borrowed from Martin Luther King. He talked about human endeavour "bending the arc of history".[427] Bending that arc has been, and is, what the Church is engaged upon in its world-wide task. Even our critics do not deny that. We must continue to bend the arc towards Christ. Our opponents may hate us for it, but if we act with humility and not worldly power, with supernatural weapons and not merely goodness, with love shown by deeds and with renewed vision of our goal in heaven, the Church will continue to be, as it always has been, the road sign; the guidepost for weary travellers on their way through the sometimes dark wood of this world.

Notes

0. G. A. Studdert Kennedy, *Lies!* (Hodder and Stoughton, 1919), p.128

1. G. M. Trevelyan, *An Autobiography and Other Essays* (Longmans, Green & Co., 1949), p. 69. By permission of Pearson Education Ltd.

2. Trevelyan, *An Autobiography*, p. 204.

3. George Philip Baker, *Book of Battles that Determined the Course of Civilization* (Cassell, 1935), p. 245.

4. Marilynne Robinson, *When I was a Child I Read Books* (Virago, 2012), p. 95.

5. C. S. Lewis, *The Allegory of Love* (Oxford University Press, 1958), p. 8. Extracts from the works of C. S. Lewis Copyright C. S. Lewis Pte Ltd.

6. H. A. L. Fisher, *A History of Europe* (Arnold, 1936), p. v.

7. John Middleton Murry, *Heaven—and Earth* (Jonathan Cape, 1938), p. 19.

8. John Cowper Powys, *The Pleasures of Literature* (Cassell, 1938), p. 56; italics in original.

9. Trevelyan, *Autobiography*, p. 155. By permission of Pearson Education Ltd.

10. Professor Davies' letter appeared in *The Times*, 19 July 2006.

11. A. C. Grayling, "Even Christianity is Not Really Christian", *The Times*, 26 April 2014.

12. Christopher Hitchens, *God is not Great* (Atlantic, 2007), p. 5.

13. Hitchens, *God is not Great*, p. 3; italics in original.

14. Hitchens, *God is not Great*, p. 4.

15. Hitchens, *God is not Great*, p. 5.

16. Hitchens' estimates of Dietrich Bonhoeffer and C. S. Lewis in his opening chapter, for instance, are demonstrably wrong and insupportable.

17. John Carey (ed.), *The Faber Book of Reportage* (Faber and Faber, 1987).

18. Episode 3, "Medieval Death", first broadcast September 2010 (BBC Four).

19. Davies' letter in *The Times*, 19 July 2006.

20. Matthew 7:20.

21. William Shakespeare, *Julius Caesar*, III.ii.77–78.
22. William Blake, *Jerusalem*, Plate 55, l.60.
23. Philip Yancey, *What's So Amazing About Grace?* (Zondervan, 2007), p. 268.
24. G. K. Chesterton, *Generally Speaking* (Fountain Library, 1937), p. 187.
25. C. S. Lewis, *Fern-seed and Elephants and Other Essays* (Fontana, 1975), p. 35.
26. Richard Fletcher, *The Conversion of Europe, 371–1386 AD* (Fontana, 1997), pp. 10–11.
27. G. G. Coulton, *Social Life in Britain from the Conquest to the Reformation* (Cambridge University Press, 1918), p. 521.
28. William Shakespeare, *Julius Caesar*, III.ii.77–78.
29. Richard Dawkins, *The God Delusion* (Bantam, 2006), p. 51.
30. Thomas Hardy, *Late Lyrics and Earlier* (Macmillan, 1922), p. viii.
31. George MacDonald, *The Princess and Curdie* (Blackie, n.d.), p. 201.
32. 2 Peter 3:16.
33. Clement, *Epistle to the Corinthians*, xlii.
34. Anon., *Didache*, 8.2.
35. H. W. Bettenson, *Documents of the Christian Church* (Oxford University Press, 1967).
36. Matthew 28:19–20.
37. J. R. H. Moorman, *A History of the Church in England* (A & C Black, 1958), p. 88.
38. Genesis 1:1
39. S. G. Evans, *The Social Hope of the Christian Church* (Hodder & Stoughton, 1965).
40. Robinson, *When I was a Child I Read Books*, pp. 70–71.
41. S. G. Evans, *The Social Hope of the Christian Church*, p. 18, quoting W. Rauscenbusch, *Christianity and the Social Crisis* (New York, 1907), p.8.
42. Isaiah 1:16–17.
43. Ezekiel 22:25–31.
44. Psalm 82:2–4.
45. Luke 4:18–21.
46. Exodus 20:5.
47. Alexander William Kinglake, *Eothen* (J. M. Dent, 1908), p. 19.
48. Quoted in Robinson, *When I was a Child I Read Books*, p. 110.
49. Collect for Good Friday, *Book of Common Prayer*.
50. Genesis 3:1.

51. Edith Hamilton, *Spokesmen for God* (W. W. Norton & Co., New York, 1962), p. 99.

52. J. P. V. D. Balsdon, *Roman Women, Their History and Habits* (John Day, 1963), p. 283.

53. Cowper Powys, *The Pleasures of Literature*, p. 54.

54. Romans 16:7, 1–2.

55. 1 Timothy 2:12.

56. Ephesians 5:22, 24.

57. Galatians 3:28.

58. 1 Corinthians 6:9.

59. Isaiah 42, 45, 2.

60. Luke 20:21.

61. Romans 10:12; Galatians 3:28; Acts 10:34–5.

62. Philippians 2:7.

63. Micah 6:8.

64. J. W. Wenham, *The Enigma of Evil* (Zondervan, 1985), p.120.

65. A discussion of such views by four theologians can be found in C. S. Cowles, *Show Them No Mercy* (Zondervan, 2003).

66. Wenham, *The Enigma of Evil*, p. 127.

67. See "A Philosophical Enquiry into the Origin of our Ideas of the Sublime and Beautiful, 1757", in *The Writings and Speeches of Edmund Burke*, ed. Paul Langford (Oxford University Press, 1997), pp. 240–241.

68. Robinson, *When I was a Child I Read Books*, p.104.

69. 2 Timothy 3:16.

70. Colossians 1:15.

71. Colossians 2:9.

72. Hebrews 1:2–3.

73. Hebrews 1:1.

74. John 5:39.

75. See, for instance, his sermon "Free Grace", preached at Bristol in 1740.

76. Charles Williams, *The Descent of the Dove* (Faber and Faber, 1950), p. 19.

77. 1 Timothy 4:13.

78. James 2:18.

79. James 2:26.

80. 1 Peter 2:12.

81. 1 Peter 1:17; 1 Peter 2:1.

82. 1 Peter 2:13.

83. 2 Timothy 3:12.

84. 1 Thessalonians 4:12.

85. 2 Corinthians 9:13.

86. Philippians 2:5.

87. Galatians 5:14.

88. Ephesians 4:1.

89. Colossians 3:13; 2 Corinthians 5:19; 1 Thessalonians 5:15–16.

90. Ephesians 5:25.

91. Philippians 2:3.

92. Galatians 5:23.

93. Tacitus, *The Annals of Imperial Rome*, XV:43.

94. Suetonius, *Claudius*, XXV:4.

95. Suetonius, *Nero*, XVI.

96. Diarmaid MacCulloch, *A History of Christianity* (Allen Lane, 2009), p.158.

97. A translation of this fascinating lengthy letter can be found in *Letters of the Younger Pliny* (Penguin, 1969), pp. 293–295.

98. Tertullian, *Apologeticus 4*.

99. *Martyrium Polycarpi* IX.

100. C. S. Lewis, *Mere Christianity* (Harper Collins, 2002), p. 78.

101. G. K. Chesterton, *Orthodoxy* (The Bodley Head, 1939), p. 184.

102. William Shakespeare, *Twelfth Night*, II.iii.111–2.

103. MacCulloch, *A History of Christianity*, p. 208.

104. M. A. Smith, *The Church under Siege* (Inter Varsity Press, 1976), p. 211 ff.

105. Middleton Murry, *Heaven—and Earth*, p. 15.

106. Chesterton, *Orthodoxy*, p. 290.

107. Ephesians 2:19–20.

108. Patrick Leigh Fermor, *A Time To Keep Silence* (John Murray, 2004), p. 90.

109. Peter Shaffer, *The Royal Hunt of the Sun* (Longman, 1966), p.1.

110. In J. H. Plumb, *The Horizon Book of the Renaissance* (Collins, 1961).

111. Williams, *The Descent of the Dove*, p. 170.

112. Ben Hoyle, "Historian Lifts His Sword Against Accepted View of First Crusade", *The Times*, 14 October 2011.

113. William Shakespeare, *Othello*, III.iii.202–203.

114. Francis Bacon, *Essays* (J.M. Dent, 1906), p. 11.

115. Bacon, "Of Unity in Religion", in *Essays*, p. 11.

116. *Encyclopedia Britannica*, Eleventh Edition (1911), Vol. 7, p. 550.
117. H. A. L. Fisher, *A History of Europe* (Edward Arnold, 1936), p. 235.
118. Steven Runciman, *A History of the Crusades*, Vol. III (Cambridge University Press, 1952–1954), p. 480.
119. Jonathan Riley-Smith, *The Knights Hospitaller in the Levant* (Palgrave Macmillan, 2012), p. 9 ff.
120. In *The Collected Poems of Wilfred Owen,* ed. C. Day Lewis (Chatto and Windus, 1974), p. 53.
121. C. S. Lewis, *The Four Loves* (Geoffrey Bles, 1960), p. 41.
122. *The Times,* July 17 2015.
123. Noted by Tim Montgomerie in *The Times,* July 23 2015.
124. Mary Warnock, *Dishonest to God: On keeping Religion out of Politics* (Continuum, 2010), p. 161.
125. See his article "Church and State Should Help Europe Grow", *The Times,* 21 July 2007.
126. Luke 4:6.
127. Luke 4:14.
128. 1 Peter 3:15.
129. Bartholeme de Las Casas, *A Short Account of the Destruction of the Indies*, ed. Nigel Griffin (Penguin, 1992), p. 128 et seq.
130. C. S. Lewis, *Prince Caspian* (Puffin, 1970), p. 185. Quoted in Rowan Williams, *The Lion's World* (SPCK, 2012), p. 23.
131. John Brinsley, *The Grammar Schoole,* ch. XXIX, "Punishments", § 289.
132. Charles Taylor, *A Secular Age* (Harvard University Press, 2007), pp. 40–41 et seq.
133. MacCulloch, *A History of Christianity*, p. 408.
134. Jaime Contreras and Gustav Henningsen, "Forty-four Thousand Cases of the Spanish Inquisition (1540–1700): Analysis of an Historical Data Bank", in *The Inquisition in Early Modern Europe: Studies in Sources and Methods* (Northern Illinois University Press, 1986), pp. 100–129.
135. Henry Kamen, *The Spanish Inquisition: A Historical Revision* (Phoenix, 1998), p. 203.
136. David Cecil, *Library Looking-Glass* (Constable, 1975), p. 83.
137. Carey (ed.), *The Faber Book of Reportage*, pp. 159–163; p. 164; pp. 193–198.
138. William Shakespeare, *Macbeth*, I.iii.126–128.
139. Arthur Miller, *The Crucible* (Penguin, 1973), p. 42.
140. Evans, *The Social Hope of the Christian Church*, p. 124.

141. Williams, *The Descent of the Dove*, p. 178 ff.

142. Sarah Bakewell, *How to Live* (Vintage, 2011), p. 322.

143. Bacon, "Of Unity in Religion", in *Essays*, p. 9.

144. Susan Hill, *Howards End is on the Landing* (Profile Books, 2009), p. 156.

145. Helen Moore and Julian Reid (eds.), *Manifold Greatness: The Making of the King James Bible* (Bodleian Library, 2011).

146. Melvyn Bragg, *The Book of Books: The Radical Impact of the King James Bible 1611–2011* (Hodder & Stoughton, 2011).

147. C. S. Lewis, "The Literary Impact of the Authorised Version", in *Selected Literary Essays* (Cambridge University Press, 1969), pp. 126–145.

148. William Shakespeare, *Twelfth Night*, II.iii.58.

149. William Shakespeare, *Twelfth Night*, II.iii.71.

150. Rabbi Jonathan Sacks, *The Great Partnership: Science, Religion and the Search for Meaning* (Hodder & Stoughton, 2011), ch. 13.

151. Antonia Fraser, *Cromwell: Our Chief of Men* (Phoenix, 2002), p. 55 fn.

152. Quoted by Andrew Lownie, *John Buchan, The Presbyterian Cavalier* (Constable, 1995), p. 188.

153. John Buchan, *Oliver Cromwell* (Hodder and Stoughton, 1934), p. 525; p. 352; p. 353; p. 346.

154. Bakewell, *How to Live*, p. 177.

155. Trevelyan, "Cromwell's Statue", in *An Autobiography*, p. 160. Permission given by Pearson Education Ltd.

156. Buchan, *Oliver Cromwell*, p. 339.

157. Buchan, *Oliver Cromwell*, p. 520.

158. Quoted in S. B. Canfield's *A Lecture on the Life of Oliver Cromwell* (Cleveland Press, 1850), p. 111.

159. Speech to General Assembly of the Church of Scotland, 1650.

160. Trevelyan, *An Autobiography*, p. 170. Permission given by Pearson Education Ltd.

161. Fraser, *Cromwell*, p. 142.

162. Fraser, *Cromwell*, p. 438.

163. Fraser, *Cromwell*, p. 444.

164. Fraser, *Cromwell*, p. 424–425.

165. See MacCulloch, *A History of Christianity*, pp. 639–644.

166. John Morrill, *Cromwell* (Oxford University Press, 2007), p. 114. By permission of Oxford University Press.

167. Morrill, *Cromwell*, p. 97.

168. Tom Reilly, *Cromwell: An Honourable Enemy* (Brandon, 1999), p. 3.

169. Reilly, *Cromwell*, p. 6.

170. *Encyclopedia Britannica*, Vol. 7, p. 493 .

171. Rene Descartes, "A Discourse on Method" (1637), in *The Portable Age of Reason Reader*, ed. Crane Brinton (Viking, 1972).

172. John Locke, *An Essay Concerning Human Understanding* (Fontana, 1964), pp. 425, 427.

173. David Hume, *David Hume's Political Essays*, ed. Charles W. Hendel (Bobs-Merrill, 1953), p. 56.

174. Williams, *The Descent of the Dove*, p. 198.

175. Keith Fieling, *A History of England* (Macmillan, 1966), p. 695.

176. 2 Timothy 3:2–5.

177. John Wesley, *John Wesley's Journal*, ed. Nehemiah Curnock (Epworth Press, 1952), p. 229.

178. Augustine Birrell, *Selected Essays* (Nelson, 1909), p. 113.

179. Wesley, *Journal*, p. 394.

180. Wesley, *Journal*, pp. 1–5.

181. Wesley, *Journal*, p. 3.

182. Moorman, *A History of the Church in England*, p. 297; my italics.

183. Wesley, *Journal*, pp. 9–10.

184. Wesley, *Journal*, pp. 7–8.

185. Wesley, *Journal*, p. 17.

186. Wesley, *Journal*, p. 19.

187. Wesley, *Journal*, p. 27.

188. Wesley, *Journal*, pp. 35–37.

189. Wesley, *Journal*, p. 51.

190. Augustine, *Confessions*, Book VIII:12.

191. Martin Luther, *Preface to the Latin Writings*.

192. Romans 7:21.

193. Wesley, *Journal*, p. 51.

194. Romans 8:3.

195. From the hymn "And can it be . . .", in *Hymns and Psalms* (Methodist Publishing House, 1983).

196. John Wesley, *The Works of the Reverend John Wesley A.M.*, ed. J. Emory (New York, 1831), p. 479.

197. J. W. Bready, *England: Before and After John Wesley* (Hodder & Stoughton, 1939).

198. Wesley, *Journal*, p. 367.

199. Wesley, *Journal*, p. 286.

200. Bready, *England: Before and After John Wesley*, p. 242.

201. Bready, *England: Before and After John Wesley*, p. 243.

202. Wesley, *Journal*, p. 261.

203. Wesley, *Journal*, p. 96.

204. Wesley, *Journal*, p. 134.

205. Wesley, *Journal*, p. 232.

206. Wesley, *Journal*, p. 242.

207. Wesley, *Journal*, p. 393.

208. Wesley, *Journal*, p. 286.

209. Winston Churchill, Speech before the House of Commons, 20 July, 1910.

210. Richard Blake, *Evangelicals in the Royal Navy 1775–1815: Blue Lights and Psalm-Singers* (Boydell Press, 2008). See also Blake's *Religion in the British Navy 1815–1879* (Boydell Press, 2014).

211. MacCulloch, *A History of Christianity*, p. 755.

212. Wesley, *Journal*, p. 348.

213. Evans, *The Social Hope of the Christian Church*, p. 142.

214. Evans, *The Social Hope of the Christian Church*, p. 143.

215. Wesley, *Journal*, pp. 228–229.

216. F. L. Cross (ed.), *The Oxford Dictionary of the Christian Church* (Oxford University Press, 1974), p. 1467; Evans, *The Social Hope of the Christian Church*, p. 141 ; Kate O'Brien, *Impressions of English Literature* (Collins, 1944), p. 202.

217. Wesley, *Journal*, p. 96.

218. R. H. Tawney, *Religion and the Rise of Capitalism* (Transaction Publishers, 1998), p. 272; Bragg, *The Book of Books*, pp. 335–344.

219. See his chapter "Religion", in *England in 1815* (Ernest Benn, 1949).

220. Moorman, *A History of the Church in England*, p. 308.

221. MacCulloch, *A History of Christianity*, p. 754.

222. Birrell, *Selected Essays*, p. 122.

223. *The Cambridge Modern History*, Vol. VI (Cambridge University Press, 1902–1912), p. 77.

224. Matthew 26:30.

225. Cross (ed.), *The Oxford Dictionary of the Christian Church*, p. 1466; Moorman, *A History of the Church in England*, p. 305; MacCulloch, *A History of Christianity*, p. 750.

226. Bernard L. Manning, *The Hymns of Wesley and Watts* (Epworth Press, 1942), p. 13.

227. John Wesley, "Preface To A Collection Of Hymns For Use of The People Called Methodists, 1779", in *The Methodist Hymn Book* (Methodist Conference Office, 1933), p. v.

228. Wesley, "Preface To A Collection . . . ", p. v.

229. Wesley, "Preface To A Collection . . . ", p. vi.

230. A. N. Wilson, *The Victorians* (Hutchinson, 2007), p. 59.

231. See p. 12 of the 1892 edition by Chapman & Hall Ltd.

232. Luke 1:52–53, *Book of Common Prayer*.

233. J. A. Froude, *Carlyle's Life in London,* Vol. II (Longmans, Green & Co., 1897), p. 20.

234. G. K. Chesterton, *Autobiography* (Hutchinson & Co., 1937), p. 143.

235. Matthew 10:25, 12:24; Luke 4:23, 7:34.

236. Williams, *The Descent of the Dove*, p. 211.

237. Lewis, *Mere Christianity*, p. 184.

238. Alister McGrath, *The Twilight of Atheism* (Rider, 2004), p. 82.

239. J. Bronowski, "Unbelief and Science", in *Ideas and Beliefs of the Victorians* (Sylvan Press, 1950), p. 165.

240. Bronowski, "Unbelief and Science", p. 168.

241. Ludwig Feuerbach, *The Essence of Christianity* (Otto Wigand, 1841).

242. Eliot's version was the first English translation of the work.

243. Ernest Renan, *Life of Jesus* (1863).

244. Humphry House, *The Dickens World* (Oxford University Press, 1942), pp. 106–132.

245. Matthew Arnold, *Literature and Dogma* (T. Nelson, n.d.), p. 19.

246. Arnold, *Literature and Dogma*, p. 290.

247. Froude, *Carlyle's Life in London*, p. 282.

248. Ralph Waldo Emerson, *Selected Essays* (T.Nelson, n.d.), pp. 305–306.

249. D. C. Somervell, *English Thought in the Nineteenth Century* (Methuen, 1929), p. 235.

250. Arnold, *Literature and Dogma*, pp. 44, 373, etc.

251. Arnold, *Literature and Dogma*, pp. 46–47.

252. *Encyclopedia Britannica*, Eleventh edition (1911), Vol. XVIII p. 585.

253. *Encyclopedia Britannica*, Eleventh edition (1911), Vol. XVIII p. 585.

254. *Encyclopedia Britannica*, Eleventh edition (1911), Vol. XVIII p. 585.

255. *Encyclopedia Britannica*, Eleventh edition (1911), Vol. XVIII p. 586.

256. *Encyclopedia Britannica*, Eleventh edition (1911), Vol. XVIII p. 586.

257. Oscar Wilde, *The Complete Plays*, ed. H. Montgomery Hyde (Methuen, 1999), p. 15.

258. Geoffrey Moorhouse, *The Missionaries* (Eyre Methuen, 1974), p. 131.

259. Moorhouse, *The Missionaries*, p. 23.

260. Moorhouse, *The Missionaries*, p. 27.

261. David Livingstone, *Missionary Travels* (Ward, Lock & Co.,1913), pp. 4; 4; 575; 579; 579; 580.

262. Livingstone, *Missionary Travels*, pp. 577 (my italics); 579; 574.

263. Julian Pettifer and Richard Bradley, *Missionaries* (BBC, 1990), p. 83.

264. John Buchan, *Nelson's History of the War*, Vol. XXI (Nelson, 1917), pp. 132–133.

265. J. C. Lambert, *The Romance of Missionary Heroism* (Seeley and Co., 1907).

266. Steven Pinker, *The Better Angels of our Nature: Why Violence Has Declined* (Viking, 2011).

267. Livingstone, *Missionary Travels*, p. 486.

268. Richard Blake, *Religion in the Navy 1815–1879*, (Boydell Press, 2014), fn p. 157.

269. Moorhouse, *The Missionaries*, p. 89.

270. Pettifer and Bradley, *Missionaries*, pp. 134–143.

271. If, by contrast, we are looking for a heroism in a remote place (after a comparable struggle to reach her destination) that was effective in a more modern era, who better to choose than Gladys Aylward, overlooked in books of mission history, but singled out by Ranulph Fiennes in his book *My Heroes* as the "smallest but most resolute" of all his heroes in her epic journey with a hundred orphaned children in China fleeing from the Japanese in 1940. Her story should live for ever.

272. Matthew Parris, "As an Atheist I Truly Believe Africa Needs God", *The Times*, 27 December 2008.

273. Alison Morgan, *The Wild Gospel* (Monarch, 2004), pp. 329, 335.

274. Ben Macintyre, What's Black and White and Red on Maps?, *The Times*, 29 November 2011.

275. Darwin outlines some of the complexity in Chapter 1 of his *Unfinished Empire: The Global Expansion of Britain* (Penguin, 2012).

276. Kwasi Kwarteng, *Ghosts of Empire* (Bloomsbury, 2011).

277. H. M. Stanley, *In Darkest Africa* (Sampson Low, Marston, Searle & Rivington, 1890), p. xviii (my italics).
278. Moorhouse, *The Missionaries*, p. 322.
279. Mentioned by Moorhouse, *The Missionaries*, p. 322.
280. Pettifer and Bradley, *Missionaries*, p. 98.
281. Moorhouse, *The Missionaries*, p. 333.
282. Moorhouse, *The Missionaries*, p. 334.
283. In C. S. Goldman (ed.), *The Empire and the Century* (John Murray, 1905), p. 170.
284. Goldman (ed.), *The Empire and the Century*, p. 162.
285. Carey (ed.), *The Faber Book of Reportage*, pp. 316–319.
286. Kinglake, *Eothen*, pp. 166–167.
287. Ralph Waldo Emerson, *Selected Essays* (Nelson, n.d), p. 228.
288. Wilson, *The Victorians*, p. 130.
289. *Encyclopedia Britannica,* Eleventh edition (1911), Vol. XXV, p. 471.
290. Wade Davis, *Into the Silence* (Bodley Head, 2011), p. 230.
291. J. B. Lightfoot, *St Paul's Epistles to the Colossians and to Philemon* (Macmillan, 1900), p. 327.
292. Jonathan Hill, *What Has Christianity Ever Done For Us?* (Lion, 2005), p. 176.
293. John Wesley, *Thoughts upon Slavery* (Dublin, 1774), pp. 20; 26; John Wesley, "Serious Address to the People of England with Regard to the State of the Nation" (1777), quoted in Bready, *England Before and After Wesley,* p. 228.
294. Quoted in Bready, *England Before and After Wesley*, p. 302.
295. William Wilberforce, *An Appeal to the Religion, Justice and Humanity of the Inhabitants of the British Empire* (London, 1823), p. 3.
296. Evans, *The Social Hope of the Christian Church*, p. 265.
297. Romans 8:21.
298. William Wilberforce, *A Practical View of the Prevailing Religious Systems of Professed Christians* (T. T. and J. Tegg, 1834), p. 259.
299. Bready, *England Before and After Wesley*, p. 301.
300. BBC 2 series, November and December 2010.
301. Arnold, *Literature and Dogma*, p. 356.
302. Arnold, *Literature and Dogma*, pp. 359–360.
303. Peter Hitchens, *The Rage against God* (Zondervan, 2010), pp. 8–98.
304. Quoted by Bready, *England Before and After Wesley*, p. 300.
305. Lord Ashley, *Speech in the House of Commons* (Seeley and Co., 1841), p. 18.
306. Wilson, *The Victorians*, p. 130.

307. A. C. Dawson, *Ideas and Beliefs of the Victorians* (Sylvan Press, 1950), p. 30.

308. Wilson, *The Victorians*, p. 246.

309. Elie Halevy, *England in 1815* (Ernest Benn, 1949), p. 387. His 100-page chapter "Religion" is a superb picture of its impact on England which was unparalleled on the continent.

310. Quoted in Bready, *England Before and After Wesley*, p. 180.

311. Philip Yancey, *What's So Amazing About Grace?* (Zondervan, 1997), p. 253.

312. G. A. Studdert Kennedy, *The Unutterable Beauty* (Hodder & Stoughton, 1927), p. 131.

313. A. B. Macaulay and F.. J. Paul, *Up Against It, or Questions Asked by the Soldiers* (Hodder & Stoughton, 1919).

314. *The Collected Poems of Wilfred Owen*, p. 53.

315. Davis, *Into the Silence*, pp. 187; 195.

316. Vera Brittain, *Testament of Youth* (Fontana, 1979), p. 218. Quotations from Vera Brittain's *Testament of Youth* (first published 1933) are included by permission of Mark Bostridge and T J Brittain-Catlin, Literary Executors for the Estate of Vera Brittain, 1970.

317. *The Collected Poems of Wilfred Owen*, p. 31

318. Quoted in Jon Stallworthy, *Wilfred Owen: A Biography* (Oxford University Press, 1977), p. 77.

319. Siegried Sassoon, *Memoirs of an Infantry Officer* (Faber and Faber, 1930), pp. 264; 268.

320. *The Collected Poems of Wilfred Owen*, p. 177.

321. Robert Graves, *Goodbye To All That* (Penguin, 1960), p. 237.

322. Richard van Emden with Harry Patch, *The Last Fighting Tommy* (Bloomsbury Publishing Plc, 2007). Copyright Richard van Emden with Harry Patch.

323. *The Collected Poems of Wilfred Owen*, pp. 52–53

324. Patch, *The Last Fighting Tommy*, p. 137.

325. Brittain, *Testament of Youth*, pp. 23; 215; 650.

326. Graves, *Goodbye To All That*, pp. 197–198.

327. Max Arthur, *Forgotten Voices of the Great War* (Ebury Press, 2003), pp. 166; 138; 172; 198; 221.

328. Studdert Kennedy, *The Unutterable Beauty*, p. 1.

329. Rose Macaulay, *Non-Combatants and Others* (Methuen, 1986), p. 144.

330. Sassoon, *Memoirs of an Infantry Officer*, p. 260.

331. Stanhope feels this in discussion about the German trenches with Osborne.

332. *The Collected Poems of Wilfred Owen*, p. 69.

333. G. A. Studdert Kennedy, *The Word and the Work* (Longmans, Green and Co., 1925), pp. 57–58.

334. Studdert Kennedy, *The Unutterable Beauty*, p. 132.

335. Macaulay and Paul, *Up Against It*, p. 80.

336. Macaulay and Paul, *Up Against It*, pp. 83; 85; 86; 87; 91.

337. Macaulay and Paul, *Up Against It*, pp. 94; 97.

338. Macaulay and Paul, *Up Against It*, pp. 141; 155; 155.

339. Macaulay and Paul, *Up Against It*, pp. 101–117.

340. Sassoon, *Memoirs of an Infantry Officer*, p. 250; my italics.

341. *The Collected Poems of Wilfred Owen*, p. 167.

342. Siegfried Sassoon, *Poems Newly Selected 1916–1935* (Faber and Faber, 1940), p. 12.

343. Wilfred Owen, "Spring Offensive", in *The Collected Poems of Wilfred Owen*, p. 53.

344. *The Collected Poems of Wilfred Owen*, p. 176.

345. Graves, *Goodbye To All That*, p. 125.

346. Brittain, *Testament of Youth*, p. 163.

347. Brittain, *Testament of Youth*, p. 218.

348. Graves, *Goodbye To All That*, p. 305.

349. Davis, *Into the Silence*, p. 189.

350. Davis, *Into the Silence*, p. 454.

351. Siegfried Sassoon, *The Weald of Youth* (The Right Book Club, 1943), p. 274.

352. Thomas Hardy, "The Convergence of the Twain", in *Selected Shorter Poems of Thomas Hardy*, ed. John Wain (Macmillan, 1972), p. 45.

353. Wilson, *The Victorians*, p. 318.

354. Hitchens, *The Rage Against God,* p. 80.

355. E. H. Gombrich, *A Little History of the World* (Yale University Press, 2008), p. 276.

356. Daniel Finkelstein, "It's Easy to Mock Religion, but Then What?", *The Times*, 15 February 2012.

357. Matthew 3:9.

358. See in particular Chapter 11, "People and Race".

359. MacCulloch, *A History of Christianity*, pp. 941–942.

360. J. G. Lawler, *Were the Popes against the Jews? Tracking the Myths, Confronting the Ideologues* (Eerdmans, 2012). His "Introduction", pp. viii–xviii, makes this clear from the start.

361. Ben Macintyre, "Heroes of the Moral Resistance against Adolf Hitler", *The Times*, 5 January 2010.

362. Matt Ridley, "The Church Wins the Award for Intolerance", *The Times*, 21 February 2012; Michael White, "The Righteous Battle of a 'Brave Minority'—or Just Intolerance?", *The Guardian*, 2 December 2011.

363. Alain de Botton, *Religion for Atheists: a Non-Believer's Guide to the Uses of Religion* (Hamish Hamilton, 2012).

364. Statistics calculated by 100people.org, and widely quoted: see http://100people. org/statistics_100stats.php?section=statistic

365. Joseph Stiglitz, *The Price of Inequality* (Penguin, 2013); see "Preface to the Paperback Edition", under "Global Perspectives".

366. Joanna Bourke, *What It Means to be Human* (Virago, 2011).

367. Janice Turner, "I Have no Faith in These Unholy Warlords", *The Times*, 18 September 2010.

368. David Aaronovitch, "Intelligent Atheists Should Want Good Religion", *The Times*, 9 September 2010.

369. Jonathan Sacks, "Credo", *The Times*, 28 January 2012.

370. Thomas Cranmer, *Book of Common Prayer*, "General Confession".

371. Peter Tatchell, "I've Joined my Foes to Defend Our Right to Insult Each Other", *The Times*, 16 May 2012.

372. Cullen Murphy, *God's Jury: The Inquisition and the Making of the Modern World* (Penguin, 2013).

373. "The Monday Interview", *The Independent*, 27 September 2010.

374. See p. 32 of the Report.

375. Jim Dobbin and Gary Streeter, *The Daily Telegraph*, 26 February 2012.

376. See p. 40 of the Report.

377. "Executive Summary"(Evangelical Alliance, February 2012), p. 3

378. Oliver Kamm, "Narnia is a Risible Rant Against the Modern World", *The Times*, 4 January 2012.

379. Humphrey Carpenter, *The Inklings* (Allen & Unwin, 1978), p. 230.

380. Nevill Coghill, in *Light on Lewis*, ed. Jocelyn Gibb, (Bles, 1965), p. 65.

381. Colin Duriez, *C. S. Lewis: A Biography of Friendship* (Lion, 2013), p. 111.

382. Williams, *The Lion's World*, p. 20.

383. Paul Coleridge, *The Welfare of the Family is of Paramount Importance, Surely?* 24 September 2009, paragraph 1.

384. See BBC News website entry for 10 November 2011.

385. Rosemary Bennett, "Plunge in Number of Children Living With Both Parents", *The Times*, 28 November 2014. Data from the MCS may be accessed through the website of the Centre for Longitudinal Studies.

386. Coleridge, *The Welfare of the Family*, section: "What underlies the changes?"

387. Coleridge, *The Welfare of the Family*, section: "Education".

388. Figure from the National Audit Office Report "Children in Care".

389. Figure from the *Who Cares Trust* website.

390. See his letter to *The Times*, 12 April 2010.

391. Frances Gibb, "Revealed: Shocking Cost of Divorce for Children", *The Times*, 24 November 2014.

392. Froude, *Carlyle's Life in London* Vol. 1, p. 96.

393. A phrase used by him in his Witney constituency on 15 August 2011.

394. See the *British Medical Journal,* 2 March 2012.

395. John Humphrys, *Beyond Words* (Hodder & Stoughton, 2006), pp. 65–66.

396. Humphrys, *Beyond Words*, p. 68.

397. Hitchens, *The Rage Against God*, pp. 122–123 etc.

398. On 26 August 2011, a leader in *The Times* quoted a figure of 60,000 pupils leaving school in 2011 without a GCSE pass at grade C or above.

399. "Unpaid Work Schemes Ruled Lawful as High Court Rejects Poundland Case", *The Guardian*, 6 August 2012; "Graduate's Poundland Victory Leaves Government Work Schemes in Tatters", *The Guardian,*12 February 2013.

400. James Quinn Wilson, *The Moral Sense* (Free Press, 1993).

401. Richard Dawkins, "Hear the Rumble of Christian Hypocrisy", *The Times*, 29 January 2010.

402. See Professor Andrews' letter to *The Times*, 30 January 2010, and also Edgar Andrews, *Who Made God? Searching for a Theory of Everything* (EP Books, 2009).

403. In *The Less Deceived* (Faber and Faber, 1955).

404. McGrath, *The Twilight of Atheism*, p. 263.

405. *IDEA,* The Evangelical Alliance, July/August 2011

406. *Time* magazine, 18 April 2005, under "Heroes and Icons".

407. Rudyard Griffiths (ed.), *The Munk Debates: Hitchens v. Blair* (Black Swan, 2011), p. 24.

408. Figures supplied by The Evangelical Alliance. See their leaflet *Big Society Kingdom Opportunity*.

409. The Education Act, 1944, Part II, Section 7.

410. Prof. David Jesson, *Strong Schools for Strong Communities* (Church of England Archbishop's Council Education Division, 2009), p. 5.

411. Rowan Williams in *The Times*, 22 April 2011.

412. Alice Thomson, "Banning Faith Schools is Ideologically Wrong. But in Practice it is Worse—it is Barbarism", *The Times*, 14 June 2014.

413. John Mickelthwait and Adrian Wooldridge, *God is Back: How the Global Rise of Faith is Changing the World* (Penguin, 2010).

414. "Christians: A Series for Holy Week", *The Times*, 18–23 April 2011.

415. Michael Burleigh, "Faith in the 21st Century", *The Times*, 23 April 2011.

416. *A Handbook of Prayer for the Persecuted Church* (Open Doors, 2011 edition).

417. John Pontifex and John Newton (eds.), *Persecuted and Forgotten?* (Aid to the Church in Need, 2011).

418. Michael Binyon, "A Persecuted Minority", *The Times*, 22 April 2011.

419. Melanie Philipps, "The Murder of Christians is Our Guilty Secret", *The Times*, 17 November 2014.

420. Todd M. Johnson and Kenneth R. Ross (eds.), *The Atlas of Global Christianity* (Edinburgh University Press, 2009).

421. Philip Pullman, *The Good Man Jesus and the Scoundrel Christ* (Canongate, 2010), p. 199.

422. Robert Crampton, "Death is Miserable Enough for All Involved, Why Would I Want to Break the Taboo to Talk About it?", *The Times*, 15 May 2012.

423. *Collected Poems of W. B. Yeats* (Macmillan, 1933), p. 401.

424. Dawkins, *The God Delusion*, p. 356.

425. C. S. Lewis, *The Last Battle* (Puffin, 1964), p. 165.

426. C. S. Lewis, *Perelandra* (The Bodley Head, 1943).

427. Barack Obama, Election Victory Speech, Chicago, 4 November 2008.